Seeking Meaning

A Process Approach
to Library and Information Services

Second Edition

Carol Collier Kuhlthau

LIBRARIES
UNLIMITED
A Member of the Greenwood Publishing Group

Westport, Connecticut • London

Library of Congress Cataloging-in-Publication Data

Kuhlthau, Carol Collier, 1937–

    Seeking meaning : a process approach to library and information services / Carol Collier
Kuhlthau.—2nd ed.

      p. cm.

    Includes bibliographical references and index.

    ISBN 1-59158-094-3 (alk. paper)

    1. Reference services (Libraries). 2. Reference services (Libraries)—United States—Case
studies. 3. Library research. 4. Library research—United States—Case studies. 5.
Information retrieval. 6. Search behavior. I. Title.

    Z711.K84   2004

    025.5'2—dc22   2003060198

British Library Cataloguing in Publication Data is available.

Library of Congress Catalog Card Number: 2003060198
ISBN: 1–59158–094–3

First published in 2004

Libraries Unlimited, Inc., 88 Post Road West, Westport, CT 06881
A Member of the Greenwood Publishing Group, Inc.
www.lu.com

Printed in the United States of America

The paper used in this book complies with the
Permanent Paper Standard issued by the National
Information Standards Organization (Z39.48-1984).

10 9 8 7 6 5 4 3 2 1

In memory of my father, Fred R. Collier, 1913–2003

Contents

List of Illustrations

Figures

Tables

xi

Preface

It has been ten years since the first edition of *Seeking Meaning* was published in 1993 and twenty years since the Information Search Process model was first proposed from the findings of the initial study of high school students. The positive reaction to the theoretical framework and concepts presented in the first edition has encouraged me to produce a second edition that incorporates some of my more recent work. This book represents my rethinking of the original work in light of advances in information technology and related research in the field of library and information science over the last decade and my recent studies of the Information Search Process in education and the workplace. On the tenth anniversary of the publication of *Seeking Meaning* this new edition is a comprehensive explanation of the Information Search Process and its process approach to library and information services

I have been particularly gratified that librarians, researchers, and students alike have found these concepts useful for gaining insight into the user's perspective on information seeking. There has been considerable development of library services applying these concepts, particularly in user education and reference services. A number of researchers have verified the findings in their own studies and extended the concepts in other contexts. However, this edition does not present a summary of all the excellent applications of the Information Search Process that librarians have implemented in numerous libraries around the world. Nor does it provide a review of all the research that the Information Search Process has engendered in the past ten years. The book presents my own research, reflection, and, in some cases, restatement of the process approach to librarianship. It incorporates the original work presented in the first edition with my recent studies in the contexts of education and the workplace.

Although we have a better understanding of the constructive process of seeking meaning than we did when this book was first published, the work is not completed. More research is needed for further insight into the user's experience in information seeking as a basis for implementing a process approach in library services and information systems. These insights and concepts call for ongoing investigation and verification within the changing library profession and the expanding field of library and information science. The new studies reported in this second edition of the implementation of the process approach in education reveal important indicators of learning in the information age school that are in critical need of attention. In addition, initial investigation into the Information Search Process in the workplace indicates an extremely fruitful arena for further study and application. We are off to a good start, but there is more work to be done to respond to the urgent need for intellectual access from the user's perspective.

Many interesting, thoughtful, and creative people continue to influence my thinking as I discuss this work in the international community of library and information science. I am constantly amazed by the innovation and competence of the people in this field. Information Seeking in Context (ISIC), the biannual international conference, has been an important source of new ideas and inspiration. And of course, the faculty in the School of Communication, Information and Library Studies at Rutgers University continues to provide a rich collaboration in interdisciplinary ideas.

Introduction

The objective of library and information services is to increase access to sources, information, and ideas. Basic access is provided through selection, acquisition, and organization of sources, what Shera (1972) called the operational aspects of librarianship. Increased or enhanced access is provided primarily through two services, reference and instruction. Enhanced access encompasses intellectual as well as physical access. Physical access addresses the location of sources and information. Intellectual access addresses interpretation of information and ideas within sources. This book is about library and information services for intellectual access to information and ideas, and the process of seeking meaning.

Library and information science is in transition and in a theory-building phase. A theory is a conceptualization of a complex combination of facts. As psychologist George Kelly (1963) explained, "A theory may be considered as a way of binding together a multitude of facts so that one may comprehend them all at once" (p. 18). Theory enables us to rise above the seemingly random confusion of everyday life to see patterns and to understand principles on which to base purposeful, productive action. "A theory provides a basis for an active approach to life" (Kelly, 1963, p. 18).

The emerging theory of librarianship, like that of other practice-oriented fields, such as law, medicine, management, and education, is firmly entrenched in library and information practice. In practice-oriented fields, theory directly informs practice and is, therefore, extremely practical. Theory enables the practitioner to base practice on general principles rather than depending solely on hunches and intuition. Experience solidly grounded in an understanding of theory is the basis for making sound diagnoses and designing services that respond to dynamic needs of clients and users.

The most useful theories are generic to human nature and not situation specific. One way to build theory is to look to other fields and disciplines addressing similar problems and situations for theoretical perspectives that may be applied to a particular situation. There is strong evidence that theories are merging and becoming less discipline specific, providing a rich climate for creative, broad understanding of human endeavors. For librarianship, established theories in thinking and learning offer insight into users' experience and behavior in information-seeking situations. Borrowed theory is only a beginning, however. Only after rigorous testing and investigation in the particular situations of concern can a statement of theory be accepted. A theoretical statement for a particular endeavor, in this case information seeking, transforms the borrowed theory into a framework to apply to practice.

This book proposes a process approach for library and information services. It describes how the theory emerged from a hunch and some borrowed theory through investigation in a series of studies, to a conceptual statement and a framework for services. A theoretical framework for a process approach to library and information services was developed in a series of studies of the Information Search Process of users. An expanded counseling role for the library and information professional became apparent and called for strategies for designing and implementing interventions into the user's process of learning from information access and use. The process concept as described in the model of the Information Search Process has been useful for understanding the user's perspective on information seeking and has offered insight into pressing problems of seeking meaning in an overabundance of information. This book incorporates the original research that underlies the model of the Information Search Process, the articulation of an uncertainty principle for library and information services, and the concept of a zone of intervention for implementing a process approach contained in the first book with the author's research and thinking over the past ten years since the first book was published.

This new edition provides a full description of the research on the Information Search Process. It presents the original series of studies that led to the model of the Information Search Process, the principle of uncertainty for library and information services, and the concept of zones of intervention with strategies for implementing a process approach to library and information services. In addition, two new chapters describe my recent studies on the implementation of a process approach to library and information services in education and investigation of these concepts in the workplace. The book concludes with a summary of the conceptual perspective, with recommendations for further research and development of process-oriented services and systems that enable the constructive process of users seeking meaning not just information.

The book is divided into eleven chapters. Chapter 1 describes a shift in library and information science from a bibliographic paradigm to users' problems and process, revealing the need for building a process theory for library and information science. Chapter 2 discusses the constructivist theory of learning and suggests that information seeking may be studied within this view. The writings of John Dewey provide a historical and philosophical perspective. George Kelly's theory of personal constructs offers a psychological perspective, and Jerome Bruner's research and writings verify and expand an integrated perspective.

Chapter 3 describes an extensive qualitative study of library users, revealing information seeking as a process of construction, and presents a six-stage model of the Information Search Process. Chapter 4 describes verification of the model of the Information Search Process in two large-scale quantitative studies. Chapter 5 discusses further verification and expansion of the model in two longitudinal studies.

Chapter 6 introduces an uncertainty principle, which is a theoretical statement proposing a process theory for library and information services. Chapter 7 discusses implications for library and information services and redefines reference service and user education in five levels of intervention. Chapter 8 presents the concept of a zone of intervention as a way to diagnose users' problems to determine the level of mediation needed and suggests ways of intervening in the users' process of learning from information.

Chapter 9 describes implementation of the process approach in educational settings and discusses the results of two studies that identified elements that contribute to successful implementation. Chapter 10 describes two studies investigating the Information Search Process in the workplace and raises questions for further research and implementation. Chapter 11 summarizes the theoretical basis of the process approach and raises challenges for librarians, system designers, and researchers for meeting the needs of users in their quest for seeking meaning.

The Constructive Process in Library and Information Science Theory

Traditionally, library and information services have centered on sources and technology. Libraries have developed sophisticated systems for collecting, organizing, and retrieving texts and have applied advanced technology to provide access to vast sources of information. This bibliographic paradigm of collecting and classifying texts and devising search strategies for their retrieval has promoted a view of information use from the system's perspective. For the most part, library and information science has concentrated on the system's representation of texts rather than on users' tasks, problems, and processes in information gathering.

Although there is no question that the difficulties of controlling increasing quantities of information must continue to be creatively addressed, the individual's process of getting and using information is a vital aspect that cannot be overlooked. Expertly organized library collections, even the most advanced digital collections, may remain untouched without proper linkage to users' problems and processes. As Wilson (1977) pointed out in his insightful work, *Public Knowledge, Private Ignorance*, "It is not the difficulty of access but the time, effort, and difficulty of using documents that are the major deterrents to library use" (p. 123). The difficulty of using information is of increasing concern to information providers.

Theoretical Foundations of Library and Information Services

Although the bibliographic paradigm has been the traditional basis of the library and information profession, the major writings on the theoretical foundations of library and information services have recognized the user's perspective as a critical component in information provision. Shera's (1972) classic text, *The Foundations of Education for Librarianship,* began with a chapter entitled, "Communication and the Individual," which included an extensive discussion of learning. In *Public Knowledge, Private Ignorance,* Wilson (1977) directly confronted the issue by juxtaposing the provision for access to what he called "public knowledge" with the individual's need to learn from information referred to as "personal ignorance." Public knowledge is the view of the world that is the best we can collectively construct at a given time. Personal ignorance, which is our individual need for information, prompts us to tap into the sources of public knowledge in one way or another. Wilson proposed that libraries and information systems be tailored to the way people use information in their daily lives. "Any policy for library system development should be based on an understanding of individual information gathering behavior" (p. 1). Connections must be made between the way people use information and the way libraries and information systems provide information. Vickery and Vickery (1981), in *Information Science in Theory and Practice,* addressed the information needs of everyone by discussing such problems as selective attention and transfer of meaning and by devoting an entire chapter to "People and Information."

In *Library Services in Theory and Context,* Buckland (1983) introduced the notion of the process of "becoming informed" and discussed barriers to the process. Along with physical and intellectual access, he included linguistic and conceptual access that is commonly considered outside the purview of the library or information system. In *Information and Information Systems,* Buckland (1991) described how information technology expands physical access and has extraordinary power for dealing with information-as-thing. However, many challenges in providing intellectual access and viewing information-as-process remain. Buckland described the difficulty of providing intellectual access in this way, "What results is a troublesome paradox: information systems exist so that users may become beneficially informed, yet information systems cannot simply be evaluated on their ability to inform beneficially because becoming informed depends, in part, on factors that are situational and external to the information system" (1991, p. 109). Buckland considers libraries as an information system particularly adept at providing physical access, but cautions that physical access does not equate with informing. He explains that, "physically receiving a text of information does not guarantee that the recipient becomes informed" (p. 113). The challenge of providing intellectual access as well as physical access requires an understanding of the process of construction in becoming informed.

Taylor (1991), in a chapter in *Progress in Communication Science,* offered a framework for analyzing the information problems and what constitutes a solution to these problems of particular sets of people in various contexts. In his book, *Information Tasks: Toward a User-Centered Approach to Information Seeking,* Allen (1996) applied a generic project management model to information system design using the steps of needs, task and resource analysis, user modeling, and designing for usability. Allen aimed at a generic approach to addressing the information needs of people in a variety of situations. These conceptual models, although not research-based, are helpful for taking a user-centered approach to library and information services. An important international initiative concerned with the context of users and uses is Information Seeking in Context (ISIC), a biannual conference initiated in 1996 that brings together scholars from around the world to present their work and publish proceedings. Although these publications and initiatives reveal heightened awareness of and interest in the user's perspective, the bibliographic paradigm and system approach for providing physical access remains predominant.

Toward an Understanding of the User's Perspective on Information Seeking

The authors of these texts acknowledged the necessity for considering intellectual access and the use of information, but each noted that more empirical research is needed in this area to provide a basis for a theory of users' information processes. The body of research is growing, with international research groups forming to share studies of users and uses within a wide variety of contexts. Dervin and Nilan's (1986) article in *ARIST* set the agenda when they found that most studies remain constrained by the system's definition of needs, with the menu of responses coming from the system's world and not that of the users. Dervin and Nilan called for researchers to address the user's perspective on information use to provide a solid research base on which to build a conceptual framework for both practice and research.

On the whole, user studies, which make up the largest single body of research in librarianship, have been constrained by a narrow view of information use (Dervin and Nilan, 1986). For the most part, information is viewed as a thing or product to be given out, the right answer and the right source, rather than as an impetus for learning and changing constructs. Too often assessments have been confined to a single incident or an answer to a specific question measured in terms of accuracy. Evaluations of outcome based on measures of precision and recall are being recognized as inadequate for assessing the complex learning process in which individuals often engage as they search for information. Such judgments may be effective for evaluating a response to a single question, but when a person is involved in the dynamic process of becoming informed, relevance does not remain static. What is relevant at the beginning of a search may later turn out to be irrelevant, and vice versa. Therefore, the concept of relevance as a static entity severely limits understanding the dynamic process of formulating a problem or learning about a subject.

In extensive conceptual research, Dervin (1983, 1999) has developed sense-making as a theoretical perspective for information seeking and use. The sense-making triangle encompasses a situation in the time and space context of everyday life, a gap or barrier to moving ahead, and uses information as a bridge to the gap that enables sense-making. A person in a situation that reveals a gap in the ability to make sense seeks information to fill the gap. The sense-making approach has opened new understanding of why people seek information and how they use it that has provided a rich theoretical framework for librarians and researchers alike.

In the active personal process of constructing and learning, an individual's judgments of relevance are difficult to predict and frequently do not match the system's determination of relevance (Saracevic, 1975). Relevance may vary not only from person to person but also from time to time for the same person. Saracevic, Mokros, and Su (1990) suggest that the concept of usefulness is more appropriate for assessing services within the natural process of information seeking. The 1990s were an active time for expanding the concept of relevance, including the reexamination of relevance to consider context and situation by Schamber, Eisenberg, and Nilan (1990); Harter's (1992) introduction of psychological relevance; Barry's (1994) research into criteria beyond topicality; Spink, Greisdorf, and Bateman's (1998) study of relevance feedback in different situations; Saracevic's (1996) framework incorporating various aspects of relevance; and Vakkari and Hakala's (2000) study of changes in relevance criteria and problem stages. There remains a need for further study of the changes in relevance, meaning, and understanding within the process of information seeking from the user's perspective.

Research related to human interaction in information systems reveals some shift in emphasis from concentration on the bibliographic paradigm of document or text representations and associated search techniques to the study of users in information-seeking situations (Belkin and Vickery, 1985; Borgman, 1984; Ingwersen, 1992). The approach centers on the user's problem in the process of information seeking and the user's evaluation of the usefulness of the information for the resolution of the problem (Belkin, 1990; James, 1983; Ingwersen, 1992; Ellis, 1992). The effectiveness of information provision must consider the integration of results within the user's own experience. The personal meaning that the user seeks from the information becomes as critical a consideration for library and information services as the content represented in texts (Hollnagel and Woods, 1983; Dervin, 1982; Bates, 1989; Ingwersen, 1996).

Turning our attention to the user's perspective on information seeking, we become aware of an active personal process. The process of construction within information seeking involves fitting information in with what one already knows and extending this knowledge to create new perspectives. Patrick Wilson (1977) defined this type of information use as being motivated by a concern involving a commitment to action that gives structure to information seeking. "A commitment to action automatically provides a basis for classification of information into more, less, or not at all relevant" (p. 44). It is the individual formulation of a personal perspective or focus from the information gathered to create something new, at least for oneself, that fits with the notion of construction.

The constructive process of learning in the library requires services that enable individuals to relate new information to what they already know and extend that knowing to form new understandings. According to Wilson (1977), "What sets a good library off from other sources of documentary material is its provision not merely of simple summaries for shallow interests but of a complex array of sources from which the individual can piece together for himself what may never yet have been explicitly summarized" (p. 98). Library services based exclusively on a source-location premise are constrained in situations that call for mediation in the constructive process of users.

Cognitive Process in Information Seeking

The literature of library and information science offers convincing evidence that information seeking is an intellectual process. Research reveals information needs as evolving from a vague awareness of something missing and as culminating in the location of information that contributes to understanding and meaning. Central to the cognitive point of view is what DeMey (1977) referred to as the information processor's model of the world, determined by prior experience and education. Some researchers refer to the constructs held by individuals as knowledge structures (Ingwersen, 1992); others describe them as cognitive models that shift according to conceptual development (Hall, 1981; Meadow, 1983). Stages in the process have been described as occurring in three phases: information seeking, information gathering, and information giving (Krikelas, 1983).

Concentrating on cognitive aspects, Belkin, Brooks, and Oddy (1982) described the constructive process of information seeking in terms of the ASK (anomalous state of knowledge) hypothesis. An information search begins with the user's problem. The gap between the user's knowledge about the problem or topic and what the user needs to know to solve the problem is the information need. The user's state of knowledge is dynamic rather than static, changing as he or she proceeds in the process. Belkin, Brooks, and Oddy describe a scale of levels in the ability to specify an information need as beginning with a new problem, in a new situation, in which connections can be made with existing knowledge and as ending with a defined problem in a well-understood situation with an identifiable gap in knowledge. The user's ability to articulate requests to the information system can be expected to change according to his or her level of understanding of the problem. At the lower levels of the specificity scale, questions are most appropriate and experiential needs most apparent. At the upper levels of the specificity scale, requests can be made as commands of *informative* need (Belkin, 1980). In the initial stages of a problem, specifying precisely what information is needed may be nearly impossible for the user.

Taylor's benchmark work on levels of information need and his latter writings on value-added information and information use environments place the user's cognitive process in the forefront of considerations of information provision (Taylor, 1962, 1968, 1986, 1991). He describes four levels of information need evident in users' queries: *visceral,* an actual but unexpressed need for information; *conscious,* a within-brain description of the need; *formalized,* a formal statement of need; and *compromised,* the question as presented to the information system.

Taylor also found that, in the initial stages of a search, users are most likely to express their need for information in the form of questions that make connections with their existing knowledge. Only in the latter stages, after specific gaps in knowledge have been identified, can users' requests be expected to be expressed in the form of commands for specific information. However, users seem to employ a less straightforward strategy in actual information-seeking situations. Although a continuum may be seen as proceeding from questions, to problems, and to sense making, there do not seem to be definite boundaries between these activities (MacMullin and Taylor, 1984). An intricately interwoven process comprising mental, physical, and perceptual activities moves the user toward the goal state of sense-making.

Affective Experience in Information Seeking

The classic triad of thoughts, actions, and feelings central to any constructive process is rarely taken into consideration in study or discussion of information-seeking behavior. The user's action taken to gather information has been established as essential for solving information needs. The cognitive process is increasingly accepted as a significant component for understanding information use. However, affective experience continues to be overlooked in the literature, with a few notable exceptions. There has been little acknowledgment that the feelings expressed by users may have some import in study and understanding of information-seeking behavior.

MacMullin and Taylor (1984) conclude that a model representing the user's sense-making process in information seeking ought to incorporate three realms of activity: physical, actual actions taken; affective, feelings experienced; and cognitive, thoughts concerning both process and content. A person moves from the initial state of information need to the goal state of resolution by a series of choices made through a complex interplay within these three realms. The criteria for making these choices are influenced as much by environmental constraints, such as prior experience, knowledge, interest, information available, requirements of the problem, and time allotted for resolution, as they are by the relevance of the content of the information retrieved. According to Bates (1986), the search process, particularly during the entry and orientation phases, is more subtle and more complex on several grounds than current models assume.

A holistic view of the information user encompassing affective experience as well as cognitive aspects is needed. T. D. Wilson (1981) states that interaction between the user and the information system may be guided by both affective needs and cognitive needs. Although purely cognitive conceptions of information need are adequate for some research purposes, consideration of the affective dimension of users' problems is necessary for a model to address a wider, holistic view of information use.

Anxiety and Uncertainty in Information Seeking

A number of studies have shown that anxiety accompanies information seeking. Library anxiety (Mellon, 1986), revealed in studies of academic library users, and technology anxiety, revealed in studies of computer users (Borgman, 1984), suggest an association between common feelings of discomfort and information use, particularly in novice users. Both lines of research, however, attribute feelings of anxiety to a lack of familiarity with sources and technology. More may be going on here. Anxiety may be an integral part of the information-seeking process, resulting from uncertainty and confusion. Uncertainty is a necessary critical element in any process of construction. When the information search process is viewed as a process of construction, uncertainty and anxiety are anticipated and expected as part of the process.

Another basic characteristic of the process of construction, which offers insight into the anxiety and uncertainty in information seeking, is that we each enter the process with a system of personal constructs built on past experience. Learning in libraries involves a vigorous process of using information in which the learner is actively engaged in seeking meaning from the information he or she gathers as a search progresses. The topic or problem changes and emerges in a series of stages or levels of understanding, which are dependent upon not only the information he or she encounters but also the individual's perspective, background, and knowledge. Therefore, the user uniquely creates each search within the framework of his or her personal constructs related to the problem at hand and to his or her larger worldview. The concept of an ideal search in an objective sense does not fit into this dynamic, personal, constructive view of information use. Rather, each search is fundamentally different and subjective. The user's personal perspective determines what he or she selects to learn along the way; that perspective directs the search through personal choices of relevance.

Uncertainty Principle

The bibliographic paradigm is based on certainty and order, whereas the user's constructive process is characterized by uncertainty and confusion. Several researchers (Whittemore and Yovits, 1973; Bates, 1986) have proposed an uncertainty principle for library and information science. Van Rysbergen (1996) proposed a logical model of uncertainty and introduced seven types of uncertainty—ignorance, incompleteness, undecidability, complexity, randomness, vagueness, and imprecision—to be considered within a probabilistic approach. This concept of an uncertainty principle as a theoretical statement needs further development to include the users' perspective on information seeking. Leading in this line of research, Wilson (2002), and his colleagues have studied uncertainty within the Wilson problem-solving model (1999), stressing the importance of gaining a more general understanding of human behavior that is the basis of the design and development of information systems.

A more holistic view of information seeking incorporates the experience of interacting thoughts, actions, and feelings in the process of construction. Uncertainty initiates the process, and anxiety and an unsettling discomfort may be expected in the early stages. The principle of uncertainty may include the uncertainty of choices of each individual user within a search for information. It can be concluded then that an information search is a learning process in which the choices along the way are dependent on personal constructs rather than on one universal, predictable search for everyone.

Chapter 6 proposes an uncertainty principle as a conceptual framework for library and information services. While building on the concept of an uncertainty principle, as previously suggested, this proposal concentrates on the constructivist theory of learning (see Chapter 2) and the findings of the studies of the information search process of library users (see Chapters 3 through 5).

Theory to Practice

Two well-established library services for mediating with information users are reference service and instruction. In recent years, each of these services has shown evidence of (1) change to accommodate more than simply locating information and (2) exploring ways to mediate in the use of information, although the bibliographic paradigm remains the primary orientation of library and information services. However, further theoretical underpinnings for constructive mediation are being developed.

Reference Services

For the most part reference services are based on a source orientation of location as the goal. Preparation for reference service consists of a comprehensive overview of reference sources and guidance in collection development, with an introduction to the reference interview. Katz, long considered an authority on reference services and the author of a text commonly used to educate new librarians for professional practice, places considerable emphasis on the communication aspects of the interview. He suggests that the core of the interaction centers on open and closed questions: "The open query is general and one which begins with a broad topic. . . . The closed question is restrictive and normally implies an equally specific reply" (1987, p. 49). He considers open and closed questions in terms of the user asking the question and of the librarian responding to the user. Katz recommends that in the reference interview the librarian turn a tight, closed question into a relaxed conversation about the topic.

Katz described three levels of reference service: conservative or minimum service, which may consist of pointing out where a source may be found; moderate or middling service, in which the librarian makes an effort to instruct select patrons in the use of the library while answering their questions; and liberal or maximum service, in which the librarian consistently comes up with the answer or with the sources of the answer. The librarian only offers liberal or maximum service when such help is requested (pp. 53–54).

The reference services described by Katz are firmly established in a source orientation and in the bibliographic paradigm. As Durrance (1989) noted, library and information services have a long way to go toward being fully responsive to the information needs of regular library users, without any consideration for the vast unserved. Furthermore, reference services in libraries have, for a century, served primarily to explain a bibliographic apparatus, help users find library materials, and increase access to the information within the library. Durrance asks, "Has the time come to reinvent reference service so that it is more responsive to user needs?" Researchers have begun to question the design of traditional reference service and the messages it sends to library users. The present model, developed when libraries were far more concerned with materials than with people, suffers from a lack of user orientation" (p. 166). Dewdney and Ross (1994) found that users' questions are extremely misleading and confounding if taken at face value. Dervin and Dewdney (1986) recommended neutral questioning that goes beyond open questions to address the actual problem of the user underlying the reference query.

Comparisons with interview techniques of other professionals, such as physicians, have revealed basic differences in the environment in which the interaction takes place. Lynch (1977) pointed out that the reference interview is conducted in public, that there is rarely any privacy, and that time considerations often force the librarian to cut the interview short: "The context of the reference interview makes it resemble the interview of a sales clerk rather than the interview of the physician or attorney or personnel officer" (pp. 136–137). Durrance (1995) furthered the notion of professional interaction by introducing the act of the user returning to the same librarian for further advice and consultation as a standard for evaluating quality of reference service. By the end of the 1990s technology was changing the environment of the reference interview, with an increase in presearch conferences that were scheduled in advance, required a substantial block of time, and were conducted in relative privacy. As direct access to databases became more prevalent, reference librarians noted a distinct change in their interaction with users. Unfortunately many reference librarians were reporting that much of their time was being spent in assisting in the use of machines. There is a need to rethink reference services to respond to users' need to find meaning and enable intellectual access in a vast information environment.

Instruction

Bibliographic instruction in academic libraries has evolved through three models or approaches, described by Tuckett and Stoffle (1984): a library tool approach, a conceptual frameworks approach, and a theory-based approach. Library and information skills instruction in school library media centers has evolved through three similar approaches: a source approach, a pathfinder approach, and a process approach (Kuhlthau, 1987). The tool or source approach centers on aiding students to use their particular library and its specific sources by improving their location skills. The conceptual frameworks or pathfinder approach, based on the pioneering work of Patricia Knapp, centers on teaching a search strategy concentrating on both locating and using sources. The Knapp (1966) program was designed to teach students about the library as a system of ways: "whoever would use the system must know the 'way' to use the system. Knowing the way means understanding the nature of the total system, knowing where to plug into it, knowing how to make it work" (p. 80). The pathfinder approach is designed to lead students through a sequence of sources in a search to help them to understand the relationship among the sources in the library. Unfortunately, the tool/source approach and the conceptual/pathfinder approach have limited potential for transference to other situations of information seeking. This is due largely to the fact that while source use and location skills are emphasized, the reasoning process that underlies independent learning is not developed. Both approaches "do not typically deal with evaluation of sources or the analysis of information need and do little to create flexible problem solving abilities" (Tuckett and Stoffle, 1984, p. 60).

A new model for instruction concerned with inquiry and learning is emerging. The theory-based process approach involves using, interpreting, and learning from information. Knapp (1966) found that students "have a basic misconception of the function of information inquiry, that they look for and expect to find 'the answer to the question' instead of evidence to be examined" (p. 283). The underlying concept proposed by the Knapp project centers on "the intellectual processes involved in retrieval of information and ideas" (Lindgren, 1981, p. 28). The concept of teaching library resources as evidence to be examined for shaping a topic rather than finding a quick answer to a question is the key idea behind learning how to learn in the library: "We must concentrate on uniting the processes of gathering information with the uses of information" (p. 31). A concept paper by Mancall, Aaron, and Walker (1986) provided the rationale for incorporating the development of thinking skills into library instruction. They emphasized that, "Information management skills instruction . . . must be broad and more process oriented. Focus must go beyond location skills and 'correct answers' and move to strategies that will help students to develop insight and facility in structuring successful approaches to solving information needs" (p. 22). Recent research on student learning in school libraries substantiates this position (Harada, 1999; Limberg, 1997; Todd, 1995).

George's (1990) review of the literature of bibliographic instruction for the prior thirty years disclosed a serious lack of theoretical underpinnings and some strides in acknowledging the necessity for moving in a more theoretical direction. Several papers delved into the work of Bruner (1973, 1975, 1977, 1986) for a theoretical foundation applicable to practice. George also noted that two new theories pertaining to instruction have come from research rather than from pure reasoning. One is Mellon's (1986) recognition of library anxiety, derived from qualitative studies using students' research logs and interviews. The other is the work reported in Chapter 2 on the information search process. George (1990) cautions that research that focuses on cognitive development, long-term learning retention, and creativity needs to supplement traditional data-gathering techniques that take snapshots but not movies.

During the decade of the 1990s information literacy became the major initiative of instruction both in the school library and in the academic library instruction communities. Information literacy standards that describe what a student needs to know and be able to do to be information literate were developed and published by both professional associations (AASL, 1998; ACRL, 2002). Although the standards are useful for defining information literacy, as specific objectives for instruction they may not accomplish the intended purpose of developing information literate students. Engaging students in inquiry that embeds information literacy in authentic learning may be more helpful for preparing them to apply their knowledge to the information tasks in their lives.

When information seeking is placed in the context of learning, the complex constructive process of using information becomes apparent. Critical questions related to library and information services for providing helpful intervention include: "What do people actually experience in a search for information?" "What are their expectations, purposes, motives, and constructs?" and "What thoughts and feelings prompt their actions as they progress, and how do these interact to form the whole experience of information seeking?"

Before we can address these questions in an empirical way, a more extensive theoretical framework is needed on which to base the analysis of data collected on the user's perspective in information-seeking situations. At present, the theory base in library and information science is not sufficient to explain fully the user's experience. In this theory-building phase, a borrowed theory from a similar area of human endeavor provides a way of expanding the theory base for analysis. A borrowed theory frequently sparks a revelation of a new way of viewing a problem and initiates fresh insights. The next chapter presents the theory of learning as a process of construction and recommends ways of applying the borrowed theory for investigating users in the process of learning from information in libraries.

Learning As a Process

2

Information seeking is a primary activity of life. People seek information to deepen and broaden their understanding of the world around them. When information seeking in libraries is placed in a larger context of learning, the user's perspective becomes an essential component in information provision. When the user's experience in the process of learning from information does not match the way the system is designed to provide information, serious problems arise. We need to understand the user's perspective to design more effective library and information services.

A sound theoretical foundation is necessary for developing effective practice. A theory is a conceptualization of a complex combination of concepts. It offers an articulation of underlying complexity that can be understood, discussed, and acted upon. In practice-oriented fields, theory provides the basis for responsible action. Theory enables us to rise above the seemingly random confusion of everyday life to see patterns and to understand principles on which to base purposeful, productive action.

To understand the user's perspective on information seeking, it is helpful to delve into the theory of other allied fields, particularly the psychology of learning. This chapter presents a theory borrowed from psychology that explains people's experience in the process of learning. We begin with this borrowed theory because we find a lack of theory within library and information science to explain fully the user's perspective on information seeking. The related borrowed theory offers insight into similar human endeavors and provides the basis for developing a grounded theory specifically for information seeking. The borrowed theory offers a frame or lens for viewing the information-seeking behavior of library users.

The constructivist view of learning, which offers insight into what the user experiences, is a particularly valuable way to understand information seeking from the user's perspective. Two basic themes run through the theory of construction. One is that we construct our own unique personal worlds, and the other is that construction involves the total person incorporating thinking, feeling, and acting in a dynamic process of learning. This chapter considers these themes from both a philosophical and a psychological position within both historical and contemporary contexts. The chapter presents a selected view of constructivist theory that provides the theoretical frame of reference for a series of studies of the user's experience in the information-seeking process and for the model that emerged from the findings.

Three prominent theorists on construction are John Dewey, George Kelly, and Jerome Bruner. The particular aspects of their work that relate most directly to information seeking are presented here rather than a complete summary of their writings. Each theorist offers a somewhat different perspective of the issue and thus fills in the picture from several vantage points. John Dewey provides the philosophical foundation for viewing learning as a constructive process. From the historical perspective, his writings form the foundation for later, more empirical work in psychology. George Kelly, a clinical psychologist, verified and refined the theory of construction from the psychological perspective. His publications in the 1950s and 1960s provided an alternative explanation to the behaviorist description of learning, which was pervasive at the time. He expanded the theory by defining a series of feelings associated with the phases of construing and reconstruing. Psychologist Jerome Bruner further verified constructive theory in his research on perception. His writings offer an integrated perspective on learning as a constructive process. This chapter discusses the compatible concepts within their work and the relation of those concepts to the process of learning from information.

John Dewey: A Philosophical and Historical Perspective

In the early decades of the twentieth century, John Dewey developed a philosophy of education that was uniquely American. Dewey's constructivist theory of learning was established from a philosophical perspective based on the earlier writings of John Locke. Although Dewey was principally a philosopher not an educator, he recognized the critical role that education plays in a democracy and turned his attention to developing the philosophical foundation of education in a free society. His work has had extensive and lasting impact on educational theory and practice, although some applications of his theories, in the form of progressive education, have not been totally successful. Rereading Dewey's writings today, one finds the ideas refreshingly enlightening and surprisingly relevant.

Dewey (1944) recognized that the basic nature of a democratic society is change and that the principal function of education is to prepare people for change: "A society which is mobile, . . . with change occurring anywhere must see that its members are educated for personal initiative and adaptability. Otherwise they will be overwhelmed by the changes in which they are caught and whose significance of connections they do not perceive" (p. 88). We have certainly witnessed that the change from an industrial economy to an information society affects those who do not have the knowledge or skills to adapt and who are overwhelmed by the changes in which they are caught. Zuboff's (1988) studies of the automated workplace revealed a radical change in the skills that all types of workers need. The information age is characterized by the availability of vast amounts of information and rapid changes of events. This dynamic environment calls for people needing abilities beyond basic skills in reading, writing, and computing. They need the higher-level skills of thinking and problem solving.

This leads us to the question: "What is it to be literate in an information society?" Although there is no formal consensus on this matter, many would respond that knowing how to learn is at the heart of education. Learning how to learn may be understood as individually internalizing a constructivist approach to learning.

Acting and Reflecting

Dewey (1944) described learning as an active individual process, not something done to someone but rather something that a person does. "Education," he said, "is not an affair of telling and being told but an active and constructive process" (p. 41). The axiom "learning by doing" is often attributed to Dewey. However, that is only half of the equation. The other, critical half is thinking or reflecting. Learning takes place through a combination of acting and reflecting on the consequences, which Dewey called reflective experience or reflective thinking. Through reflection we seek connections between our actions and the results. In this way, we achieve a deep understanding that is transferable to a range of situations. Transference is the ultimate objective of education. Education is "the power to retain in one's experience something which is of value in coping with the difficulties in a later situation" (Dewey, 1944, p. 44). Dewey described learning as a continuous process of reflective experience in which the person is actively constructing his or her view of the world.

Consideration for the whole child was another of Dewey's postulates. Learning takes place within the context of a whole experience in which the learner is completely engaged. A whole experience goes beyond the narrow, one-dimensional, passive incident to encompass actively all aspects of the new. Although Dewey (1934) did not explicitly define the interplay of thoughts, feelings, and actions, his concept of the whole child projects this view. His description of reflective thinking inseparably interweaves three aspects: thoughts, actions, and feelings.

Phases of Reflective Thinking

In *How We Think*, Dewey (1933) explained the interrelatedness of actions and thoughts. He described what he called reflective thinking as occurring in five phases: suggestion, intellectualization, guiding idea (hypothesis), reasoning, and testing by action (pp. 106–114).

The first phase, suggestion, is a state of doubt due to an incomplete situation, and is characterized by perplexity, confusion, uncertainty, and hesitation. The difficulty is spread throughout the situation and infects the situation as a whole. Direct activity is temporarily arrested. The conditions of hesitation and delay are essential to the job of reflecting on the difficulty.

The second phase, intellectualization, involves conceptualizing the problem, interpreting the given elements, and anticipating possible solutions and suggestions. The third phase, the guiding idea or hypothesis, is a tentative interpretation of the suggestion that is used as a hypothesis to initiate or guide the collection of factual material. A careful survey incorporating examination, inspection, exploration, and analysis is made to define and clarify the problem at hand. Acts of searching for, hunting for, and inquiring about information characterize this phase.

In the fourth phase, reasoning, the hypothesis is made more precise and more consistent by familiarity with a wider range of facts. An elaboration of the idea emerges through reasoning. The fifth phase, testing by action, involves taking a stand on the projected hypothesis, doing something to bring about results (and thereby testing the hypothesis by overt or imaginative action), and concluding with a resolution of doubt. The result is settling and disposing of the perplexity.

In the five phases of reflective experience (see Table 2.1), Dewey (1933) describes the dynamic role that the individual plays in the process of using information for learning. Extensive thinking and reflection are an integral part of the information-seeking process, for as he wrote:

> If we knew just what the difficulty was and where it lay the job of reflection would be much easier than it is. . . . As the saying goes, a question well put is half answered. In fact, we know what the problem exactly is simultaneously with finding a way out and getting it resolved. Problem and solution stand out completely at the same time. Up to that point, our grasp of the problem has been more or less vague and tentative. (p. 108)

Dewey explains that facts, data, and information arouse ideas that enable the learner to make inferences. In these "leaps from the known" the learner is "going beyond the information given" (p. 158), a phrase later adopted by Bruner.

Table 2.1. Dewey—Phases of Reflective Thinking

PHASES	DEFINITION
Suggestion	Doubt due to incomplete situation
Intellectualization	Conceptualizing the problem
Guiding idea (hypothesis)	Tentative interpretation
Reasoning	Interpretation with more precise facts
Action	Idea tested by overt or imaginative action

George Kelly: A Psychological Perspective

Whereas Dewey's writing was primarily philosophical, George Kelly's work in the 1950s and 1960s verified and defined constructivist theory from a psychological perspective. As a clinical psychologist, he built his theory from extensive investigation of real people acting in a real world. Personal Construct Theory is the legacy he left in his insightful, provocative writings, in particular the classic *A Theory of Personality: The Psychology of Personal Constructs* (1963).

Personal Construct Theory proposes that constructs are built out of a person's experience to anticipate future events. Constructs are the patterns that one formulates to make sense of the world. These patterns provide guidelines or frames of reference, which determine the choices one makes. Individuals devise their own construct systems, which establish a personal orientation toward the events they encounter. Therefore, behavior is determined by the constructs one holds. It is highly individual rather than in response to stimuli, as the behaviorist would explain. In Kelly's (1963) terms, "a person's processes are psychologically channelized by the ways in which he anticipates events" (p. 46).

Forming new constructs and reconstruing old ones are continual processes throughout life. All learning takes place in this way. Underlying Personal Construct Theory is the endless opportunity for change. Kelly assures us that no one needs to paint himself or herself into a corner. We continue to learn throughout our lives. That is to say, we adjust our constructs to better match our environment and to improve our predictions upon which to base our actions. "All our present interpretations of the universe are subject to revision" (Kelly, 1963, p. 15). (Maher [1969] and Bannister [1977] compiled Kelly's other important papers after his untimely death.)

The constructs that we have formed are not easily discarded, however. While we continually seek to improve these patterns, we are hampered by the damage to our existing system that results from alteration. Adjusting a construct may be a major psychological experience and entail considerable anxiety and threat.

Kelly (1963) describes the process of forming new constructs as progressing through a series of psychological phases. His descriptions of experience in the phases of construction are strikingly similar to Dewey's stages of reflective thinking. Actually, he was greatly influenced by Dewey's concept of reflective experience and built his psychological theory on Dewey's philosophical outlook. Kelly expanded on Dewey's model by emphasizing the disruption of new information to the person's system of constructs and the resulting increase in apprehension within the early phases of the process of construction. He found the threatening effect of the unknown to be a natural part of the constructive process.

Phases of Construction—Interplay of Thinking and Feeling

Kelly (1963) classified common experience in constructing individual worlds as "a full cycle of sensemaking." Although a person's constructs of the world are highly personal and individual, the process of construction has certain common features and characteristics that are experienced generally. Kelly elaborated on this basic premise of construct theory. The constructs that one builds are unique, but people experience the constructive process in certain common ways.

One of the major contributions of Kelly's work was his emphasis on the influence of feelings in the process of construction. He described the process of construction as naturally evolving through a series of phases and identified the predominant feelings commonly experienced in each phase.

A sequence of phases is commonly experienced in the process of constructing new information into one's system of personal constructs (see Table 2.2). When a person is initially confronted by a vague new idea, his or her system of constructs is either able to incorporate the idea or is inadequate to assimilate it. If the idea cannot be assimilated into the existing system of constructs, it is perplexing and the person experiences confusion. Kelly asserts that "almost everything new starts with confusion" (Maher, 1969, p. 151). As individuals become more involved they find the new information is often inconsistent and incompatible with existing constructs; this increases their sense of confusion and uncertainty. The new information may be so disruptive that the person becomes threatened by the prospect of the unknown. This brings us to a critical turning point in the process of construction. At that point, the individual may choose to reject the new idea. Kelly describes this phase as "the threshold between confusion and certainty, between anxiety and boredom . . . (when) we are most tempted to turn back" (Maher, 1969, p. 152). We have another choice, however. At this turning point, the person may choose to formulate a hypothesis to move the investigation of the idea toward assimilation.

Table 2.2. Kelly—Five Phases of Construction

PHASES	DEFINITION
Confusion and doubt	New experience
Mounting confusion and possible threat	Inconsistent/incompatible information
Tentative hypothesis	A direction to pursue
Testing and assessing	Assessing outcome of undertaking
Reconstruing	Assimilating new construct

By using the term *hypothesis,* Kelly adopts the metaphor of a scientist, whose ultimate aim is to predict and control. The hypothesis is a focus or a theme that gives a direction to pursue. Kelly asserts that a hypothesis can enable a person "to break through his moment of threat to get on with the task of testing to confirm or reject the hypothesis" (Maher, 1969, p. 151). The final phases of the cycle involve assessing the outcome of the undertaking and reconstruing or assimilating the new construct into the existing system (Bannister, 1977, pp. 14–15).

Feeling and Formulating

Feelings interplay with thoughts and actions, engaging the whole person in a complete experience of learning. Lack of consideration of any one of the three offers not only an incomplete but also an inaccurate picture. By directly addressing the impact of feelings on the process of construction, Kelly contributes the critical missing link for understanding the person's experience in any constructive process.

In Personal Construct Theory, hypothesis formulation plays an instrumental role, as it does in Dewey's model of reflective thinking. Like Dewey, Kelly uses the term *hypothesis* not in its formal scientific sense but in a less structured psychological sense. Formulating is closely related to the feelings experienced within the constructive process. Formulating a "hypothesis" is a way to move beyond uncertainty and the associated, inhibiting feelings of confusion, doubt, and threat. Kelly offers a way of viewing a hypothesis and the instrumental part it plays in the process of construction. He describes two types of hypothesis statements, those in the invitational mood and those in the indicative mood (see Table 2.3) (Maher, 1969). A hypothesis stated in the invitational mood allows one to "suppose or behave as if the facts were known" (p. 149); "An invitational hypothesis is not asserted as a fact but serves rather to make

Table 2.3. Two Types of Hypothesis Statements

MOOD (Affective)	CHOICES (Cognitive)	ACTIONS (Physical)
Indicative	Predicting closure	Confined to prescriptive task
Invitational	Predicting expansion	Posture of expectancy for formulative task

an unrealistic conclusion tenable for a sufficient period of time for a person to pursue its implications as if it were true" (p. 152). The indicative mood, on the other hand, has a prescriptive nature that dictates the direction to be taken.

The hypothesis establishes a frame of reference for the prediction of what is to follow. The invitational mood assumes the posture of expectancy and enables one to take risks and to profit from mistakes. The indicative mood limits the predictions that one can make and tends to close down or confine the task at hand. Both types of hypotheses move the process of construction from the initial state of confusion toward understanding. In information seeking, these moods may be envisioned either as styles and traits that are habitually followed or as strategies and states that arise from a particular problem or stage of the process.

Predicting and Choosing

Prediction plays an essential role in the constructivist theory of learning. Individuals form constructs with which to predict future events (Kelly, 1963, p. 14). Predictions lead to action, which confirms or rejects the construct. We continually assess our constructs and reconstrue them to better match our world. The accuracy of our predictions determines the effectiveness of our actions. Through the reconstruction of constructs, predictions change and, as a result, behavior is altered.

Kelly (1963) describes the process of construction as a series of choices based on prediction of the outcome or result of the choice. He states, "a person chooses that which will extend and define his system" (p. 64). The choices that one makes are directed toward finding meaning and making sense of the world. Construction is a highly individual process based on one's system of prior personal constructs.

Kelly (1963) introduces the concept of elaborative choice, which is a choice that broadens understanding (p. 65). Although all choices may hold this promise, choices that are truly elaborative change perspectives or provide clarification. Elaborative choices in the process of construction provide a pivotal point of greater understanding and clarity.

Although Kelly's explanation of prediction may seem overly systematic and structured, when he describes an individual's experience within the process of construction, a dynamic, uncertain process is revealed. When he depicts people working through the process by a series of choices from alternatives, these choices are anything but obvious and straightforward, particularly in the early phases.

Jerome Bruner: An Integrated Perspective

Bruner's research and writings are grounded in the earlier work of Dewey, Jean Piaget (see Elkind, 1976), and Vygotsky (1978) as well as William James, Kenneth Goodman, and Frederick Bartlett. Three themes in Bruner's work center on consideration of the nature of the (1) knowledge, (2) knower, and (3) knowledge-getting process. Although libraries have traditionally attended to the first, we will concentrate here on the latter two.

Bruner's studies of perception further verify and refine the constructive view of the nature of human thinking and learning. Bruner was influenced by Bartlett's work as well as Piaget's research on the concept of schema, which is similar to the notion of construct. Bruner (1973) defined schema as "that integrated, organized representation of past behavior and experience which guides individuals in reconstructing previously encountered material which enables people to go beyond evidence, to fill in gaps, to extrapolate" (p. 5). The constructive nature of thinking underlying schema theory has provided the conceptual underpinnings for Bruner's study of a wide variety of activities involving perception.

Bruner's (1973) research confirms that we are actively involved in making sense of the world around us rather than being passive receivers of information: "The individual is seen not as a passive, indifferent organism but rather as one who actively selects information, forms hypotheses and on occasion distorts input in the service of reducing surprise and of attaining understanding" (p. 3). This active process of learning is similar to that described earlier by Dewey and Kelly. Bruner stresses our ability, indeed our compulsion, to go beyond the information at hand to create a personal understanding. He describes perception as "an act of categorization which is based on an inferential leap from cue to class identity and allows us to go beyond the properties perceived to prediction" (p. 14). Like Kelly, he sees the person interpreting or making sense of new information to make more accurate predictions for action.

The Interpretive Task

Bruner's research and writing corroborate and elaborate on the basic concepts in the constructive sequences of both Dewey and Kelly. Bruner (1986) also describes construction as involving hypothesis generation, which he views as a process of interpreting and creating. He notes that: "We can create hypotheses that will accommodate virtually anything we encounter" (p. 51). Again, a hypothesis is not viewed in the strict scientific sense but as an imaginative story that allows us to "consider possible alternative personal perspectives on the world" (p. 54). The concept of choosing between possible alternatives corresponds to that of Kelly's work. Bruner suggests that we move along in the process of construction by suspending disbelief to consider possible worlds.

The interpretive task is central to the constructive process (see Table 2.4). It is not enough merely to gather information. Bruner (1986) explains that: "If we are to understand it (new information), it will not be by means of a positivist archaeology in which everything particular about it and everything leading up to it are finally dug up, labeled, and collated. However much we dig and delve, there is still an interpretive task" (p. 53).

Table 2.4. Bruner—The Interpretive Task

PHASES	DEFINITION
Perception	Encountering new information
Selection	Recognizing patterns
Inference	Joining clusters and categories
Prediction	Going beyond the information given
Action	Creating products of the mind

Interpreting involves creating. The interpretive task of "going beyond the information given" is a central concept in Bruner's work. Information is interpreted to create what Bruner calls products of mind. This mysterious capacity to interpret and create is at the core of what it means to be human. Bruner strives to understand the ways that human beings construct their worlds, and he wonders, "How we come to experience them as real, and how we manage to build them into the corpus of culture as science, literature, history, whatever" (Bruner, 1986, p. 45). The interpretive task is based on constructs built from past experience. This enables us to go beyond the information given to create something uniquely our own.

Interplay of Thinking, Feeling, and Acting

The process of construction is not a systematic, orderly procedure, but rather it is the confusing, uncertain, threatening process that Kelly revealed. As Bruner (1986) cautions:

I have rendered it all too gray and orderly. World making of this type rides from time to time on wild metaphors. . . . They are crutches to help us get up the abstract mountain. Once up, we throw them away (even hide them) in favor of a formal, logically consistent theory that (with luck) can be stated in mathematical terms. (p. 46)

Bruner decries the habit of drawing heavy conceptual boundaries around the classic triad: thought, action, and emotion. He warns of the misunderstanding that can result from making too sharp a distinction among the three: "Emotion is not usefully isolated from the knowledge of the situation that arouses it.

Cognition is not a form of pure knowing to which emotion is added and action is a final common path based on what one knows and feels. The three constitute a unified whole" (p. 117).

Bruner's work confirms Dewey's stages of reflective thinking and Kelly's phases of construction, which incorporate feelings with thoughts and action (see Table 2.5). When we add the dynamic affective component to the constructive process, the full range of experience becomes apparent. Interpreting, choosing, and creating the inconsistent, often incompatible information encountered is likely to cause profound feelings of uncertainty, confusion, anxiety, and even threat. The critical impact of feelings in information seeking is illustrated by the conflict in any constructive process caused by encounters with unique or redundant information.

Table 2.5. The Constructive Process—Phases and Definitions

Dewey—Phases of Reflective Thinking

PHASES	DEFINITION
Suggestion	Doubt due to incomplete situation
Intellectualization	Conceptualizing the problem
Guiding idea (hypothesis)	Tentative interpretation
Reasoning	Interpretation with more precise facts
Action	Idea tested by overt or imaginative action

Kelly—Five Phases of Construction

PHASES	DEFINITION
Confusion and doubt	New experience
Mounting confusion and possible threat	Inconsistent/incompatible information
Tentative hypothesis	A direction to pursue
Testing and assessing	Assessing outcome of undertaking
Reconstruing	Assimilating new construct

Bruner—The Interpretive Tasks

PHASES	DEFINITION
Perception	Encountering new information
Selection	Recognizing patterns
Inference	Joining clusters and categories
Prediction	Going beyond the information given
Action	Creating products of the mind

Uniqueness and Redundancy

All new information is not treated equally in the constructive process of learning. There is a tension between the uniqueness and the redundancy of the information encountered within a new experience. Humans have a limited capacity for an overabundance of either the new or the familiar. This basic principle of human ability is important for understanding the interplay of affective experience with cognition and action in the process of construction.

Bruner's work reveals our inclination for seeking redundancy in new information. Our ability to recognize familiar patterns and to draw inferences leads to action. These familiar patterns are internal models or theories, similar to Kelly's constructs, which enable us to make predictions and to act (Bruner, 1986): "Internal models or theories are built by redundancy, the ability to recognize similarity; inference, the ability to classify and categorize similarities, and generic coding systems, the mental models which allow one to go beyond the present by using probability and prediction" (p. 222).

As in Kelly's work, Bruner sees prediction or expectancy as an important component in recognizing redundancy. The basic principle of expectancy is revealed in his studies of perception: "Thresholds, the amount of time and input necessary for seeing or recognizing an object or event, are closely governed by expectancy. The more expected an event, the more easily it is seen or heard" (Bruner, 1986, p. 55). Too much familiarity, however, can cause attention to lag and lead to boredom.

Uniqueness, on the other hand, places our system on alert. Unexpected new information startles and surprises. There is a limit to the amount of unique information that the human system can take in. According to George Miller (1956), the capacity is 7 +/– 2 slots, known as "the magic number." Bruner points out that you can get a lot of redundant, expected information into seven slots, but much less unique, unexpected information.

The notion of surprise explains the vigorous impact of uniqueness on the individual (Bruner, 1986): "Surprise is a response to a violated presupposition. If what impinges on us conforms to expectancy, to the predicted state of the model, we may let our attention flag a little. . . . Let input violate expectancy and the system is put on alert" (p. 46).

Kuhn's (1970) paradigm shift speaks to this problem. A paradigm shift incorporates a vast amount of unique information that startles, confuses, and disrupts. We experience the tension between uniqueness and redundancy as the balance between anxiety and boredom. Our feelings play a critical role in motivating and directing our learning. Bruner refers to this as the affective threshold, which is explained in the Yerkes-Dodson Law, an established principle in psychology related to learning and motivation. The law states that: "The stronger the drive, up to a point, the faster learning will be. But beyond that point, increased drive will make an organism go out of control and will slow down learning. . . . The effect of too much drive is to create a state that disrupts or otherwise interferes with effective cognition" (Bruner, 1986, p. 111).

Bruner suggests that if we label this disruption "emotion" and use the concept to pursue the question of how cognition and emotion interact, the law suggests an economy of functioning based on a trade-off principle. "When need is high, the time given t o information processing declines and the depth of that processing declines. Preoccupation with the goal smothers occupation with the means to it" (Bruner, 1986, p. 113). The concept of an affective threshold sheds light on the complex interplay of thoughts, actions, and feelings in the process of construction.

Learning is not a simple, straightforward cognitive process of assimilating new information. Affective experience of uncertainty and confusion complicates the process. Bruner (1986) finds "linkages between emotion, arousal, drive on the one side and learning, problem solving, thinking on the other. Such linkages bear upon the question of how we construct and construe the worlds in which we operate" (p. 113).

Let us consider the tension between uniqueness and redundancy within the constructive models of Dewey and Kelly. In the early phases, when thoughts are vague and unfocused, the level of uniqueness would be expected to be high and redundancy low. At this point, it would be easy to exceed the affective threshold by introducing too much uniqueness. On the other hand, too much redundancy could result in lack of interest and boredom. The affective experience of the user is likely to have a profound effect on the process of construction.

Summary of the Constructive Process

These constructivists view learning as an active, engaging process in which all aspects of experience are called into play. We each construct our own personal worlds, which may or may not agree with those of others around us. The process of construction is dynamic and driven by feelings interacting with thoughts and actions. People commonly experience the process of construction in a series of phases or stages with distinct changes in feelings, thoughts, and actions.

Personal Construct Theory describes the experience of individuals involved in the process of constructing meaning from the information they encounter. New information is assimilated in a series of phases, beginning with confusion, which increases as inconsistencies and incompatibilities are confronted within the information itself and between the information and the constructs presently held. As confusion mounts, it frequently causes doubt in the validity of the new information. The disruption caused by the new idea may become so threatening that the new information is discarded and the construction abandoned. At this point, however, another alternative is to form a hypothesis that can be tested and assessed to move toward incorporating the new construct into the existing system of personally held constructs. Forming a tentative hypothesis is the critical turning point in construing and reconstruing.

Taken together the theories of Dewey, Kelly, and Bruner provide a vivid explanation of construction. Affective experience plays a significant role in directing cognition and action throughout the process of construction. There is a delicate balance between uniqueness and redundancy in the information encountered. An overwhelming intrusion of the new and unique may bring about feelings of uncertainty and anxiety on the one hand. A profusion of redundancy causes lack of interest and boredom on the other.

Thinking in the form of reflection is closely allied with acting throughout the process. Reflection leads to prediction, which is a key component of construction. A prediction is an anticipation of an outcome. The process is driven by a desire to make accurate predictions. The choices that people make and the actions that they take are based on the predictions they form from the constructs they hold.

Reflection also leads to formulation, another critical component of the constructive process. A tentative predictive formulation, called a hypothesis by all three theorists, moves the individual out of uncertainty by providing a direction or a guiding idea, to borrow Dewey's term. Changes in feelings are associated with formulation, bringing the three aspects of human experience into the constructive process. From a tentative formulation, individuals move beyond the information given to interpret and create something of their own. The process of construction incorporates a cycle of acting and reflecting, feeling and formulating, predicting and choosing, and interpreting and creating.

Kelly's Phases of Construction and Taylor's Levels of Information Need

By imposing Kelly's (1963) phases of construction on Taylor's (1968) levels of information need we can begin to visualize some elements of the constructive process, particularly the affective experience, that we may expect to observe in users' information-seeking behavior (see Table 2.6). The visceral level of need is an actual, but unexpressed, need for information, which may be only a vague sort of dissatisfaction. The earliest phase of construction is characterized as a confusing, perplexing reaction to a vague new idea. The conscious level of need is an ill-defined area of indecision, which may be expressed in an ambiguous, rambling statement. Kelly describes the state of confusion and doubt as continuing to mount until the person may become quite threatened by the lack of understanding. At the level of formal need the area of doubt may be described in concrete terms. Kelly states that a person can formulate a hypothesis, enabling him or her to break through the moment of threat to get on with the task of investigating the new idea. At the compromised level of need the person has translated his or her need into what the files can deliver in terms of the information system available. The final phases of construction are testing the hypothesis, assessing the results, and construing or reconstruing to assimilate the new idea. In this way, levels of information need may be thought of as a continuum within the process of construction.

Table 2.6. Comparison of Levels
of Need and Phases of Construction

Taylor—Levels of Need	Kelly—Phases of Construction
Visceral—Q1	Confusion and doubt
Conscious—Q2	Mounting confusion and possible threat
Formal—Q3	Hypothesis formulation
Compromised—Q4	Testing, assessing, reconstruing

Having summarized the borrowed theory and highlighted those aspects that seem particularly applicable to understanding the user's experience in information-seeking situations, succeeding chapters discuss empirically testing the borrowed theory in information-seeking situations. The following three chapters describe a series of studies of library users in actual information-seeking situations. The data gathered from the participants in these studies were analyzed within the frame of reference of the constructivist theory of learning summarized in this chapter. The findings of these studies provide the foundation for a grounded theory for library and information services articulated in later chapters.

3

The Information Search Process

Chapters 3 through 5 describe a series of five studies of library users in the process of seeking information for the completion of extensive projects. The studies were designed to observe people involved in information seeking over a period of time and to elicit their perceptions of what they were doing, thinking, and feeling in the process. Chapter 3 describes a small-scale qualitative study of high school seniors who were assigned research papers. A model of the information search process was developed from the common patterns that emerged within the context of the constructivist theory of learning. Chapter 4 describes two large-scale studies of library users to verify the model of the information search process. Chapter 5 describes further verification and expansion of the model in longitudinal studies of the same students who participated in the first study when they were at high school. Taken together these studies provide a basis for making the theoretical statement in the form of an uncertainty principle in Chapter 6 and further frameworks for designing practice in Chapters 7 and 8.

This research into the information search process grew out of three vantage points. First is the evidence in the literature of library and information science of the inadequacy of the bibliographic paradigm for addressing users' information problems, as discussed in Chapter 1; second is an understanding of learning as a constructive process as it might be applied to learning from access to information contained in libraries as discussed in Chapter 2; and third is the author's direct, professional experience as a librarian.

Direct personal experience as a practitioner was a critical element in understanding the basic problem for study. Students in the daily course of seeking information for the completion of assignments were observed experiencing great difficulty regardless of the topic of the assignment or their ability level. Under the bibliographic paradigm they should have been able to proceed in a straightforward manner, retrieving information from an organized collection of materials. Quite the contrary was the case. They were confused, anxious, and hurried, and frequently uninterested, annoyed, and frustrated. All of these are symptoms that any experienced teacher recognizes as potentially disruptive to the learning process. Why, after being given clear instructions on how to locate information and how to receive ample assistance in using sources as they proceeded, were students experiencing such negative feelings, particularly at the beginning of a project?

When these students' symptoms were placed within the context of the first and second vantage points, two basic questions occurred to this researcher. Is information seeking a process of construction in which students may expect to be confused and anxious? Is the bibliographic paradigm inadequate for mediation within the constructive process? Out of these speculations and reflections came the hypothesis that information seeking is a process of construction, with all the accompanying dynamic complexities.

To investigate this hypothesis, the author applied exploratory methods to reveal the process for study and analysis. The initial study was a qualitative exploration of the search process of twenty-five academically capable high school seniors (Kuhlthau, 1985a, 1988a).

Application of Methods in Library and Information Services

The methodology described in this chapter and the following two chapters was designed for empirical research and was intended to be applied and adapted in further research into information-seeking behavior. The development of this work offers an example of how theory may be built in a sequence of studies.

The methods may be utilized in developing a process approach to library and information services. There are two ways that these methods may be applied in library practice. One is as tools for action research. The methods and instruments described in this chapter provide ways of revealing the user's information search process and may be used in many different information settings for assessing and evaluating users' perspectives of services and their experience in the process of information seeking. In this way, these methods may be used as tools for assessing existing services and for identifying the need for a process approach as well as for measuring the effectiveness of process interventions.

Another use of the methods is as a means of developing self-awareness in users. As these methods open the process for the observation of the researcher they also reveal the process to the user. The methods may be applied and adapted as interventions with users that enable them to understand the information search process as a process of learning from having access to information. At various points in this discussion of methodology, ways to use particular methods as process interventions are noted.

A Qualitative Beginning

The initial study addressed the problem of understanding the user's experience in the process of seeking information. A number of research questions were addressed, but the primary ones were: Do users have common experiences in the process of information seeking that can be articulated and described? Do users' experiences resemble the phases in the process of construction?

The study was a qualitative exploration of students' experiences in completing assigned library research. Research methods were employed to seek the fullest description of the situation from the perspective of those directly involved; this foundation provided a base for grounded theory. Glaser and Strauss (1967) recommend the use of rigorous techniques to collect data that overlap and that offer multilayered descriptions providing an empirical basis for findings. In this way, an emerging theory was grounded in a real-life situation.

The study was conducted in a large, eastern, suburban high school with a group of twenty-five academically capable high school seniors (Kuhlthau, 1983). Academic capability was determined by standardized test scores above 90 percent, using national percentiles and grade point averages. The students selected were expected to be the most proficient in the high school population at using the library for completing research assignments. The objectives were to investigate the search process of *successful* students and to observe the strategies they used to work through the process. Subjects were chosen based on their ability and willingness to recall and discuss the library search process as they experienced it.

The students were studied in the natural setting of their school library media center. Two research papers were assigned in their English course, one each semester of the school year; they were given considerable latitude in selecting topics.

Instruments and methods were designed to reveal aspects of the search process that would otherwise be hidden from an observer. Developing methods for observing the search process was an important aspect of the initial study. Each method and instrument was assessed for its effectiveness in eliciting the user's perspective of the process of information seeking. The qualitative methods used were journals, search logs, short written statements, case study interviews and conceptual maps, and the teacher's assessment of focus in the students' papers. A questionnaire to elicit perceptions was the beginning of the development of more quantitative instruments.

Journals

The students kept journals during their progress in the first assignment in which they were asked to record their feelings as well as the thoughts and actions related to their library search. They were directed to record thoughts and conversations they had about their topics outside of the library, as well as within it. Students submitted the journals, together with their papers, at the completion of the assignment.

Journals gave students an opportunity to include personal content and what they considered to be important about their search without placing restrictions on the format or length of the entries. Although some students made fuller, more consistent entries than others, all recorded the progression of their thoughts and feelings. The students displayed highly individual styles in keeping their journals: Some consistently made descriptive entries, while others summarily recorded their actions or made only an occasional, incomplete entry. Many students made several entries at once rather than recording their search separately on each day. All journals reflected changes in student understanding of the topic from the time that they first selected that topic.

Search Logs

While working on the second assignment, students kept search logs in which they recorded the names of the sources they used; procedures for finding sources; and whether sources were useful, highly useful, or not useful (see Figure 3.1).

Topic: Transcendentalism & Emerson

Date	Title	Call No.	Located In	Not Useful	Somewhat Useful	Most Useful
3/3/82	B EME Ralph Waldo Emerson Portrait of a Balanced Soul AUTHOR Edward Wagenknecht PUBLISHER DATE Oxford University Press NY 1974		Public Library		X	
3/5/82	American Transcendentalism: An Anthology of Criticism Brian M. Barbour, ed. University of Notre Dame Press 1973 141 BAR		Media Center			X

Figure 3.1. Search Log.

Search logs were effective for tracking the sources used and for making relevance judgments as the search progressed. Unlike the unstructured writing of the journal, the search log did not offer an opportunity to include feelings. It did, however, provide data on the decisions made about the relevance of the sources consulted during a search, and the log offered another way of examining the progression of thoughts and actions. Further study is needed to develop and analyze the search log method. An interesting outcome was that some of the sources considered not useful early in the search were included in the bibliography of the papers. This may indicate a change in decision of relevancy as a search progresses, or it may simply be a result of padding the bibliography. Based on these findings, further research into decisions of relevance and pertinence at various points in a search is warranted. The responses on the search logs were charted to track patterns of choices made during the progress of the search. Patterns of "somewhat useful," "most useful," and "not useful" were expected to be evident. The results were inconclusive, but the method shows promise for further development.

Short Written Statements

Participants were asked to write a paragraph about their topic two weeks after the assignment was made and again after they had submitted their papers. It was assumed that the ability or inability to express a central idea in writing would indicate the state of their thinking about the topic. The method was analyzed for effectiveness in revealing the formulation of a focus.

Writing a paragraph about the topic at the middle and again at the end of the search proved effective for revealing the students' thoughts at a particular point. All of the students wrote a paragraph about their topic or focus in the two writing sessions. A change in all of their writings was apparent between the first and second writing. However, some had difficulty expressing a central theme or focus for their topic in the written statements even in the second session.

Case Studies

Although there is not a proliferation of case studies in library and information science research, there are substantial precedents for the use of the method. Some examples of case study research are Ford's (1986) study of psychological determinants of information needs of higher education students and Blackie and Smith's (1981) study of situational influences and constraints on undergraduate information seekers. Prentice (1980) presents case studies to describe information seeking of persons from various backgrounds. She summarizes differences and similarities in an approach not unlike the one reported in this work. Case study methods are becoming more prevalent in library and information science as researchers seek to gain insight into the user's perspective on information seeking. Vakkari and Serola's (2002) longitudinal case study of graduate students preparing a research proposal is an example.

Case studies offered an important, if not essential, way of collecting data on users' experiences, perceptions, and choices affecting the information search process. Interviews allowed subjects to explain their actions and to elaborate on perceptions and predictions that lie behind action. The students had an opportunity to tell how the search process works as they see it. Case studies provided a potential method for checking on the researcher's assumptions and findings in the realm of personal experience.

Six of the twenty-five students volunteered to be case study subjects to clarify and explain the data collected in the journals, logs, writings, and questionnaires of the total sample. Case studies provided in-depth insights into not only what was happening but also why it was. These subjects were interviewed in forty-five-minute taped sessions on separate occasions during completion of the two research assignments. The interviews were designed to examine the particular stage of the process that participants experienced at the time. The following are examples of the prompts and questions to which the students responded:

- Describe how you felt when the teacher announced the research assignment.

- Describe how and why you chose your topic.

- Describe any focus your topic has taken.

- Describe any choices you have made in your search that gave you just the information you were looking for, changed your mind about your topic, led you to new understanding, or gave you direction.

- How did you know when your search was completed?

- Describe the conclusion of your search and how you feel about your work.

- What did you find most difficult about your search?

Interviews were an exceedingly effective method for investigating the students' interpretations and explanations of what had occurred during the search process. Students were asked similar questions but were urged to elaborate on personal experiences. They were cooperative and willing to participate in these discussions during the six interviews. Their responses were analyzed for both individual approaches and common experiences.

Conceptual Maps

Two other methods, flowcharts and timelines as conceptual maps of the search process, were used to collect data on the six interview subjects. Concept mapping is the general term for the method of graphically depicting mental relationships, logic, or strategies. Flowcharting, widely used in systems analysis and programming, can be adapted as one technique for capturing a person's concept or mental map. In research on information use, flowcharting has been applied most frequently as a method of data analysis. Dervin, Jacobsen, and Nilan

(1982) used timelines as a research technique, and Taylor (1968), among others, employed flowcharting. In this study, however, flowcharts and timelines were used as methods of data collection since users diagrammed their own perceptions of the information search process.

At the end of the first assignment, the six students were asked to describe the progression of their search by drawing a timeline including all important decisions. They drew timelines, after having completed the research project, by referring to their journals to document particular dates and events. They were given a paper on which a horizontal line was drawn and told that the beginning of the line represented when they had received the assignment and the end when they began to write their paper. They were asked to fill in a timeline of what had taken place in the search that they had just completed.

At the end of the second assignment, they were asked to draw flowcharts of the process they had followed. The subjects were given instructions similar to those for the timeline. In this instance, however, the upper-left corner represented when they had received the assignment and the lower-right corner when they began to write their paper.

Timelines and flowcharts were ways of mapping and diagramming the progression of a search. All six interviewees identified a sequence of steps and strategies on the timelines and flowcharts. The timelines were analyzed for revealing stages in the search process and the evolution of the topic. The flowcharts were analyzed for patterns of prediction and choice in the search and evidence of a process taking place.

Teachers' Assessment

At the end of each assignment, in addition to assigning a grade, the teacher characterized each student paper as having a vague, general, or clear focus. It was assumed that those students who understood the process in which they were involved and knew strategies for using the library to work through the search process would have clearly focused papers.

Perceptions Questionnaire

The perceptions questionnaire was an early attempt at developing a quantitative instrument to elicit users' perceptions of information seeking in libraries. Perceptions are difficult to observe and are not normally seen by merely watching individuals while they use a library. The development of a questionnaire to elicit perceptions of users was an important aspect of the study. Rather than testing knowledge of sources, a method was sought to identify perceptions of the process of a search that would influence the way that students approach a search. A questionnaire was designed to examine students' perceptions of six areas of library use: general library use, topic selection, research assignments, focus formulation, procedures for gathering information, and role of mediators. Thirty statements were developed in the areas of library use under investigation and were intermixed on a questionnaire, using a 5-point Likert scale, with 5 being "almost always" and 1 becoming "almost never" (see Table 3.1, p. 36).

Table 3.1. Perceptions Questionnaire I

		Almost Always	Often	Sometimes	Seldom	Almost Never
1.	I use more than one library to research a topic.					
2.	I prefer research topics suggested by the teacher.					
3.	I use the library to gather information on my own, not connected to an assignment by a teacher.					
4.	I use more that two libraries to research a topic.					
5.	I prefer research topics that I choose myself.					
6.	I get help from a teacher when choosing a research topic.					
7.	When researching a topic I need the librarian's assistance.					
8.	I talk to others about possible topics before making a final choice of a research topic.					
9.	The card catalog is the first place I check when researching a topic.					
10.	I try to select a topic that relates to another paper I have written.					
11.	My teacher helps me to gather information.					
12.	I talk to others about my topic.					
13.	I use reference books when gathering information about a topic.					
14.	I select a topic that I know little about.					
15.	I have difficulty finding information on a topic.					
16.	I spend free time in the library.					
17.	I become more interested in a topic as I gather information.					
18.	I use periodicals when researching a topic.					
19.	I have difficulty selecting a topic for a research paper.					
20.	A central theme evolves as I gather information on a topic.					
21.	I use indexes in the back of books to find information on a topic.					
22.	When I first choose a topic I have a clear idea about what I will find and write about.					
23.	Research assignments add to what I learn in a course.					
24.	Researching a topic takes more time than I anticipate.					
25.	When selecting and developing a research topic I use information from television.					
26.	My topic changes as I gather information about it.					
27.	I change my topic according to the materials that are available.					
28.	I ask a librarian for help before I have chosen my topic.					
29.	I use the library when I want to select books to read.					
30.	I ask a librarian for assistance after I have chosen a research topic.					

The questionnaire was analyzed for ease of administering, students' willingness to participate, time for administering, and effectiveness for revealing perceptions of the group as well as those of individuals.

The questionnaire took approximately twelve minutes to administer, with students completing their responses in six to ten minutes and the instructions given in approximately two minutes. The questions were easily understood and able to be answered without undue deliberation. The scale was appropriate for the content and type of questions that the students were asked. The questionnaire was suitable for surveying a group of students. The responses indicated students' impressions, which provided the basis for making inferences about the perceptions they held.

Analysis of Qualitative Data

The objective of analyzing the collected data was to test the constructivist approach to learning within the information-seeking activity of students in the process of doing library research. Evidence was sought to support the theoretical assumption that students' experiences in the search process would match those in the phases of construction and document similar accompanying feelings.

The students' experiences in the assigned library research were analyzed to develop a model of the stages of the search process that they completed; these stages included feelings, thoughts, and actions. Content analysis was used with categories derived from the theory base, particularly Kelly's phases of construction. The search was thought of as a process with a beginning, middle, and end. The students' descriptions of the beginning of a search were grouped together, as were their descriptions of the middle and the end of a search. The data collected were analyzed to discover patterns of common experience at particular points in a search.

A description of the search process was sought through the data collected from the application of the methods designed in the study. The students' journals, search logs, and writings as well as the case study subjects' interviews, timelines, and flowcharts were examined for evidence of stages in the search process and the characteristics that might be common to each stage. Six categories of characteristics were sought for each stage: task, thoughts, feelings, actions, strategies, and mood.

The task of each stage in the search process was analyzed as the students commonly interpreted the task. The tasks were identified within the process of accomplishing the ultimate goal of writing a research paper.

The thoughts and feelings that accompany the action of the search for information were examined. Whereas source or system orientation of library use would concentrate on the actions of a library search, process or user orientation needs to consider the thoughts and feelings that prompt actions. Thoughts and feelings that were commonly experienced were sought within the stages of the search process.

Students' expressions of their thoughts were examined to determine their state of understanding of the topic under investigation and to discover evidence of developing clarity and focus. The feelings that accompany the search process were analyzed within the frame of reference of Kelly's phases of construction: confusion and doubt, threat, hypothesis formulation, testing and assessing, and reconstruing. The actions of each stage were examined for the underlying predictions and choices made by students that determined the direction of their actions. Students' choices were analyzed within Kelly's categories of choices for extension and for definition to determine if either type were characteristic of specific stages in the process. Evidence of choices that were particularly significant or had an "elaborative effect" on the search was sought.

The function of a focus as an elaborative choice in the process was an important consideration in the study. The focus in the search process was expected to parallel the role of the hypothesis in the phases of construction. As the hypothesis was crucial to the phases of construction, the user's perception that a focus must be formed within the search process was considered as a critical element for moving the search to completion. The descriptions of the middle of the search were analyzed for evidence of a turning point, as were the teacher's assessment of a focus in the students' papers.

Evidence of the presence of an invitational mood or an indicative mood was sought as indication of how attitude and stance might affect the search process. Characteristics of the search process were sought to develop a model of the process that would demonstrate the common experience of users.

Patterns in the Constructive
Process of Information Seeking

Common patterns in the experience of this small, specialized group of library users were noted where they were articulated and could be documented. Although the pace of a search varied among individuals, certain aspects in the experience and the sequence remained relatively constant. Six stages in the search process were identified from the students' description of their experience; these stages match the phases in the process of construction. The following is a description of the patterns noted in students' experiences, are illustrated by some of their comments.

The first stage was task initiation. When the students received the assignment, they expressed feelings of uncertainty and apprehension. They needed to prepare for the decision of selecting a topic by understanding the assignment and relating it to prior experience. One student revealed, "When I first hear about an assignment, personally I just get upset." Another person described feeling "a spontaneous kind of fear." A student noted this to be a common experience among fellow students: "In the real beginning I guess I was like everyone else. I didn't know what I wanted to do. . . . I felt anxious."

The uncertainty continued until a topic was selected; this was identified as the second stage of the process. If a topic was not chosen quickly, apprehension increased: "I felt anxious when I didn't have a topic. I was upset because even though I knew that the paper was due a long way off, everybody else seemed to be working and I wasn't," explained one student. When a topic had been selected, a sudden feeling of optimism was commonly expressed: "Once I have my topic I usually feel a great deal better and the idea of a research paper doesn't seem so cumbersome."

The third stage involved exploring information on the general topic to gain a focus. For many of the students this was the most difficult stage of the process. As they found information on their topics they frequently became confused by the inconsistency and incompatibility they encountered, which is the reaction the theory of construction would anticipate. One student declared, "I was so confused up until the 25th. I had no idea what direction I was going in." As another person recalled, "I felt kind of blind because I didn't know what I was looking for." A third student said, "It seemed there was so much to do, it really scared me."

For some, the confusion became so threatening that they wanted to drop their topic at this point. "I went to look for a total change because I was really sick of it, the whole Elizabethan period. I had trouble with it; I was sick of it; I didn't want to do it anymore." The inclination to turn back and to abandon the quest at this point is also an expected reaction, according to the constructivist theory of learning.

Focus formulation is identified as the fourth stage. For many students this was the turning point in their research. The following example, from a student's journal, traces the thinking underlying focus formulation.

11/5: Decided to do a critical analysis of Mark Twain's Huck Finn.

11/8: Hope to find the theme that caused Huck Finn to be banned.

11/11: How Mark Twain's life in Mississippi affected his writings.

11/23: In the book were real events in Sam Clemens' life. I took great interest in the Colonel Sherburn chapters.

11/29: I am definitely doing Colonel Sherburn.

[The next journal entry described her feelings.]

OPTIMISM—I might be able to do this paper by Christmas.

The focus gave direction to the library search, and students expressed more confidence once they had reached this point: "I felt relieved: it makes things a lot easier once you have a basis for where you are going."

When students did not form a focus during the search process, they commonly experienced difficulty throughout the remainder of the assignment. One student elaborated on the difficulty that she had experienced:

I had a general idea not a specific focus, but an idea. As I was writing, I didn't know what my focus was. My teacher says she doesn't know what my focus was. I don't think I ever acquired a focus. It was an impossible paper to write. I would just sit there and say, "I'm stuck." There was no outline because there was nothing to complete. If I learned anything from that paper it is, you have to have a focus. You have to have something to center on. You can't just have a topic. You should have an idea when you start. I had a topic but I didn't know what I wanted to do with it. I figured that when I did my research it would focus in. But I didn't let it. I kept saying, "This is interesting and this is interesting and I'll just smush it all together." "It didn't work out."

A clear focus needed to be formed at this stage in the search process to enable students to progress to the next stage, as a hypothesis moves along a process of construction.

The fifth stage involved collecting information on the focus. Students described a sense of direction and feelings of confidence. As one student explained, "On December 9, I got my main focus. Before this I did basic research. After I got my focus, I got all of my sources to support the focus I had found." Another person declared, "After you know exactly what you are going to do it on, the research is easy."

Many students reported that their interest increased at this stage. As one student noted, "I sat down . . . and became totally interested in what I was reading." Another student added, "I didn't find this boring. I have senioritis and really didn't feel like doing it, but it was interesting what I found."

The last stage was the conclusion of the search process and the starting phase of the writing process. Students revealed different reasons for closing a search. Some ended when they encountered diminishing relevance: "You get what you want and then afterwards start getting off the topic a little." Another consideration was redundancy. "In the end you are just looking for extra things so you're sure you have everything. But it's a lot of repetition." Some concluded the search when they felt they had put forth sufficient effort. "After digging through five floors of books I said, 'This is good enough. I've done a good enough job. The material I've gotten is sufficient.' " Students were aware of time constraints and closed the search near the date the assignment was due.

An Emerging Model

The study proposed a new model for the process of information seeking encompassing the development of thoughts about a topic, the feelings that typically accompany such an evolution of thinking, and the actions of seeking and using sources. The task of each stage was categorized along with the feelings, thoughts, actions, and helpful strategies, as well as the mood found to be most productive.

The overall task was to form a perspective on the topic from the information encountered and to locate, interpret, and present information on the focused topic. Students attempted to understand the task at the onset of the assignment, but they frequently concentrated on the mechanics, such as number of pages and sources, and the format of paper and citations rather than the intellectual task of selecting a topic and forming a focus for their search. This indication of a conflict related to task became a major finding in the later studies reported in Chapters 4 and 5.

Within the search process thoughts evolved from unclear, vague uncertainty to clearer, more focused understanding, or in Belkin's (1980) terms from an anomalous state of knowledge to specificity. A series of phases or stages were evident, as predicted by the models of construction (Kelly, 1963), of reflective thinking (Dewey, 1933), and of the interpretive task (Bruner, 1986). Information need emerged through levels, as described by Taylor (1962, 1968).

An important finding was the sequence of feelings commonly experienced during the search. Students' feelings about themselves, the library, the task, and the topic evolved as their understanding of their topic deepened. The feelings that students described were predictable from Kelly's phases of construction. At the beginning of a search, evidence of uncertainty, confusion, and apprehension was evident. Indications of increasing rather than decreasing uncertainty were noted as the search progressed. In the middle of the search evidence of a sense of clarity was documented as a focus was formed. With the focus, a sense of direction and confidence was common, and that sense increased toward the end of the search.

As anticipated, the formulation of a focus was the turning point of students' feelings about their work. Before the focus was formed, they commonly felt confused and anxious. After the focus was formed, they felt more confident and had a sense of direction. In this way the focus served as an "elaborative choice" or a decision that advanced the process in a significant way. The focus served the same function as a hypothesis during the phases of construction, a step that a person takes to move out of the phase of confusion and on to the task of construing. The formulation of a focus provided a guiding idea or central theme that gave a direction to pursue on which the information seeking was centered.

The actions taken in the search also changed with the formulation of a focus. In the early stages students sought relevant information related to a general topic. After gaining the focus they sought pertinent information related to the focused topic. The concept of relevance and pertinence was adopted from Saracevic (1975). Relevance is a determination that information relates to or applies to the matter at hand and has a connection or fits with the topic under investigation. Relevant information has some bearing on the research topic and is considered useful in a search for information. Irrelevance is a determination that information does not fit or connect and does not contribute to understanding. Irrelevant information is outside of the boundaries of a topic and is considered not useful in a search for information.

Pertinence is a determination that information has a more decisive and significant relationship to a topic than relevance and is related to personal information need. Pertinent information is to the point and contributes to understanding or the solution of a problem. Pertinence is the determination that information is germane to the focus of a research topic and is considered most useful in a search for information.

The attitude or mood found to be most productive for each stage was identified in the study. The terms *invitational* and *indicative* were adopted from Kelly's Personal Construct Theory. Invitational mood would foster an open search, one ready to take in new information. An indicative mood would foster an approach seeking closure. A mood indicates the way that a person approaches a task or event. The invitational mood leaves the person open to new ideas and receptive to change and adjustment according to what is encountered. In the indicative mood a person depends on the construct that he or she presently holds and rejects new information and ideas. The indicative mood directs the person toward closure and is the opposite of the invitational mood. An invitational mood is compatible with the early stages of the search process, and opens up extending strategies. Extension is a type of choice that leads to new information and ideas. An indicative mood was revealed as compatible with later stages of the search process leading to defining strategies. Definition is a type of choice that refines an existing idea.

Criteria for Making Decisions

There were two major decision points during the search process: topic selection and focus formulation. Students use four criteria for making decisions about topic and focus: personal interest, assignment requirements, information available, and time allotted. They considered these criteria in terms of the perceptions that they held from former experience, and they predicted the outcome of each possible choice. Although their use of perceptions and prediction was not overt, when asked to explain their choices, they described reasoning based on the four criteria.

Personal interest arose from some familiarity with the topic, and interest increased after the search was well underway. Determining personal interest in a general topic at the beginning of a search appeared difficult. Students relied on hunches and vague notions: "I read something about that once." "I saw something on TV." As constructs about the topic were formed during the search process, interest intensified. The issue of interest and intellectual engagement was critical to students' approaches to the search process.

Assignment requirements are the parameters set by the teacher. At the beginning, questions of mechanics—how much and in what form—often deflected the more intellectual questions leading to construction and personal learning. The assignment was the overarching task that framed the search process, from the earliest announcement to the end of applying the findings to accomplish the task.

The information available became a critical element in decisions of topic and focus. Students considered the convenience of using information at hand and often accommodated their choices accordingly. The limitation of one all-purpose, comprehensive search became apparent for meeting the information needs emerging in the process.

The time allotted was an important element throughout the search process but became a predominant factor in the later stages. Students made miscalculations about the amount of time needed for each stage of the process, usually underestimating the time required. They frequently used the negative term *procrastination* to describe their sense of inaction during the early formative stages.

Strategies, Expectations, and Attitudes

A strategy is a tactic used to seek information or to work through a stage of the search process. Talking to a friend about a possible focus is a strategy, as well as consulting general sources before seeking specific materials. The strategies of talking, writing, and thinking seemed to be as important to students as the actual sources and formal search strategies that they used. Students used talking as a strategy to assist them in making decisions in their search process. Discussing the topic was an important strategy in the early stages of the process. They frequently involved informal mediators in this way.

A mediator is a person who intervenes in the search process of another. There are informal mediators, such as friends and family, and formal mediators, such as librarians and teachers. Formal mediators hold a professional position in which they are responsible for intervention, such as reference assistance or planned instruction. The study revealed a limited role for formal mediators; that role primarily centered on locating sources in the library collection. Several students expressed a desire for intervention in the process of their search and some frustration with the guidance received from formal mediators that did not go beyond location.

Students' expectations of the search process frequently did not match the process they were experiencing during the study. They did not expect to encounter uncertainty in the early stages and did not have a clear understanding of a sequence of tasks within the search process. The methods used to reveal the process for study helped students become aware of their own process and to discover that their experiences were common to other students. As one commented,

"It helped to know that others were having trouble, too." Tolerating uncertainty and intentionally seeking a focus were strategies that students found to be particularly helpful in the process.

Model of the Information Search Process

The model of the information search process incorporates three realms: the affective (feelings), the cognitive (thoughts), and the physical (actions) common to each stage. The task considered most appropriate to move the process on to the subsequent stage is also included as well as some strategies that students used. Following is a description of the six stages of the search process as revealed in the findings of the initial study (see Figure 3.2).

Stage 1: Task Initiation

The first stage is task initiation, when a person first recognizes that information will be needed to complete the assignment (see Table 3.2). When, for example, students first receive an assignment, they typically express feelings of uncertainty and apprehension. They think over the assignment to comprehend the task before them, to recall previous projects in which they have gathered information, and to identify possible alternative general topics. Actions frequently involve discussing possible topics and approaches.

Table 3.2. First Stage of the Search Process—Task Initiation

TASK	THOUGHTS	FEELINGS	ACTIONS	STRATEGIES	MOOD
Stage 1—Task Initiation					
To prepare for the decision of selecting a topic	Contemplating assignment Comprehending task Relating prior experience and learning Considering possible topics	Apprehension at work ahead Uncertainty	Talking with others Browsing library collection	Brainstorming Discussing Contemplating possible topics Tolerating uncertainty	Primarily invitational

Stages	Task Initiation	Topic Selection	Prefocus Exploration	Focus Formulation	Information Collection	Search Closure	Starting Writing
Feelings	uncertainty	optimism	confusion, frustration, doubt	clarity	sense of direction/ confidence	relief	satisfaction or dissatisfaction
Thoughts	ambiguity -> specificity						
				Increase interest			
Actions		seeking relevant information -> seeking pertinent information					

Figure 3.2. Initial Model of the Information Search Process.

Stage 2: Topic Selection

Feelings of uncertainty continue until the second stage of the process, when a general topic is selected (see Table 3.3). During topic selection, the task is to identify and select the general topic to be investigated and the approach to be pursued. Feelings of uncertainty often give way to optimism after the selection has been made, and there is a readiness to begin the search. Thoughts center on weighing prospective topics against the criteria of personal interest, assignment requirements, information available, and time allotted. The outcome of each possible choice is predicted, and the topic judged to have the greatest potential for success is selected. During this stage, actions may include making a preliminary search of information available, skimming and scanning for an overview of alternative topics, and talking to others about possibilities. When, for whatever reason, selection is delayed or postponed, feelings of anxiety are likely to intensify until the choice is made.

Table 3.3. Second Stage of the Search Process—Topic Selection

TASK	THOUGHTS	FEELINGS	ACTIONS	STRATEGIES	MOOD
Stage 2—Topic Selection					
To decide on topic for research	Weighing topics against criteria of personal interest, project requirements, information available, and time allotted Predicting outcome of possible choices Choosing topic with potential success	Confusion Sometimes anxiety Brief elation after selection Anticipation of prospective task	Consulting with informational mediators Making preliminary search of library Using reference collection	Discussing possible topics Predicting outcome of choices Using general sources for overview of possible topics	Primarily indicative

Stage 3: Prefocus Exploration

A third stage, prefocus exploration, is characterized by feelings of confusion, uncertainty, and doubt, which frequently increase during this time (see Table 3.4). For many students, this is the most difficult stage in the process. The task is to investigate information on the general topic to extend personal understanding and to form a focus. Thoughts center on becoming oriented and sufficiently informed about the topic to form a focus or a personal point of view.

Table 3.4. Third Stage of the Search Process—Prefocus Exploration

TASK	THOUGHTS	FEELINGS	ACTIONS	STRATEGIES	MOOD
Stage 3—Prefocus Exploration					
To investigate information with the intent of finding a focus	Becoming informed about general topic Seeking focus on information on general topic Identifying several possible focuses Inability to express precise information needed	Confusion Doubt Sometimes threat Uncertainty	Locating relevant information Reading to become informed Taking notes on facts and ideas Making bibliographic citations	Reading to learn about topic Tolerating inconsistency and incompatibility of information encountered Intentionally seeking possible focuses Listing descriptors	Primarily invitational

Information encountered rarely fits smoothly with previously held constructs, and information from different sources commonly seems inconsistent and incompatible. Users may find the situation quite discouraging and threatening, causing a sense of personal inadequacy as well as frustration with the system. Some actually may be inclined to abandon the search altogether at this stage. An inability to express precisely what information is needed makes communication between the user and the system awkward. Actions involve locating information about the general topic, reading to become informed, and relating new information to what is already known. Invitational strategies that open opportunities for extending constructs (e.g., listing facts that seem particularly pertinent and reflecting on engaging ideas) may be most helpful during this time. Strategies that foster an indicative rather than an invitational mood, such as taking detailed notes, may thwart the process by stressing premature closure.

Stage 4: Focus Formulation

Focus formulation, the fourth stage, is for many the turning point of the search process, when feelings of uncertainty diminish and confidence increases (see Table 3.5). The task is to form a focus from the information encountered. Thoughts involve identifying and selecting ideas in the information from which to form a focused perspective of the topic. The success of possible concentrations is predicted within the criteria of personal interest, assignment requirements, information available, and time allotted. Strategies for choosing a specific concentration within the general topic are reading over notes for themes and reflecting, talking, and writing about themes and ideas. The topic becomes more personalized during this stage if construction occurs. Although a focus may be formed in a sudden moment of insight, it is more likely to emerge gradually as constructs become clearer. During this time, a change in feelings is commonly noted, with indications of increased confidence and a sense of clarity. When individuals do not form a focus during the search process, they commonly experience difficulty throughout the remainder of the search and when they begin to write or present findings. A clear focus enables a person to move on to the next stage, just as a hypothesis initiates testing in the process of construction.

Table 3.5. Fourth Stage of the Search Process—Focus Formulation

TASK	THOUGHTS	FEELINGS	ACTIONS	STRATEGIES	MOOD
Stage 4—Focus Formulation					
To formulate a focus from the information encountered	Predicting outcome of possible foci using criteria of personal interest, requirements of assignment, availability of materials, and time allotted Identifying ideas in information from which to formulate focus Sometimes characterized by a sudden moment of insight	Optimism Confidence in ability to complete task	Reading notes for themes	Making a survey of notes Listing possible foci Choosing a particular focus while discarding others Combining several themes to form one focus	Primarily indicative

Stage 5: Information Collection

Information collection is the fifth stage in the process, when interaction between the user and the information system functions most effectively and efficiently (see Table 3.6). At this point, the task is to gather information pertaining to the focused topic. Thoughts center on defining and supporting the focus. Actions involve selecting information pertinent to the student's focus and taking detailed notes on that which pertains specifically to the focus, as general information on the topic is no longer relevant after formulation. The user, with a clearer sense of direction, can specify the need for relevant, focused information to librarians and systems, thereby facilitating a comprehensive search of all available resources. Feelings of confidence continue to increase as uncertainty subsides, with interest in the project deepening.

Table 3.6. Fifth Stage of the Search Process—Information Collection

TASK	THOUGHTS	FEELINGS	ACTIONS	STRATEGIES	MOOD
Stage 5—Information Collection					
To gather information that defines, extends, and supports the focus	Seeking information to support focus Defining and extending focus through information Gathering pertinent information Organizing information in notes	Realization of extensive work to be done Confidence in ability to complete task Increased interest	Using library to collect pertinent information Requesting specific sources from librarian Taking detailed notes with bibliographic citations	Using descriptors to search out pertinent information Making comprehensive search of various types of materials, i.e., reference, periodicals, nonfiction, and biography Using indexes Requesting assistance of librarian	Combination of indicative and invitational

Stage 6: Search Closure

In search closure, the last stage in the search process, feelings of relief are common. There is a sense of satisfaction if the search has gone well or disappointment if it has not (see Table 3.7). The task is to complete the search and to prepare to present or otherwise use the findings. Thoughts concentrate on culminating the search with a personalized synthesis of the topic or problem. Actions involve a summary search to recheck information that may have been initially overlooked.

People reveal different reasons for closing a search. Some stop when they encounter diminishing relevance or evidence of redundancy, while others conclude the search when they feel they have put forth "sufficient" effort. Assuming a deadline, many people cease collecting information, not because they have exhausted the available sources but because they need time to synthesize and prepare their final "product" before the due date. Organizing strategies, such as outlining, for preparing to present or otherwise use the information, are applied.

Table 3.7. Sixth Stage of the Search Process—Search Closure

TASK	THOUGHTS	FEELINGS	ACTIONS	STRATEGIES	MOOD
Stage 6—Search Closure					
To conclude search for information	Identifying need for any additional information Considering time limit Diminishing relevance Increasing redundancy Exhausting resources	Sense of relief Sometimes satisfaction Sometimes disappointment	Rechecking sources for information initially overlooked Confirming information and bibliographic citations	Returning to library to make summary search Keeping books until completion of writing to recheck information	Indicative

The results of the initial study of the small sample of library users suggested that affective symptoms associated with construct building may be a natural part of the information search process and commonly experienced by users. This study provided a window into the user's experience within the search process and offered an in-depth description of a new problem by providing many layers of data collected over an extended period of time for the purpose of developing a grounded theory. The research hypotheses and process model generated in this study required testing using quantitative methods on a larger, more diverse sample of library users in different information environments to validate and generalize the findings.

Assessing the Process

Assessment is a time of reflection after the search process has been completed and the assignment accomplished. With the students this was an important element for developing their own sense of competence in the search process. The reflection of students about what had taken place during the process and their expectations of the next time they encounter a similar task revealed their sense of process. Students were asked to assess their use of time, sources, and the librarian during their search process. This task increased their self-awareness of the stages in the process. Students were often surprised to discover stages in their search process. One student explained, "Well I guess there are three phases. . . . I never realized that I did this. I never realized I did all the work in three phases. I just thought I did all of the work the last minute and did my report." There is some question whether this is a separate stage of the search process or part of the sixth stage. In *Teaching the Library Research Process* (Kuhlthau, 1985b), a seventh stage, "assessing the process" is included as a separate stage. In this text some aspects of assessment are incorporated in the sixth stage.

Summary of Major Findings

This chapter has presented a model of information seeking derived from an intensive study of a group of high school seniors. The model describes the information search process from the user's perspective as being experienced in six stages of thoughts, feelings, and actions. The model is presented in two forms: Figure 3.2, which depicts the entire process from initiation to closure, and Tables 3.2 to 3.7, which describe each stage in the process. In the tables, the task most appropriate to move the process along is identified for each stage, as well as thoughts, feelings, action, strategies, and mood.

The major finding in this study is that the patterns of experience of these information users matched those described in the process of construction. The main contribution is the articulation of information seeking as a process of construction in the form of a model.

Several problems related to information provision began to surface in this study. One is a conflict between students' understanding of their task in information seeking and their actual experience in the process of information seeking. In many cases their expectations of the process and the tasks did not match their experience. Uncertainty and the more formulative task of the early stages were frequently met with impatience and a sense of inadequacy. An expectation of uncertainty at the beginning of the process was needed for tolerating uncertainty and assuming the task of intentionally seeking a focus to guide the search. An additional problem was students' limited perception of librarians as merely locators of sources. Such a perception was inadequate to mediate in the dynamic process of the search. The model of the information search process needed to be verified in a larger, more diverse sample of library users. The next chapter describes two large-scale studies conducted after the model had emerged from the initial study.

4

Verification of the Model of the Information Search Process

The results of the initial study of the small sample of library users, as described in Chapter 3, suggested that thoughts and feelings associated with construct building may be commonly experienced by users in the information search process. The research hypothesis and process model, however, required further study to validate and generalize the model. Two studies were conducted using quantitative methods on a larger, more diverse sample of library users in different information environments.

The Information Search Process model depicts information seeking as occurring in six stages with patterns of thoughts, feelings, and actions commonly experienced by user's involved in extensive information problems. The general research question for further verification was: Does the model of the information search process hold for a large, diverse sample of library users? The model was based on the finding that uncertainty, a natural and necessary aspect of the early stages of the search process, causes discomfort and anxiety that, in turn, affect articulation of a problem, choices made within a search, and actions taken toward addressing an information need.

Hypothesis for Further Study: A Model

Testable hypotheses were generated in the qualitative study in the form of a model of the information search process in six stages. Chapter 3 describes the findings of the initial study and the model developed from the findings. Chapters 4 and 5 discuss the findings of the subsequent four studies in the sequence that verified and refined the model.

Two approaches were taken to verify the findings of the exploratory study. One was a large-scale approach using a more diversified sample; the other was a longitudinal approach using the original sample. In the large-scale approach a diverse sample of high school students was studied as well as library users in academic and public libraries. In the longitudinal approach, the same panel of library users in the initial study was studied four years later. By combining the two verification approaches, using both quantitative and qualitative methods, general and in-depth results were obtained.

Large-Scale Verification

The verification studies were designed to collect data on the thoughts, feelings, and actions of library users in the process of an extended search for information. Although the data had certain qualitative characteristics, quantitative analysis was required for verification. Two methods were applied for preparing the data for analysis. One was that nominal-level data were treated as ordinal, assumed-level data to perform statistical measures. The other was that open-ended responses were coded into categorical data for statistical analysis.

Study of Diverse Sample of High School Seniors

Research Question: Do low- and middle-level high school seniors and other high-achieving seniors experience the information search process as described in the model?

Six high schools in New Jersey representing a diverse population were selected as sites for the study. Low- , middle- , and high-achieving seniors in homogeneously grouped English classes were selected on the basis of their grade-point averages and national percentile scores on a standardized test. There were 147 participants: 34 in the group were identified as high achievers, 73 as middle college-bound, and 40 as lower-level achievers.

Each participant was assigned an English paper requiring library research on a topic of the student's choice related to the course. The paper was limited to five pages, but the number and variety of sources were not specified. The project was to be completed in four weeks, during which time the librarians taught five predesigned instructional sessions on the search process taken from *Teaching the Library Research Process* (Kuhlthau, 1985b).

Instrument for Large-Scale Study: Process Surveys

The process surveys were designed to elicit cognitive and affective aspects of the information search process, as the journal, search log, and written statements had in the initial study. The instrument was intended to collect data from a large sample that could be analyzed and compared. The objective was to elicit experience in terms of thoughts, feelings, and actions at the beginning, middle, and end of the search process.

The surveys were made up of five questions, the first four related to thoughts (name the source you are using; what you are looking for; state the title of your project; what your topic is about) and the last two related to feelings (rate your confidence level using a scale of 1 as low to 10 as high, and write three adjectives describing how you feel). The librarians at each site administered a process survey at three points, at the beginning (initiation), in the middle (midpoint), and toward the end (closure).

Responses to the questions related to thoughts were coded by two coders as follows: 1 for general or background thoughts, 2 for more specific ideas or narrowing of the general topic, and 3 for a focused perspective of a personal point of view. A "Thoughts Index" was derived from a simple additive of nominal data treated as an assumed interval scale, with aggregate scores that ranged from 4 minimum to 12 maximum. The aggregate scores were then tested for significant change at the three points in the search process.

From the responses to the questions related to feelings, an interval confidence scale, ranging from 1 as low to 10 as high, was devised. The confidence level was compared at the three points in the search process to determine significant changes, as were the adjectives listed by participants to describe their feelings.

In addition, the teachers assessed each student paper for evidence of focus on a scale of 1 as low to 10 as high, and listed the number and variety of sources cited in the bibliography. The grades given to the papers by the teachers were also collected. Changes in confidence level as found in the process surveys were then compared to the teachers' assessments to determine if there were correlations.

Statistical analysis was made by using t-tests and analysis of variance (ANOVA) to determine significance, and Pearson product-moment measures to determine degree of correlation and measures of linear regression.

Results of Study of the Search Process of a Larger Sample of High School Seniors

The model that had been developed in a small sample of academically competent high school library users was tested in a larger sample of more academically diverse high school students. The study examined the information search process of high-, middle-, and low-achieving high school seniors (Kuhlthau, 1989) to verify the model. Three questions were addressed, two related to verifying the model and the other investigating a further issue of outcome or relation of process to product: Do other high achievers experience a process similar to those in the initial sample? Do low- and middle-level students experience a similar process? Does the search process relate to the teacher's assessment of the product?

Participants were 147 seniors, in English classes in six high schools, who were identified as high, average, and low achievers. A research paper assignment of four weeks' duration was made. Process surveys were administered at three points in the search process—initiation, midpoint, and closure—eliciting thoughts and feelings at each point. Teachers assessed the students' papers for presence of focus, quantity of sources, and normal grading. The data from forty participants identified as low achievers were incomplete and could not be analyzed in the study. There was no significant difference, however, between the high and middle achievers, with the exception of grade; the high achievers received higher grades

High- and middle-achieving high school participants showed a significant change in thoughts, during completion of the search process, moving from general background, to specific and more narrowed, to clearer and more focused. There was a similar significant difference in their confidence and feelings during the process, with confidence increasing throughout and feelings moving from confused to confident and relieved.

Participants' thoughts changed during the search process, from general and background at initiation with a mean of 5.89, to specific and narrowed at midpoint with a mean of 7.20, to clearer and focused at closure with a mean of 8.52. A single-tailed t-test showed significant differences in means from initiation to midpoint and midpoint to closure at $p < .001$. In a similar way, students' feelings changed during the search process. At initiation they reported a mean confidence level at 5.37, which increased only slightly at midpoint to 5.70, but increased significantly at closure to 6.83. Although the change is not as pronounced as that of thoughts, there was a substantial gain in the confidence of the students from initiation to closure. Figure 4.1 shows that the change in thoughts parallels a rise in confidence from initiation to midpoint to closure during the search process.

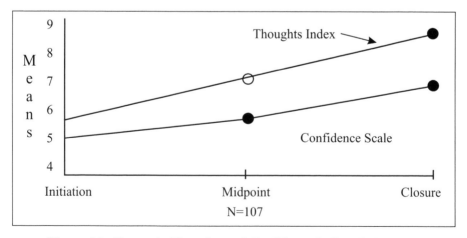

Figure 4.1. Change in Thoughts and Confidence in Search Process.

Relation of Changes in Confidence and Outcome of Search

There was some evidence of relationship between changes in feelings during the search process and the outcome of the search. Slight correlation was noted between increase in confidence and the teachers' assessment of focus in the papers, and the grade on the papers. There was, however, no correlation between increased confidence and the quantity and variety of the sources used in the papers. According to the model, an increase in confidence corresponds to an increase in clarity and focus in thoughts, and may also correspond to evidence of construction. Correlation between increased confidence and the quality of student papers indicates that there may be a connection between process and outcome, an important issue that warrants further investigation. On the other hand, within the context of the model of the search process, the quantity and variety of sources used may not necessarily indicate construction, that is, clarification of thoughts. Lack of correlation between the number of sources used and the teachers' assessment of focus in the students' papers, although not surprising within the context of this research, does not support the traditional view of information use within the bibliographic paradigm. This research questions the assumption that sources of information equate construction and learning.

These findings verify the model of the search process with high- and middle-level seniors. Information seeking is a complex learning process that involves finding meaning. Thoughts evolve, feelings change, and confidence rises as a search progresses.

Major Findings and Implications

The main finding of this study of high school seniors was that information seeking of college-bound students was revealed as a process over time in which thoughts evolved and feelings of confidence increased. The underlying concept of the model of the information search process was verified in this study, thereby indicating a process of learning that began with vague thoughts and low confidence and closed with significant clarification of thoughts and increased confidence.

A major disappointment was the inability to collect sufficient data for analysis from the lower-level students. The design of the study required that participants complete surveys at three specific points. High incidence of absenteeism caused these students to miss many of the critical days on which data were collected. Most of them simply were not in school on one of the three days designated for data collection. (Another study using flexible tracking methods and perhaps a more qualitative approach is required to investigate the search process of this population.)

An interesting aspect of the findings was an indication of some correspondence between the process that the students had experienced and the product of their search. A correlation was found, albeit a slight one, between the students' increase in confidence during the search process and the teacher's assessment of focus in their papers. This is the only study in this series to address the outcome of the search. The quality of the outcome or the product of the search is a key issue in our concern with mediation. Ultimately, we need to address the effectiveness of mediation in terms of the outcome of the search. The outcome of the information search process is learning. However, the number of sources students used did not correlate with the teacher's assessment of focus in the students' papers. This suggests that the quality of the process has more impact on learning than does the quantity of sources. Therefore, mediation in the bibliographic paradigm of locating sources is likely to be inadequate to address the process of learning from information.

Study of the Search Process of Academic, Public, and School Library Users

Research Question: Does the model of the information search process hold for a large, diverse sample of library users?

Another study in this series addressed the problem of validating the model of the search process among a wider sample of library users. Up to this point, the research had centered on studies in school libraries and had not addressed the question of whether there were similar patterns in the process of other users and in other types of libraries. Further testing of the model was conducted with 385 academic, public, and school library users at twenty-one sites (Kuhlthau, Turock, George, and Belvin, 1990). The study was conducted in field situations with actual library users, most of whom were responding to an imposed rather than a personally initiated or job-related problem.

Field sites were chosen on the basis of their location, size, receptivity to innovation, and willingness to participate in all phases of the study. In the final sample there were eight school, seven academic, and six public library sites. The librarians at each location selected up to thirty library users on the basis of the suitability of their information problem and their willingness to participate in the study. Only research-level questions that would be completed within the twelve-week period of the study were considered.

The academic library sample was composed of undergraduate students; neither faculty nor graduate students were included. The public library sample was limited to mature adults; high school and college students were not included. The school library sample was composed of tenth- to twelfth-grade students. Of the 385 library users who participated in the study, 59 percent (229) were from school library media centers, 28 percent (108) were from academic libraries, and 13 percent (48) were from public libraries.

Instruments for Study of the Information
Search Process of a Diverse Sample of Library Users

Three instruments were used to collect data—a process survey, a conceptual map, and a perceptions questionnaire—each of which was adapted from those designed in the prior studies.

Process Survey

The process survey was adapted to elicit experiences in the information search process as described in the model of a large, diverse sample of library users, as shown in Figure 4.1 (p. 60). Changes were made to facilitate comparative analysis and to test the model with more detail and precision. A nine-question survey was developed, with the first four questions eliciting open-ended responses and the others selections from a list of choices taken directly from the model. The surveys were administered to each of the participants at three points—initiation, midpoint, and closure—in their search.

Date _____   Number _____
INITIATION

1. What are you looking for?
2. Describe the topic in a short paragraph.
3. What is the title of your project?
4. Whom have you talked to about your project?
5. On the scale below indicate your confidence level at this point in the project.

	1	2	3	4	5	6	7	8	9	10	
	Low									High	

6. From the adjectives below, check those that describe how you feel at this point in the project.
    ☐ Confident   ☐ Confused   ☐ Disappointed   ☐ Doubtful
    ☐ Frustrated   ☐ Optimistic   ☐ Relieved   ☐ Satisfied
    ☐ Sure   ☐ Uncertain
    ☐ Other _____

7. What is your task now? Please check one box.
☐ To gather information pertaining to the specific topic.
☐ To investigate information on the general topic.
☐ To complete the information search.
☐ To recognize an information need.
☐ To formulate a specific topic.
☐ To identify the general topic.
☐ Other _____

8. What are you doing now? Check as many boxes as apply to you.
☐ Discussing the topic.   ☐ Making a comprehensive search of the library.
☐ Browsing in the library.   ☐ Outlining to organize information.
☐ Reading over notes for themes.   ☐ Making a preliminary search of the library.
☐ Conferring with people who know about the topic.   ☐ Asking the librarian questions.
☐ Talking about themes and ideas.   ☐ Making a summary search of the library.
☐ Skimming and scanning sources of information.   ☐ Writing about themes and ideas.
☐ Reading about the topic.   ☐ Taking detailed notes on facts and ideas.
☐ Taking brief notes of facts and ideas.   ☐ Recording bibliographic citations.
☐ Rechecking sources for information initially overlooked
☐ Other _____

9. What are you thinking now? Check as many boxes as apply to you.
☐ Organizing ideas and information.
☐ Identifying possible alternative topics.
☐ Becoming informed about the general topic.
☐ Exhausting all possible sources of information.
☐ Considering alternative topics in light of the information available to me.
☐ Choosing the broad topic that has the potential for success.
☐ Comprehending the task before me.
☐ Recognizing ways to draw the project to a close.
☐ Considering alternative topics in light of the time I have to complete the project.
☐ Choosing specific concentrations within the general topic.
☐ Considering alternative topics in light of the requirements of the project.
☐ Confronting the inconsistency and incompatibility in the information encountered.
☐ Getting more interested and involved in ideas.
☐ Defining and extending my specific topic.
☐ Gaining a sense of direction and clarity.
☐ Recalling a previous project when I searched for information.
☐ Predicting success of each possible concentration.
☐ Identifying several possible areas of concentration in the broad topic.
☐ Considering alternative topics in light of the things that are of personal interest to me.
☐ Seeking information about my specific area of concentration.
☐ Other _____

Figure 4.2. Process Survey.

The first step of the data analysis involved producing descriptive statistics, including frequency distributions and measures of central tendency. In preparation for this step, responses on the process survey were coded. The first four questions: "What are you looking for?," "Describe topic in a short paragraph," "What is the title of your project?," and "Whom have you talked to about your project?" elicited open-ended responses, resulting in categorical data, as shown in Figure 4.3. Question 5 asked the respondents to identify their confidence level on a ten-point scale at three different stages of the project: initiation, midpoint, and closure. This question was analyzed as if the data were interval.

Q1.   What are you looking for?
        1 = General information (Background)
        2 = Specific information (Relevant)
        3 = Pertinent information (Focused)
Q2.   Describe topic in a short paragraph.
        1 = General topic
        2 = Narrowed topic
        3 = Focused point of view
Q3.   What is the title of your project?
        1 = Vague concise expression
        2 = Clearer concise expression
        3 = Compromised concise expression
Q4.   Whom have you talked to about your project?
        1 = Other (Friend, family member)
        2 = Peer (Person also doing project)
        3 = Expert (Person who knows about topic)
        4 = Professional (Person who knows about sources)

Figure 4.3. Process Survey Coding.

An attempt was made to elicit the respondents' feelings with question 6, "From the adjectives below, check those that describe how you feel at this point in the project." Multiple responses were expected because no limit was put on the number that could be selected. To show both response and nonresponse, each item within these questions was entered as a separate variable, coded "1" to show that the item had been selected, or "0" to show that it had not been selected. This yielded sets of dichotomous variables, which were treated as interval-level data. Question 7, "What is your task now?" limited responses to only one choice, each of which was then coded from 1 to 7, resulting in categorical data. Question 8, "What are you doing now?," and question 9, "What are you thinking now?," elicited multiple responses, which were coded in the same manner as question 6. Frequencies and percentages were calculated from the data.

The second step of data analysis involved producing inferential statistics, including measures of significant difference and analysis of variance. Analysis of the process survey's questions 1–4 was limited to the construction of contingency tables and single sample chi-square tests. Question 5, the confidence scale, was analyzed using paired t-tests between the initiation, midpoint, and closure responses. The t-tests were performed on aggregated data by site and as repeated measures on each variable from questions 5, 6, 8, and 9.

In each instance where a t-test was performed, the more conservative separate estimate of variance and, whenever possible, the paired t-test were used. A two-tailed probability of significance was applied. ANOVA was performed on variables aggregated by site, and the Scheffe test was used to indicate significant differences between group means. The nominal-level data of items selected in questions 6, 8, and 9 were treated as assumed-interval data. However, in keeping with the actual measures involved, chi-square tests were also performed whenever any analysis of difference by group was done using interval tests, such as t-tests and ANOVA.

Conceptual Maps

Participants were also asked to depict their views of the search process in two flowcharts, one at the beginning of their extended information-seeking projects and the other as they completed their searches. Only two limitations were placed on the diagrams: space was limited to one side of a standard page, and participants were told to draw and connect boxes; no further flowcharting instructions were given. By providing only a point of entry, "Initiate project," and a point of exit, "Information Search Completed," the instrument allowed participants freedom to depict their own mental maps of the search process. Note that this activity sought to elicit users' perceptions of the information search process and not actual accounts of a search in progress.

This unstructured flowcharting resulted in a diversity of data that proved difficult for comparative analysis. The results were meaningful, however, in the context of the larger study and within the frame of reference of the model of the information search process under investigation (Kuhlthau, Belvin, and George, 1989).

Perceptions Questionnaire

Users' perceptions of the search process and the role of mediators were tested by a perceptions questionnaire, administered before and after the search, as shown in Figure 4.4. Statements on the perceptions questionnaire were based on characteristics of process orientation as defined in the earlier study. Of the twenty questions, ten were related to process and ten to the role of mediators. A four-point Likert scale of "almost always," "often," "seldom," and "almost never," was supplied for respondents.

THE INFORMATION SEARCH PROCESS

Date: _____ Code: _____	Almost Always	Often	Sometimes	Seldom	Almost Never
1. I have a clear focus for my topic before using the library.					
2. I find it helpful to talk to others about my topic.					
3. My thoughts about my topic change as I explore information.					
4. I like to find everything I will need first and then read it.					
5. The library has the information I need.					
6. A focus emerges as I gather information on a topic.					
7. The information that I find at the beginning of a search is confusing and doesn't fit in with what I know.					
8. I take detailed notes from every source of information I look at.					
9. I ask the librarian for direction in locating materials in the library.					
10. A search is completed when I no longer find new information.					
11. All the sources of information I need are listed in the card catalog.					
12. A search is completed when I find enough information.					
13. I talk to people who know about my topic.					
14. I become more interested in a topic as I gather information.					
15. The information I need is in unexpected places in the library.					
16. I make several trips to the library to research a topic.					
17. I am successful in using the library.					
18. I ask the librarian for advice on exploring a topic.					
19. I ask the librarian for assistance in identifying materials.					
20. I need materials other than books.					

Figure 4.4. Perception Questionnaire II.

Items on the Likert-scaled perceptions questionnaire ranged from a minimum value of 1 (almost always) to a maximum of 4 (almost never), with a mean of 2.5 for each item. Five questions on the perceptions questionnaire were written to elicit an ideal response of "almost never" rather than "almost always" and were reversed for coding and analysis. The responses to the perceptions questionnaire were collapsed into a dichotomous nominal variable as either matching the anticipated response or contradicting the anticipated response. Additional analysis was performed on these responses as ordinal, assumed-interval data. The t-tests were used both on the aggregated data by site and as repeated measures.

Results of Study of Search Process of Academic, Public, and School Library Users

Findings revealed a similar process across types of library users, with participants seeking background information at initiation and information related to the general topic at midpoint and closure, with some seeking information on a focused perspective of the topic at closure. Descriptions of thoughts were general and vague at initiation, narrowed and clearer at midpoint, with 50 percent of the users making focused statements of their perspective on the topic at closure. Confidence increased significantly from initiation to closure. The adjectives most used to describe feelings were confused, frustrated, and doubtful at initiation and satisfied, sure, and relieved at closure.

The first three questions on the survey elicited cognitive aspects of the search process (see Table 4.1). Responses indicated that thoughts about the topic became clearer and more focused as respondents moved through the search process seeking more pertinent and focused information. Although there was strong evidence of clearer thinking about a topic as a search progressed, many participants did not make a focused statement at all during the search process.

Table 4.1. Evidence of Cognitive Aspects

"What are you looking for?"
Response Percentage

N =	Initiation 363	Midpoint 312	Closure 316
Background	81	19	4
Relevant	9	70	17
Focused	.	4	25
Other	10	7	54

"Describe the topic in a short paragraph."
Response Percentage

N =	Initiation 341	Midpoint 312	Closure 314
General	71	11	5
Narrowed	23	80	45
Focused	. 2	9	50
Other	4		

"What is the title of your project?"
Response Percentage

N =	Initiation 336	Midpoint 305	Closure 315
No title yet	32	18	13
Vague	48	29	25
Clearer	18	42	36
Compromised	. 2	12	26

The fourth question sought to reveal those who were perceived as mediators during the search process (see Table 4.2). Responses indicated that 39 percent of the respondents consulted experts, 25 percent conferred with librarians, 20 percent reported conferring with friends and family, and 13 percent talked with peers. There was no significant change from initiation to midpoint to closure, nor was there a significant difference by type of library.

Table 4.2. Evidence of Role of Mediators

	"Whom have you talked to about your project?" Response Percentage		
N =	Initiation 348	Midpoint 305	Closure 315
No one	15	8	7
Family/Friends	15	17	20
Peer	12	12	13
Expert	39	38	38
Librarian	19	25	22

The next question addressed the affective aspects of the search process (see Table 4.3). Responses revealed that confidence steadily increased, with lowest confidence at initiation, rising significantly at midpoint, and with another significant increase at closure.

Table 4.3. Identification of Confidence Level

	"On the scale below indicate your confidence level at this point in the project" Percentage Frequency		
N =	Initiation 361	Midpoint 313	Closure 329
1 Low	4	2	1
2	5	3	1
3	10	4	2
4	12	8	4
5	14	16	10
6	8	14	9
7	16	19	15
8	15	19	23
9	7	9	26
10 High	7	6	12
Mean	5.8	6.5	7.6

Question 6, which further addressed the affective elements in the search process, listed ten adjectives, taken from the model, from which respondents were asked to select to describe their feelings at initiation, midpoint, and closure. The feelings checked by the participants matched those predicted in the model. There was a significant difference between initiation and closure for all adjectives. Confidence increased from initiation to closure, as did the responses "satisfied," "sure," and "relieved." Responses of "confused," "frustrated," and "doubtful" decreased from initiation to closure. "Optimistic" was a consistently high selection at each point for participants in all three types of libraries.

In summary, the findings indicate that participants' thoughts about their topics became clearer and more focused as they moved through the search process seeking more relevant and focused information. Feelings accompanying the changes in thoughts matched those predicted in the model, with confidence steadily increasing. Uncertainty, confusion, and frustration decreased during the process as feelings of being satisfied, sure, and relieved increased.

Differences Among the Groups Studied

There were, however, some differences among the groups of library users studied. Comparison of users in three types of libraries revealed some differences in the levels of confidence reported as they progressed through the stages of the search process. The public library users were more confident at initiation than were the academic and school participants. Whereas the academic and school library users indicated similar levels of low confidence at initiation, the college students were significantly more confident at closure than were the high school students.

Perception of Task

An important finding in the study of three types of library users was that although participants' thoughts and feelings matched the model as anticipated, their identification of task did not (see Table 4.4). The tasks predicted by the model show a progression from recognizing an information need, to identifying

Table 4.4. Comparison of Tasks in the Information Search Process (ISP)

Stages in ISP	Appropriate Task According to Kuhlthau Model	Task as Reported by Study Participants
Initiation	Recognize information need	Gather
Selection	Identify general topic	Gather
Exploration	Investigate information on general topic	Gather/Complete
Formulation	Formulate focus	Gather/Complete
Collection	Gather information pertaining to focus	Complete
Presentation	Complete information search	Write or present

a general topic, to exploring information on a general topic, to formulating a specific focus, to gathering information pertaining to the specific focus, to completing the information search. Most participants limited their responses to the tasks of gathering and completing in all stages; few, however, selected the more formative tasks at any point in the process. Whereas gathering and completing are traditional information-seeking tasks, exploring and formulating may be more compatible with thoughts and feelings commonly experienced in the early stages of the information search process.

Focused Perspective

In addition, half of the users in academic, public, and secondary school libraries studied did not show evidence of reaching a focused perspective on their topic at any time during the search process. Although a significant change in thoughts was found, only 50 percent of the participants made focused statements of their topic at the close of their search. Furthermore, while most participants were seeking background information at initiation and information relevant to the general topic at midpoint, at closure only 25 percent reported that they were seeking information on a focused perspective of the topic. These findings lead to the assumption that many people may have entered the presentation or writing phase without clearly focused topics.

For some people, organizing and writing in preparation for presenting may enable them to focus their thoughts. The result is that formulation occurs at a later point in the process than indicated in the model. On the other hand, lack of a personal perspective may be the result of the notion that the purpose of a search is to reproduce an author's view rather than to make sense within one's own frame of reference, a perception that may inhibit the process of construction during the search process.

Major Findings and Implications

The major finding was that the model of the information search process held for the library users in academic and public libraries as well as with a range of high school students. The high school sample was selected from students in grades 10 through 12 across subject areas. Further testing is indicated, however, in even more diverse groups, particularly in academic and public libraries and with lower-achieving high school students. As the academic participants were limited to undergraduates, the study did not reveal whether graduate students and faculty experience a similar constructive process in information use. Further research is also indicated with public library users and with the population of potential library and information users. Although this work provided a good beginning for research into the constructive process of information seeking, further investigation into the experience and process of novice and expert information users with diverse information problems is needed.

To summarize the findings of this series of studies on the user's perspective on the search process, the affective symptoms of uncertainty, confusion, and frustration prevalent in the early stages were associated with vague, unclear thoughts about a topic or problem. As the participant's knowledge state shifted to clearer, more focused thoughts, a corresponding shift was noted in feelings of increased confidence and certainty. Satisfaction and relief were common at the conclusion of the search process.

Some implications for mediation in different types of libraries are suggested. The low level of confidence of students, both in high school and in college, at the beginning of assignments indicates the need for guidance in the process of searching and support in the early stages of learning from gaining access to information. The higher level of confidence of the public library participants may indicate the competence of more experienced, expert library users. Further study may reveal that less competent novice public library users can benefit from similar process intervention early on.

A clear problem emerges from the study of diverse library users that also was indicated in the studies of high school students. Users perceive the task of the search process as primarily to gather information, even in the early stages of vague, unfocused thinking. Users do not clearly understand the task of forming a focused perspective from the information encountered in the early stages of the search process. Users may need guidance and counseling in the task most appropriate for moving on to the next stage. A role for information professionals in the search process is suggested beyond that of locating sources. A new kind of intervention that meets the process needs of information users is indicated.

Longitudinal Confirmation of the Information Search Process

5

As we have seen, a constructive process takes place over an extended period of time and cannot be studied within the framework of a single incident. In the initial model-building study and the large-scale validation studies, discussed in the previous chapters, the changes that accompany the process of learning from information were examined over a period of one month to one year. In this sense, each of the studies in this series has been longitudinal. Two further studies, however, were extended over a period of five years, applying the longitudinal approach as a method of data collection for comparison.

The theory of construction proposes that the way we view the world is based on the constructs we build from our personal experience. Therefore, the experiences that we have related to information use determine the way that we perceive the information-seeking process. We cannot fully know what perceptions have been formed in a particular experience until some time later when that experience has become an integral part of our system of constructs and the way that we view the world. Therefore, longitudinal studies are essential for revealing the constructs that individuals have built over time. Two such longitudinal studies of the panel of students in the original study were conducted.

Full reports of these studies have been published previously (Kuhlthau, 1988c). This chapter discusses those critical elements revealing information seeking as a process of construction.

Longitudinal Verification

Two longitudinal studies were conducted: one using quantitative methods for gathering data and statistical methods for analyzing data, and the other applying the qualitative approach of case study. The first section describes the methods used in the quantitative study.

A Quantitative Approach

Research Question: How had students' perceptions of the information search process changed after four years of college?

A longitudinal study was conducted to verify further the model by addressing the question of whether individuals with extensive experience in using libraries and an introduction to the model have perceptions that more closely match the model of the search process. The research hypotheses in this study were as follows:

- Perceptions of library use change with exposure to the model of the search process.

- Perceptions of library use change with library experience.

- The perception that a search is a process of evolving and changing thoughts contributes to the success of the outcome of a search.

This study assessed students at the beginning of their senior year in high school and after four years of college. The participants were the same students who had been selected for study when they were high school seniors during the 1981–1982 school year. All of the group subsequently attended four-year colleges and had completed college by June 1986, with the exception of two students who were intending to complete their requirements during the next academic year. The perceptions that these students had of the library research process were likely to indicate some expectations that promote productive library use. Changes during college would indicate ways that they had refined their perceptions in response to their actual experience in the process of searching for information. This study examined perceptions and did not track students in the progress of a search.

Perceptions Questionnaire

The study was based on responses to the questionnaire given to twenty-five students at the beginning of their senior year in high school and again to the same group of students more than four years later, at the end of their senior year in college. Twenty students responded to the follow-up study. The longitudinal element in the study provided a means of comparison and analysis of change in perceptions.

In high school, the questionnaire was administered directly in a class setting with the librarian giving instructions. The model of the search process was presented to them sometime later during their senior year. In college, the students were mailed the questionnaire with instructions for completion and return. They were asked three additional questions related to their library use when they were undergraduates: the number of papers they were assigned, how well prepared they were to research the papers, and what more they needed from their high school experience. They were also invited to make any further comments in writing.

An analysis of the responses was made within the six areas of library use elicited by the questionnaire. The participants' responses when they were undergraduates were compared with those they had made in high school to identify any changes in perceptions. With the expectation that the students' perceptions would change in the direction of the model of the search process, one-tailed t-tests were used to determine whether there were significant differences between the students' responses in high school and college. The comments written by the students when they were in college were examined for the extent of their library experience and how they might have been better prepared for college library use.

A Qualitative Approach

Research Question: What do longitudinal case studies reveal of students' internal views of the information search process after four years of undergraduate study?

This study provided a longitudinal perspective on four case studies that were part of the earlier study. Four students who were the subjects of case studies when they were seniors in high school were studied again after they had completed four years of undergraduate education, with the prospect of continuing the investigation through their experience in graduate study or situations of employment in future studies. The in-depth individual case study was extended over a period of four years to examine patterns and changes in personal perspectives. Where the original case study offered insight into the perceptions of the subjects over an extended search process, this study revealed their perceptions of information use at two different points in their lives as students. Changes were traced as well as consistency in styles and preferences.

The study was based on subjects' recall and introspection, not on direct interaction with a librarian or information system. The study was composed of the participants' explanations of the search process and the information system. Further, the study examined each user's perception of information seeking and information systems.

The researcher sought to remain interested but neutral during the interviews. The users' perspectives were elicited without value judgments or correction imposed by the researcher. The participants' recollections and reactions were accepted as true. The emphasis of this inquiry was on the nature of the process of seeking information, not on the location and use of specific sources. The users' recollected thoughts, actions, and feelings were the central emphasis of the study.

The subjects of the original case studies were contacted after completing four years of undergraduate study, with four of the six able to participate in interviews and cognitive mapping exercises. All four participants had achieved academic success in college and were planning to enter graduate programs. Two of the students were male and two female.

Case Studies: Interviews and Conceptual Maps

Interviews and conceptual mapping provide an understanding of an individual's personal experience in the search process. The decision was made to continue tracking the case study subjects via two methods used in the initial study, interview and conceptual mapping, and to trace consistencies and changes in their perceptions of their experience after four years of college.

A one-hour interview was conducted individually with each subject. Each interview was recorded and subsequently transcribed. The interview consisted of the following ten questions and prompts:

- How often have you been given a research assignment in college?

- Describe some of the topics of past research assignments.

- How do you feel when a research assignment is announced?

- Describe the way you chose some of the topics for your research papers.

- Describe the procedure you follow when researching for a paper.

- Describe how you use the library at the beginning of research, at the middle, and at the end (before writing the paper).

- How did librarians assist you (instruction, reference)? How could librarians be more helpful?

- What is the most difficult part of a research assignment? Why?

- How could you have been better prepared for college research?

- How do you know when a search is completed?

In addition each participant was asked to draw on a timeline the process of a search as he or she commonly experienced it. The timelines provided a conceptual map of the subjects' perceptions of the search process based on their recall of, and reflection on, their search experiences. They were not shown the earlier renditions prior to drawing the timelines after college. The college timelines chart a generic rather than a specific search. Although the timelines drawn in high school do not precisely parallel those drawn after college, they were used to reveal patterns and to make a rough diagnosis. Future studies need to refine the mapping methodology.

The interviews of each case study participant were analyzed under the following five categories: selection of topic, attitude toward research assignments, perceptions of searching, procedures for gathering and organizing information, and the role of mediators. Comparisons were made with each participant's high school case study. Each student's conceptual map was compared with the one that he or she had drawn during high school. Consistent patterns as well as evidence of change were sought in each participant's description of the search process.

The interviews and conceptual maps of the four participants were then compared with each other under the same five categories. Similarities and differences in their perceptions of the search process were identified.

In addition, the data were analyzed within the context of the original model of the information search process that had been developed in a prior study. Refinements and adjustments of the model were made.

Qualitative methods, such as longitudinal case studies, are essential for filling the gaps that quantitative studies leave and for raising new questions and hypotheses that need to be further tested quantitatively. The two forms of research build a theory base through the opening and closing cycle of questioning and testing. Dervin and Nilan (1986, p. 27) state that traditional studies of information needs and uses have examined one discrete information incident rather than taking a more holistic view of information use. Longitudinal study, combined with case study, unlike the snapshot approach, has the power to reveal the complex cognitive process that takes place over a period of time involving the whole person, emotionally as well as intellectually, and so offers a holistic view of the search process.

Perceptions of Information Seeking After Five Years

One of the longitudinal studies addressed the problem of how students' perceptions of the search process had changed after four years of college and how their perceptions compared with the six stages of the model of the information search process (Kuhlthau, 1988b). The same questionnaire eliciting perceptions, which had been administered to this group in high school, was used to provide longitudinal data on their perceptions, with twenty of the original twenty-five students responding. Although the term *perceptions* was used rather than *constructs,* for all intents and purposes the working definition is the same for both terms within this research. Responses after college were compared with those that they gave in high school, and statistically significant changes were determined.

Comparison of the panel of participants when they were in high school and after four years of college revealed certain perceptions of more experienced information users. The study showed that the model held over time for this select group of students.

The students' perceptions of information search activity changed during the four years of college in several ways. Significant changes were found in three of the six areas studied: research assignments, focus formulation, and procedures for gathering information. Perceptions pertaining to research assignments revealed that interest in a topic increases as a search progresses. Perceptions pertaining to focus formulation revealed that a topic changes as information is gathered and that a central theme evolves as information is gathered. Perceptions pertaining to procedures for gathering information showed a decreased emphasis on the card catalog as the only place to initiate a search and increased emphasis on the use of periodicals.

Perceptions of research assignments shifted significantly in two important respects. First, in college the students were found to expect to become more interested in a topic as they learned more about it in the process of a library search. As the model describes, interest increases as a search progresses. The expectation of deepening interest provides the motivation for pushing on through the confusing, frustrating, prefocus stage. Another perception that students held that changed during the four years of college related to assignments. That perception was that a library assignment adds to what is learned in a course. The students came to perceive library use as related to course work rather than as an extraneous requirement. When students realize that using information in the library extends and deepens their course learning, research assignments are attributed greater validity and purpose.

Perceptions of formulating a focus within a topic also changed during college years to match the model more closely. According to the model, focus formulation is the pivotal point in the search process, the point at which the user moves out of confusion and doubt and on to clarity and purpose. In college, the students came to expect a topic to change during a search for information. They also came to expect a central theme to evolve during a search for information. These perceptions enable users to be open to learning from the ideas that they encounter in a library search and to avoid seeking only that information that supports their preconceived notions of a topic. Some change was also noted in the perceptions of the students toward changing a topic according to the availability of materials.

There was no significant change in the perceptions in the other three areas: general library use, topic selection, and role of mediators. These students perceived themselves as library users in high school and continued this view through college. There was a slight change noted in the use of more than one library. Fewer students reported the use of more than one library when they were in college than when they were in high school, which can be explained by the common practice of using both the high school media center and the public library, whereas at college they tended to use only the campus library.

Although there was a slight gain in their preference for topics that they chose themselves over those suggested by the teacher, this was not statistically significant. Although there was no significant change in the role of mediators, this area warrants some further comment. Although the students perceived a minimal role for teachers and librarians, they disclosed that they talk to others about their topic. In high school 62 percent, and in college 80 percent, of the students responded that they "almost always" or "often" talk to others about their topic. In the questions related to their perceptions about seeking help from librarians or teachers, however, most of their responses fell into the "sometimes," "seldom," or "almost never" categories. The perception of a need to talk about their topic did not alter their perception of a minimal role for formal mediators such as librarians and teachers.

Longitudinal Case Studies

A longitudinal study also was conducted of the case study participants in the initial study to offer fuller description of changes in perceptions of the search process over time (Kuhlthau, 1988c). Four of the six original case study subjects were interviewed, in one-hour sessions, after completion of four years of undergraduate education.

The perceptions of each of the case study participants were analyzed under the following five categories: research assignments, topic selection, search process, procedures for gathering information, and role of mediators.

Research Assignments

All four participants had positive attitudes toward research assignments and saw themselves as scholars who would be using libraries for this type of work in the future. J. had the concept of contributing to the literature of a field and explained that in one assignment he had to "put (his) work back into the literature." Participants preferred research papers over other types of course requirements, namely exams and multiple-choice tests. For C., research assignments were actually a preferred way of learning: "I have better control of my grade and I learn a lot more. I remember more from those research papers I did than I did from any of the classes I have ever taken." Another person stated that, "for me, going into science and trying to get a Ph.D., writing a paper is a very important skill. . . . I am happy when I am given an opportunity to do a paper that a person will read and criticize."

Each of the students noted feelings of uncertainty and confusion that remained prevalent in the early stages of completing research assignments. C. had come to expect to be confused at the beginning of a search and had learned not to "panic." Another student explained that she "puts off going to the library but that [she] is not as bad about this as are some people." Another person explained how she had come to tolerate her feelings at the beginning by understanding the whole process: "I used to be very anxious. But now I know how to go about it. I don't get upset anymore. I know it will take x amount of time to do the research, to narrow down my topic, and to begin writing. I know how I work."

Topic Selection

When selecting a topic each of the students attempted to internalize the assignment and create his or her own personally felt information need. They preferred to choose their own topics rather than being given a topic "out of a hat" or "by a lottery." When given the opportunity, they designed topics that were meaningful to them, and ones with which they had some familiarity or a particular interest. All four students built on topics from prior research papers they had done. Although this may have been an attempt to make the task easier, it also indicated identification of an area of specialization and movement toward developing expertise in certain subjects. As students matured and had more experience with conducting library research, they sought to mold an assignment to their own area of interest and concern.

Many of the topics that the students chose for research papers related to the careers for which they were preparing. One economics major explained that he chose topics that

> weren't even on the list of one hundred possible topics that the professor gave out. Those were ideas that I had in the back of my mind that I had researched to a lesser degree and had touched on in other classes. Both dealt with the economic development of Mexico. Actually one was a continuation of the other.

A premed student who was enrolled in an engineering course explained how she accommodated a topic to her interest. In a civil engineering course on structures,

> We had to do a structural analysis of something. . . . I was trying to think of an interesting building. People were doing the Astrodome, the Brooklyn Bridge, the Coliseum, the Pantheon. It just came to me that the skeleton would be interesting. The elbow is a basic hinge joint and the hip, a ball and socket.

Choosing a topic involves a tension between alternative approaches. On the one hand, there is the opportunity for building repertoire and expanding knowledge. On the other, there is the inclination to play it safe, set up success, and conserve energy. Habitual approaches that remained consistent over time were evident in the subjects' explanations of how they selected topics. The criteria of personal interest, assignment requirements, information available, and time allotted were applied for making choices, as the model revealed. Personal interest, however, was given greater importance than in the earlier case study. As the student who chose the skeleton as a structure explained:

> I was very excited about the topic. When I had a hard time finding information I didn't want to change it. There was nothing else I wanted to do. It turned out to be a really fun paper to write. I got some pictures and sketches. I had to get materials on interlibrary loan.

Search Process

All four participants saw the search process as taking place over a period of time for which they had to plan in advance. Each had a concept of the amount of time needed for searching. However, perceptions of time differed and may have been based on preferred ways of learning generally. There was a marked difference between one student's approach to searching, taking place over a four- or five-day span, and another's approach, extending over four to six weeks.

They used metaphors to describe a purposeful, meaning making process in which they were actively seeking to increase their understanding of the problem or topic before them. One person sought "a story out of the whole thing" and another "a thread for tying the parts together. I look for a main string that runs through all of the sections." Another participant described seeking to answer all of her questions, and one of the students explained that this "focusing and narrowing were the most difficult part of the search."

Searching was not described as a strictly linear process. Both D. and C. explained how they worked their way through the literature, interspersing use of indexes and catalogs with browsing and following leads that opened up along the way. Although students perceived the process as moving from general information to specific, their descriptions of searching revealed more of a spiral of thoughts building through the information encountered rather than a neat step-by-step progression.

Frequently one source that was particularly relevant to a topic was found late in the search:

> There was one book that went through everything. That was my major source of information. That came kind of late. But it was ok because [from] the information I had gotten previously I was already familiar enough with what I wanted to concentrate on.

The "one critical source" is recognized as pertinent after considerable formulation has taken place.

By the way, one of the most noted changes was the case study participants' use of recent materials that were not considered particularly important in high school but were regarded as essential in college.

Students had personalized their determinations of closure and concept of what is enough. A search was considered completed by G. and C. when they had exhausted all sources. D. described having an internal feeling that she had everything. J. sought to find a "story" rather than to exhaust all sources. He stated that if he had wanted he could have uncovered most of the sources on a topic. However, comprehensiveness did not seem necessary to him.

Procedures for Gathering Information

Each participant had developed a system for gathering and organizing information that he or she described as his or her own personal way of approaching the research task. The students' systems, however, had marked similarities. They took few notes at the beginning of a search, and all used yellow pads. C. was the only one to use note cards, and this use was limited to recording major points. J. reported that he took no notes but, instead, underlined photocopied texts. All participants used outlining to organize for writing; they did this toward the close of the search. They developed similar methods of coding notes and articles by using symbols, such as stars, checks, and different colors.

All of the subjects were confident in their own searching ability, with G. and C. appearing the most confident and D. and J. seeming somewhat less confident. D. expressed some fear of not measuring up to past performances. J. allowed less time than the others to gather, organize, and write papers, and frequently expressed dissatisfaction with the final outcome.

Role of Mediators

Participants mentioned three types of mediators: professors, librarians, and other students. Although all four did use mediators to some extent, librarians played a minimal role in their search process. C. and G. conferred with professors and other students quite extensively. G. had worked successfully on group projects with other students.

Librarians were expected to answer location questions and little else; they were not expected to have sufficient subject expertise to recommend sources. Instruction given by librarians was described as inadequate and not tailored to the students' majors. Further discussion revealed dissatisfaction with the role that librarians had played. D. pointed out that although librarians were available, students have to go to them; they do not come to the students, and some students are reluctant to reveal their ignorance by asking a question. C. noted students need help with the process of a search. Both C. and D. had assumed the role of mediator for fellow students. J. sought independence and remained isolated in his process for the most part. All were dissatisfied with librarians as mediators, to some degree, and expressed the need for increased participation and a more proactive role for librarians.

Summary of Case Study Findings

Examination of the case study participants reveals an understanding of the search process and a tolerance for the ambiguity and uncertainty of the earlier stages. They had gained a sense of their own pace in the information search process, expected to be uncertain at the beginning, and had developed tolerance for the early uncertainties in the formative stages. They also showed a sense of ownership in the process and the strategies that they used to work through the stages, referring to "my process" and explaining that, "this is the way I do it." Although they described experiencing a sequence of stages, they related a somewhat recursive, iterative process in which they moved toward a clearer, focused perspective rather than one that was strictly linear.

For these users, the information search process had become an important way to learn rather than just a means for fulfilling requirements for a course. They showed an awareness of being involved in seeking meaning by purposefully engaging in "focusing and narrowing," and in seeking "a thread," "a story," and "answers to all my questions." Discussion of the topics that they chose for research assignments showed evidence of molding an imposed task to their own interests, building on prior searches, and developing areas of expertise.

Verification and Expansion of the Model of the Information Search Process

Analysis of the two longitudinal studies showed that the participants experienced stages similar to those identified in the original model of the search process. Although the process appears to be accurately described, the data also indicated several areas in which the original model may be refined and expanded. The longitudinal view indicated that the titles of each stage might be refined to accommodate a wider range of library users. The following discussion is limited to elaborations of the model based on the longitudinal study and is not a full description of the characteristics of each stage in the search process (see Figure 5.1).

Stage 1: Initiation

The essential element in the initiation stage is the presence of an information need. While a research assignment imposed an information need, the students internalized the task to create a personal need for meaning that motivated and directed their information-seeking activity. An assignment that invites a student to transform an imposed task into a need for meaning raises questions and problems that he or she can identify as worth pursuing. All of the participants in the study attempted to do this when given the opportunity.

Tasks	Initiation	Selection	Exploration	Formulation	Collection	Presentation
Feelings (affective)	uncertainty	optimism	confusion/ frustration/doubt	clarity	sense of direction /confidence	satisfaction or disappointment
Thoughts (cognitive)		vague ————————————→		focused		
					————————————————————→	
					increased interest	
Actions (physical)	seeking relevant information exploring		————————————————→		seeking pertinent information documenting	

Figure 5.1. Model of the Information Search Process (ISP).

Stage 2: Selection

The four criteria for selecting a topic in the original model were personal interest, requirements of the assignment, information available, and time allotted. Although the participants continued to use these criteria, this study noted that all were not of equal importance in every case. G. described approaching topic selection in two ways in different assignments. In most instances, the information available took priority over personal interest, but in one assignment she described selecting a topic of personal interest although adequate information was not available. J. repeatedly described giving priority to personal interest over the requirements of the assignment. For all four students, personal interest had become a more important criterion than it had been in high school as they moved toward an area of specialization and expertise.

Stage 3: Exploration

The subjects described the exploration stage as a search for information, from general to specific, but their explanations revealed a more heuristic process that could be quite disorderly and confusing at times rather than a neat step-by-step progression. For example, D. and C. described going back and forth from the card catalog to sources as they learned more about the topic and "browsing" the shelves to seek out "buried" information.

The conceptual maps showed that as students matured they became more aware of the essential part that thinking plays throughout the search process. After entering college, their maps include active, cognitive concepts, such as think, worry, procrastinate, decide, discuss, read, reread, and organize. When students noted that they procrastinated at the beginning of a search, they applied a negative connotation to the preparatory thinking and mulling that characterizes this stage; such a trend also was evident in the high school case studies. Participants' descriptions of information seeking at this stage reveal the tendency to use sources they had on hand before reaching out for further information. First they used sources already known or recommended, and then they sought less accessible sources.

Stage 4: Formulation

Formulation is the development of a focus that evolves from thinking and reading about a problem or topic. The focus provides direction for the collection of information. At this stage, decisions of relevance change as a result of increased personal knowledge.

The students used metaphors to express their perceptions of formulation. C. described a thread to pull the separate parts together; J. used a story within the literature that made sense. D. used the more conventional theme of a focus, as did G. in her reference to narrowing the general topic. There was a combination of chance and creativity in their descriptions of formulation. In several instances students used the term *luck,* which is more likely to be an "aha" of recognition with increased personal knowledge and understanding. G. remembered finding one particular source that pulled things together late in the process. She further noted that if she had come to the source earlier, she might not have recognized its relevance. These students described formulation occurring toward the middle or latter part of the process after they had been searching for some time.

The original model depicted stages 3, 4, and 5 as discrete and separate. The present study revealed the stages from exploration through collection as overlapping and merging. The participants described a more heuristic, spiral process in which emerging thoughts were changing and evolving, rather than a distinct formulation point. Formulation, however, was seen as part of the search process and was not postponed to the writing stage. Even though formulation remained a difficult part of the search process, as college students they had become more articulate in describing their experience in formulation than they had been in high school. Individual approaches to formulation seemed to remain consistent over time.

Stage 5: Collection

When students explained their method of collecting information they revealed a sense of ownership on an internal, intellectual, and personal level. There was an element of possession in the process as well as product. Students had devised personal systems for collecting information that did not include all of the methods commonly taught in traditional library instruction programs. Yellow pads replaced note cards for the most part. Outlining was used to organize for writing and not earlier, as is often recommended to organize for searching. Systems of coding were devised, and recall was considered as an important component of organizing.

In addition to the due date of the paper, completion of a search was determined by either the concept of exhausting sources or having enough to present. Both perspectives were based on meeting the original information need and the ability to present. The students had personal standards that they consistently used to determine closure.

Stage 6: Presentation

Outlining was an important technique for organizing information for presenting. G. described her ease in writing a paper after she had prepared a detailed outline for an oral presentation. The organization of information for giving to others was creatively approached for the most part. However, D. reported that she sometimes became bored with her topic at this point and wanted to move on to something new. There was evidence of personal ownership in the topic and a frequent need to know more and to go further with the research after an assignment was completed. As students matured, their sense of ownership in their products increased. They were actively seeking to build an area of expertise.

Major Findings and Implications for Mediation

These longitudinal studies further verified the model of the search process developed in the initial study. As students used the library throughout their college years, their perceptions of the search process became more like the model. They came to expect their topic to change and a central theme to evolve during a search for information. They expected to become more interested as the search progresses. From these studies, we cannot say what effect cognitive development, experience, or introduction to the model had on perceptions. The findings, however, provide a sound base for further research into the nature of the experience of a search for information.

The five studies, including research questions, key findings, and citations of the major papers, are summarized in Figure 5.2.

Two areas of findings are worthy of particular attention because they have implications for library and information services. These are changes in perceptions of process and of interest, both of which may be general characteristics of more experienced users. These longitudinal studies revealed changes in students' expectations of the search process as a meaning making process occurring over time. They expected a topic to change and their thoughts to evolve during the process. They anticipated uncertainty as a normal beginning for their investigation and formulation. They had a sense of closure beyond that of running out of time.

In addition, of the four criteria for making decisions about topic and focus, personal interest received priority over assignment requirements, information available, and time allotted. They expected to become more interested in their topic as the search progressed.

Each of these areas of findings indicates a direction for process intervention. One disheartening finding, however, was the perception of a minimal role for librarians and dissatisfaction expressed at the inadequate role that formal mediators played in their search process. While the students sought counseling and guidance in the evolving process from friends and family, librarians remained in the role of locator.

Study 1 (1983)

Research Question: Do users' experience in the ISP resemble the phases in the process of construction?
Key Findings: Common patterns in ISP correspond to process of construction in a 6-Stage Model.
References:
Kuhlthau, Carol C. (1985). "A Process Approach to Library Skills Instruction." *School Library Media Quarterly, 13*(1), 35-40.
———— (1985). *Teaching the Library Research Process*. West Nyack. NY: The Center for Applied Research in Education.
———— (1988). "Developing a Model of the Library Search Process: Cognitive and Affective Aspects," *Reference Quarterly, 28*(2), 232-242.

Study 2 (1986)

Research Question: How had students' perceptions of the ISP changed after four years of college?
Key Findings: Perceptions of ISP became more like the model over time, particularly regarding focus and process.
References:
Kuhlthau, Carol C. (1988). "Perceptions of the Information Search Process in Libraries: A Study of Changes from High School Through College," *Information Processing and Management, 24*(4), 419-427.

Study 3 (1987)

Research Question: What do longitudinal case studies reveal of students' internal view of the ISP after four years of undergraduate study?
Key Findings: ISP described as a purposeful, sensemaking process.
References:
Kuhlthau, Carol C. (1998) "Longitudinal Case Studies of the Information Search Process of Users in Libraries," *Library and Information Science Research, 10*(3), 257-304.

Study 4 (1988)

Research Question: Do low- and middle-level high school seniors and other high achieving seniors experience the ISP as described in the model?
Key Findings: The model was confirmed in a larger, more diverse sample of high school seniors. In addition, there was an indication of a correlation between focus in research papers and change in confidence during search process.
References:
Kuhlthau, Carol C. (1989). "The Information Search Process of High-Middle-Low Achieving High School Seniors," *School Library Media Quarterly, 17*(4), 224-228.
———— (1989). *The Information Search Process of High-Middle-Low Achieving High School Seniors.* Final Report of Study Funded by Rutgers Research Council. ERIC Clearinghouse on Information Resources, Syracuse University. (ED 310787).

Study 5 (1989)

Research Question: Does the model of the ISP hold for a large, diverse sample of library users?
Key Findings: The model was verified with academic, public, and school library users. While thoughts and feelings matched the model as anticipated, the identification of task did not.
References:
Kuhlthau, Carol C., Betty Turock, Mary W. George, and Robert J. Belvin (1990). Validating a Model of the Search Process: A Comparison of Academic, Public, and School Library Users. *Library and Information Science Research, 12*(1), 5-32.
Kuhlthau, Carol C., Betty Turock, Mary W. George, and Robert J. Belvin (1989). *Facilitating Information Seeking Through Cognitive Modeling of the Search Process.* Final Report. U.S. Department of Education, Library Research and Demonstration Grant G008720323-87, ERIC (ED 328268).

Summary of Findings:

Kuhlthau, Carol C. (1989). "Information Search Process: A Summary of Research and Implications for School Library Media Programs," *School Library Media Quarterly, 18*(5), 19-25.
———— (1991). "Inside the Search Process: Information Seeking from the User's Perspective." *Journal of the American Society for Information Science, 42*(5), 361-371.

Figure 5.2. Information Search Process (ISP): Questions and Key Findings in Five Studies.

A longitudinal view of the information search process led to the following recommendations for intervening in the process of learning from information and of designing programs of instruction:

- an emphasis on the process of a search to promote an awareness of the sequence of feelings, thoughts, and actions commonly experienced in a search for information;

- the provision for situations that promote seeking a focus during a search for information; and

- an involvement in extended library searching that offers opportunities to experience increased interest as individuals learn more about a topic.

By viewing the findings of these studies in the frame of the constructionist theory of learning, we can propose a process theory for library and information services. The process theory is articulated as an uncertainty principle in the theoretical statement (see Chapter 6).

Understanding perceptions opens the possibility of mediating directly in those areas that might be expected to cause difficulty in a search for information. Intervention can be tailored to the specific needs of an individual user or to those of a group of users. For example, people can be made more aware of the need to seek a focus for their search and be better prepared to meet the feelings of uncertainty that they might expect to experience as they progress toward a focus.

These studies indicate a deeper level of intervention needed to guide and counsel people in the process of learning from gaining access to information. Library and information services must be redefined in terms of the user's experience in the process of seeking information.

Emerging Theory of a Process Approach to Information Seeking

Chapters 3 through 5 have described a series of research studies into users' perspectives on information seeking. Methods were developed to reveal the experience of users within the search process investigating an extensive problem over a period of time. Both qualitative and quantitative methods were developed to build and verify a model of the information search process. A combination of qualitative and quantitative methods provided overlapping data that offered a comprehensive view of a complex, dynamic process. These studies initiate an area of research into the information search process for further investigation, verification, and refinement.

The two main assumptions on which the methodology was based are that a longitudinal approach is necessary for studying the search process and that field studies are essential for eliciting real-life experience. The methods were developed to study real people with real problems in real libraries. Therefore, the methods are particularly appropriate for application as tools for action research in library and information systems. In addition, these methods were intended to open the search process for observation and may be adopted as process interventions to enable users to become aware of and to understand their own search process.

From the findings of these five studies on the information search process viewed within the perspective of the constructivist theory of learning emerges a theory of a process approach to information seeking in library and information services. This emerging theory is articulated as a principle of uncertainty in the next chapter.

6

Uncertainty Principle

This chapter proposes a theory for library and information services based on the constructivist view of learning and grounded in the findings of the series of studies in the information search process of library users described in various articles and summarized in this book. We began with a borrowed theory, tested that theory within the context of information-seeking situations, and now proceed to make a theoretical statement specific to information-seeking behavior. When the borrowed theory was empirically examined within the frame of library users' experience, information seeking was revealed as a process of construction. The constructivist view could then be formulated as a theory for library and information services. The process is specifically articulated and proposed as a premise on which to base interventions with users of library and information systems.

A process theory for library and information services addresses the common experience of uncertainty and anxiety. An uncertainty principle has been introduced into information science by several other researchers.

Bates (1986) recommended that uncertainty be used as one of three design principles, the others being variety and complexity. The mechanistic assumption is that there is an ideal indexing system with one perfect description of a document that will produce the best match with the user's information need and query. Bates maintains that the ideal is impossible in principle because of fundamental human traits that make indexing behavior and information searching behavior varied and individual. Therefore, a principle of uncertainty is posited to allow for the indeterminate range of mental associations that characterize human thought.

Whittemore and Yovits (1973) also proposed an uncertainty principle for the fundamental theory of information flow. They summarize the three levels of communication research identified by Shannon and Weaver (1949) by posing three questions: "What is the message?," "What does the message mean?," and "What are the effects of the message on the recipient?" Concentrating on the third level, their research addresses the effectiveness and meaning of information to the user for decision-making, referred to as pragmatic information. Addressing the problem of the way that information is used once it is transmitted and received, they set out to evaluate information in terms of the reduction of uncertainty for the decision maker. According to Shannon and Weaver (1949):

Uncertainty is the critical link between information and decision-making. To effect a meaningful analysis of pragmatic information, one must look in detail at that which makes decision making such a challenging and oftentimes agonizing activity: uncertainty. (p. 224)

Uncertainty involved in decision-making enlivens learning and makes selection into a dynamic process (Yovits and Foulk, 1985). As understanding of the situation changes over time, attitude toward uncertainty changes as well. In the decision-making process, confidence increases as the person obtains results that he or she predicts:

The confidence that the decision-maker has in his current model clearly affects the manner in which his state of knowledge is altered by the learning process and is an important factor in choosing a course of action. (p. 64)

Testing the premise that information always reduces uncertainty, Yovits and Foulk (1985) found that in some situations information may make a person more, not less, uncertain of his or her appraisal of a particular situation. They noted that typical decision models address those who are assumed to have reached a rather advanced state of knowledge about the decision situation in question. Information science, however, must cover all levels of decision-making, novel situations in which a sequence of related decisions are required over a period of time as well as advanced decision situations.

Van Rysbergen (1996) proposed a logical uncertainty principle to consider the dynamic nature of information retrieval interaction that ties together the notions of logic, uncertainty, and information through a mathematical approach.

In a series of collaborative studies Wilson and his colleagues (2002) found that the concept of uncertainty could be operationalized so that information seekers can express the degree of uncertainty they have regarding the stages of the problem-solving process, although some preferred to use the term *issue* rather than *problem*.

Building on the recognition of the importance of uncertainty introduced by these researchers, our emerging theory is further developed and articulated. Research into the users' actual experience in the process of using information for seeking meaning, gaining a deeper understanding, and learning reveals pervasive patterns of uncertainty. Studies of the user's perspective of information seeking suggest an underlying persistence of uncertainty that describes and shapes the way that the process is commonly experienced. An uncertainty principle is proposed as a basic premise in the process of learning from information access and use.

Personal Construct Theory As an Example of Theory Building

Kelly's presentation of Personal Construct Theory offers a prototype for theory building that is composed of a fundamental postulate elaborated by a series of corollaries. The corollaries explain and elaborate the fundamental postulate but are not presented in any particular hierarchical or priority order.

By adopting Kelly's prototype, an uncertainty principle, based on the findings of the series of studies into the user's perspective on the information search process, can be formulated. The central principle, as the fundamental postulate, is supported and expanded by six corollaries that are also drawn from the findings of the studies. The uncertainty principle is presented as a proposal for an emerging theory of intervention that is further developed and discussed in Chapters 7 and 8.

This theoretical statement is meant to stand alone as an underlying principle for the development of process-oriented library and information services. Some of the discussions may seem to reiterate concepts presented in Chapter 2 that discuss constructivist theory. This chapter, however, is a redefinition of constructivist theory as it directly applies to library and information services. The uncertainty principle is stated as a theoretical underpinning for the process approach to services.

Uncertainty Principle

The findings of the studies of the information search process have been described in a six-stage model. The same findings are articulated in this chapter as a principle of uncertainty for library and information science. An uncertainty principle is stated in Figure 6.1 (p. 92) and elaborated in six corollaries.

Uncertainty Principle

Uncertainty is a cognitive state that commonly causes affective symptoms of anxiety and lack of confidence. Uncertainty and anxiety can be expected in the early stages of the information search process. The affective symptoms of uncertainty, confusion, and frustration are associated with vague, unclear thoughts about a topic or question. As knowledge states shift to more clearly focused thoughts, a parallel shift occurs in feelings of increased confidence. Uncertainty due to a lack of understanding, a gap in meaning, or a limited construction initiates the process of information seeking.

Figure 6.1. The Uncertainty Principle.

Uncertainty is a cognitive state that commonly causes affective symptoms of anxiety and lack of confidence. Uncertainty and anxiety can be expected in the early stages of the information search process. The affective symptoms of uncertainty, confusion, and frustration are associated with vague, unclear thoughts about a topic or question. As knowledge states shift to more clearly focused thoughts, a parallel shift occurs in feelings of increased confidence. Uncertainty due to a lack of understanding, a gap in meaning, or a limited construct initiates the process of information seeking.

Process Corollary

The process of information seeking involves construction in which the user actively pursues understanding and seeks meaning from the information encountered over a period of time. The process is commonly experienced as a series of thoughts and feelings that shift from vague and anxious to clear and confident as the search progresses.

Users experience the active process of information seeking as a process of construction, much the way that the theorists have described. Dewey's phases of reflective experience, Kelly's phases of construction, and Bruner's interpretive task provide a theoretical basis for understanding individual experience in using information. The studies of the users' perspective described in Chapters 3, 4, and 5 indicate that people commonly experience a series of phases or stages as they seek information over an extended period of time. Within the stages of the search process, people construct their own perspective or understanding of a topic or problem. The stages are experienced as an increase in understanding, interest, and confidence from the initiation to the conclusion of the process.

The process involves the total person and incorporates thinking, feeling, and acting in the dynamic process of learning. From the user's point of view, information seeking is a holistic experience with thoughts, actions, and feelings interweaving in a complex mosaic rather than as separate, distinct entities. Thoughts unfold through actions and feelings evolve throughout. The holistic process of information seeking has not been fully recognized in library and information services. Although information seeking is recognized as a cognitive process, the affective process is rarely considered as interacting with the cognitive as part of a whole experience. Within the traditional bibliographic paradigm, we have attended almost exclusively to actions with source identification and location as the central objective. Recently, more consideration has been given to the cognitive aspects of information use, with thinking and interpretation as a goal. Incorporation of the affective, essential for fully understanding the experience of information seeking, has not yet occurred on any significant scale.

Information searching is traditionally portrayed as a systematic, orderly, and rational procedure rather than the uncertain, confusing process that users commonly experience. After the search is completed, the topic understood, and the problem solved, it is all too easy to look back and deny the chaos and confusion that was actually experienced in the process, but at what cost?

Bruner (1986) warned of a poverty bred by making too sharp a distinction among cognition, affect, and action, what he calls "tripartism." Consideration of all three in unison offers new approaches and insights to long-standing issues and problems in information provision.

The information search process may not always be as clear-cut as the six-stage model might imply. The model is more of a metaphor for common experience in the search process than a prescription or a precise replication of individual experience. For example, the studies reported in this text examine problems with a distinct beginning and end. The beginning and end of the information search process is often difficult to isolate and define. The level of the user's uncertainty, rather than the age of his or her problem, may be a better indicator of the point in the process that the user is experiencing. The concept of beginning and end is both fluid and elusive. However, this is a task model that is based on users with a specific objective to be accomplished that defines the initiation and close of the information-seeking process.

Another factor influencing uncertainty is expertise. The novice may not experience uncertainty in the same way as the expert. The expert is rarely at the true beginning, as is a novice who holds only a few constructs on a topic. The expert in one area, however, may be a novice in another. Many doctoral students have identified with this process as matching their experience in dissertation research and writing. Practicing professionals have noted a similar process in preparing reports, lectures, sermons, briefs, papers, presentations, and articles, as discussed in Chapter 10.

The model of the information search process is useful for describing a series of feelings and thoughts commonly related to the tasks in an evolving search process. However, the process is extremely complex, dynamic, and individual. The user's experience is complicated by two levels of process; the process of construction for meaning overlays the process of information seeking. Although the sequence of constructive experience described accurately emulates the search process, the pace of the process may vary greatly from individual to individual and search to search. The process may be more cyclical than the model implies, with stages recurring in a persistent quest for decreased uncertainty and increased understanding.

Formulation Corollary

Formulation is thinking, developing an understanding, and extending and defining a topic from the information encountered in a search. The formulation of a focus or a guiding idea is a critical, pivotal point in a search when a general topic becomes clearer and a particular perspective is formed as the user moves from uncertainty to understanding.

Formulation, a central concept in this work, is thinking and forming thoughts during the process of a search. Understanding develops through extending and defining a topic from the information encountered. Thoughts change from vague and general to clear and specific. A personal perspective or point of view is formed from the information gathered. Formulation is based on former constructs and is, therefore, unique and personal. A consensus or an agreement may be made or some common ground established among information users, but this is not necessarily the expected outcome of information seeking.

The information search process involves using information, not merely locating it. Using information involves interpreting and creating or, to adopt a phrase from Dewey and Bruner, "going beyond the information given." Formulation is the thinking that leads to interpreting and creating from the information encountered in the search process. The interpretive task, as Bruner described it, is critical to information seeking. No matter the amount or the quality of the information gathered, the problem is not solved or the topic understood until the information has been interpreted. The person actively creates possible alternative ways to interpret information in the process of seeking information.

Interpretation is highly individual. Different people can pursue the same general topic or problem and each come up with quite different perspectives and solutions. There is no one perfect paper, as there is no one perfect formulation, interpretation, or creation. There are many ways to view the world, and many formulations contribute to our collective understanding. There is no one way out of uncertainty, but rather there is an individual process of construction within the information search process. A certainty approach to information seeking, which promotes a single right answer to a specific question, obscures the central task of formulation for moving from uncertainty to understanding in complex issues.

Formulation, as the central task in the search process, is frequently misunderstood. In the study of the information search process of users in three types of libraries, nearly 50 percent of the participants did not reach a focused topic at any point in their search process. In addition, most users identified their task as gathering and completing, even in the early stages of information seeking. The case studies provided an elaboration of the user's experience when very little formulation took place during the process of the search. A lack of formulation resulted in significant writing blocks and great difficulty preparing to present the topic. One participant explained that when there was no focus, there was nothing to center on and nothing to complete; therefore, the paper was impossible to write. The concept of formulation provides a way of understanding and articulating the user's task in the search process.

Formulation of a focus is a critical pivotal point in a search when the general topic becomes clearer and a particular perspective is formed. Although the focus may be conceived of as a hypothesis, it may be quite tentative and fluid. A focus serves as a guiding idea that gives the search direction, narrows the search, and provides a basis for collecting information and making relevance judgments. A focus may emerge slowly or be a sudden moment of insight. When little formulation has been made within the search process and no focus formed, difficulty is commonly experienced in writing and presenting the topic.

Disconcerting feelings are commonly associated with the exploration that leads to formulation. Users often find the period preceding formulation of a focus the most difficult phase in the search process. Uncertainty commonly increases, rather than gradually decreasing, during this time. Users experience anxiety and frustration as they encounter information from many different perspectives, much of which is not compatible with their own constructs. Some may be tempted to turn back and drop the quest altogether. We have no way of knowing just how many searches have been abandoned at this point. The connection between feelings and formulating is evident from the rise in confidence that parallels increased clarity as formulation unfolds.

Exploration is key for formulating a focus during the search process. However, users often attempt to move directly from selecting a general topic or area to the task of collecting information, skipping the important stage of exploration altogether. Exploratory acts uncover information for formulating new constructs, whereas collecting acts gather information for documenting established constructs. Formulation, which takes place through acting and reflecting, is better facilitated by exploring than it is by collecting.

Tolerance for uncertainty is important for formulation within the search process. Some practical strategies that lead to formulation are talking, writing, browsing, reading, and reflecting. Mediators, frequently family and friends, play an important part in a person's formulation in the process of understanding information. Libraries and information systems, which have been devised primarily for collection rather than exploration, too often actually inhibit strategies that foster formulation. New forms of mediation that encourage and engage exploration are needed.

Kelly (1963) describes certain choices as elaborative, leading to clarification or expansion and bringing new understanding and direction. Elaborative choices in the process of information seeking give the search a focus or a theme, enabling the user to move ahead with greater certainty and confidence toward closure. Such elaborative choices occur after considerable exploration and formulation have taken place. For example, a particular source may be seen as critical in triggering the formulation. However, if the source had been encountered earlier in the process it may have been considered relevant to the topic but not recognized as pertinent to the constructed focus. Formulation provides a framework for judging relevance of information. A shift may be noted, after a focus has been formed, from seeking information that is relevant to the general topic to choosing information that is pertinent to the focused perspective of the individual. The formulation of a focus is an elaborative choice that moves the search from uncertainty to understanding.

Redundancy Corollary

The interplay of seeking what is expected or redundant and encountering what is unexpected or unique results in an underlying tension in the search process. Redundant information fits into what we already know and is promptly recognized as being either relevant or irrelevant. Unique information does not match our constructs and requires reconstruction to be recognized as useful. Redundancy may be expected to increase as uncertainty decreases. The lack of redundancy at the beginning of the search process may be an underlying cause of anxiety related to uncertainty.

The significant impact of emotion on the constructive process of information seeking is illustrated by the problem of redundancy versus uniqueness encountered in a search. Redundancy is that information which fits into what we already know and is promptly recognized as being relevant to our topic. Uniqueness is that information which does not match our former constructs and prompts us to construct new ideas and learn new concepts. The interplay of seeking what is expected or redundant on the one hand and encountering what is unexpected or unique on the other is little understood within the information search process.

Redundancy verifies what we know. Uniqueness extends what we know. The balance of redundancy and uniqueness is critical in a search for information. Too much redundancy results in boredom; too much uniqueness causes anxiety. There is a distinct linkage between emotion and thinking that bears upon the actions that we take and the choices that we make. Relaxing and a tolerance for the learning process seem to be important for comfortable progression. However, as the Yerkes-Dodson Law reminds us, although too much tension causes one to spin wheels, too little causes one to lose interest.

The individual information user does not treat all information equally. Rather, a person selectively attends to certain aspects of the information encountered and ignores others. Selective attending patterns do not remain stable throughout a search but change and evolve as understanding increases.

In this way, the balance of redundancy and uniqueness shifts during the stages of the information search process. Early in the process the amount of uniqueness is likely to be much greater than later in the process. At the beginning, familiar information or redundancy is a reassuring sign that there is something that fits in with what we already know and that we are on the right track. Uncertainty and anxiety can be expected as a result of the large amount of uniqueness encountered. Tolerance for uniqueness, which does not fit with our constructs, is essential in the early stages. Toward the midpoint of the information search process, some of the initial uniqueness takes on meaning as we build new constructs.

At this point, thoughts become clearer and more focused and selections of relevance become more pertinent. At the end of the process, the amount of redundancy in the information encountered and gathered can be expected to be much greater than the amount of uniqueness. Much of the initial uniqueness has been reconstructed into the familiar. The shift to encountering mostly redundant information lessens anxiety and raises confidence.

There is much we do not know about how individuals construe and reconstrue during information seeking. These studies do indicate, however, that the process is not purely cognitive. Feelings of anxiety are prevalent early in the search, and levels of confidence increase considerably during the process.

There are different degrees in the amount of information that can be understood at different stages in the process. Therefore, information overload is a dynamic, not a stable, concept. An understanding of the affective aspects of the search process seems to result in a tolerance for stages that commonly cause discomfort. One of the case study subjects in an interview noted that he never can have too much information because he has learned to tolerate uniqueness and the feeling of uncertainty that accompanies more information than can easily be assimilated or reconstructed at one time. The studies of the search process of users indicate that an understanding of the feelings commonly experienced and a tolerance for the anxiety commonly associated with uncertainty are important concepts for users to have. A misreading of feelings as a signal of failure is likely to occur when users do not have an understanding of the affective component of the constructive process of information seeking.

Mood Corollary

One critical way that emotion affects the process of information seeking is by the stance or mood that the user assumes. A mood may be thought of as an attitude that determines one's approach to the task at hand. Kelly (1963) describes two moods in any constructive process: invitational and indicative.

Mood, a stance or attitude that the user assumes, opens or closes the range of possibilities in a search. An invitational mood leads to expansive actions, whereas an indicative mood leads to conclusive actions. The user's mood is likely to shift during the search process. An invitational mood may be more appropriate for the early stages of the search, and an indicative mood better suited to the latter stages.

Assuming a single mood, either invitational or indicative, throughout the entire information search process may obstruct progress at certain points. The ability to alter mood as the search progresses allows for the accommodation of the different tasks in each of the various stages.

At initiation, an invitational mood opens the possibilities within the comprehensive topic or problem and keeps at bay any tendency toward early closure based on insufficient information. At selection, however, when the task is to choose the general direction or topic, a more indicative stance prompts the decision to be made. When users are overly invitational at this point, they are likely to have difficulty settling on a general topic to get their search underway. On the other hand, when they are excessively indicative they tend to choose topics without sufficient investigation and reflection, which frequently result in obstacles later on. At the exploration stage, an invitational mood opens the search for accomplishing the task of investigating and learning about the general topic to form a focused perspective. An indicative mood at this point prompts the person to collect rather than to explore. In this time of extension, a productive strategy is to relax, read, and reflect, and to list ideas rather than to take copious notes. At the formulation stage, an indicative mood fosters the closure essential to accomplish the task of narrowing and focusing the general problem area. The indicative mood is also effective in the collection stage when the task centers on gathering information specific to the focused perception of the topic. The indicative mood aids the user to seek closure in preparation for presenting the information during the last stage, presentation.

In general, the invitational mood is likely to be most effective in the earlier stages of the search process, and the indicative mood is more appropriate for the tasks at and after midpoint. An invitational mood throughout may result in a lack of focus and closure. An indicative mood throughout may result in a lack of new construction and learning. The ability to shift stance to match the task at hand during the search process is a strategy of experienced searchers.

The question of whether moods assumed by users are actually styles that persist across searches is important to consider. Are moods attitudes that may be easily changed, or styles with persistent patterns of habits? The studies described in this text did reveal evidence of styles that users assumed; however, the styles did not seem so fixed that they could not be adjusted when the users became aware of them as a result of extensive search experience.

The case study participants were examined for research styles that persisted over time. It was noted that two case studies showed evidence of more invitational mood tendencies and two showed evidence of tendencies that could be identified as more indicative. During their high school information-seeking situations these tendencies impeded their process at various points in the search, as described above. Those displaying invitational mood tendencies had difficulty in selecting topics, forming focuses, and closing the search for presentation. Those with indicative tendencies tended to choose topics without sufficient preliminary investigation and to focus without forming constructs from the information they encountered. The tendency toward one style was modified during college to accommodate both invitational and indicative moods to better address the tasks of the different stages of the search process.

The bibliographic paradigm projects an image of the task of information seeking that is primarily to gather and collect information rather than a series of tasks within a constructive process. In this way, the traditional approach to information seeking fosters an indicative mood. A misconception of tasks seems to pervade users' understanding of what they are about in information-seeking situations. In the study of the users in three types of libraries, described in Chapter 5, the one area of responses that did not match the model of users' experience in the search process related to perception of a changing task throughout the process. The model describes the following series of tasks:

- Initiation—to recognize an information need

- Selection—to identify a general topic

- Exploration—to investigate information on the general topic

- Formulation—to formulate a focus

- Collection—to gather information pertaining to the focus

- Presentation—to complete the information search

The users in the study chose "to gather and complete" from a list of tasks for all stages in the search process. They did not identify any of the other less indicative tasks for the earlier, more invitational stages of the process, even though they reported experiencing these stages differently.

In light of this finding, mediators may expect users to be impatient with the more invitational aspects of information seeking. They feel they are procrastinating when they reflect during the early phases of construction. They have a tendency to move from selection to collection, leaping over the critical invitational stages of exploration in preparation for formulation. They use indicative strategies, such as copious note taking, when more invitational tactics, such as listing interesting ideas, would be more appropriate. An exclusively indicative approach to information seeking is in conflict with the actual experience of users.

Prediction Corollary

The search process may be thought of as a series of choices based on predictions of what will happen if a particular action is taken. Predictions are based on expectations derived from constructs built on past experience. Since each of us constructs our own unique personal worlds, the predictions and choices made in the search process may vary widely from user to user. Predictions may change during the search process, as the user moves from uncertainty to understanding.

One of the basic principles of construction theory is that each of us constructs our own unique personal world. When two people encounter similar information, the interpretation each makes may be quite different. Kelly (1963) explains this as happening through prediction based on personal constructs: "Individuals form constructs with which to predict future events" (p. 14). Since no two people hold precisely the same constructs, the predictions underlying their actions may vary widely.

In Kelly's terms, the predictions that users make during a search direct the information-gathering process. Only the action is observable. The underlying prediction remains hidden unless brought to the surface by a question or other intrusive probe.

Predictions are based on an expectation of what will result if a certain action is taken, "If I choose this, this is likely to happen." Predictions can be wrong when they are not based on solid evidence or misleading when based on incomplete experience.

The concept of predicting outcome brings insight to the issue of relevance judgments. Relevance is not absolute and cannot be considered as constant from person to person. Choices within the search process are highly individual and may be expected to vary considerably. One of the most stable characteristics of relevance judgments is that they are not uniform. For this reason, objective measurements of the accuracy of information retrieval do not suffice for determining effective performance.

The search process involves a series of choices of what users find relevant or irrelevant. Kelly (1963) states that a person chooses that which will extend and define his or her system. In the process of a search users seek information that will extend and define the topic or problem. As constructs related to the topic being investigated in the search process are formed and clarified, choices of what information will extend and define also change. What was relevant at the beginning of a search may not be relevant later, and information not considered relevant early on may become pertinent in the later stages. To better understand the predictions that drive choices, it may be necessary to elicit what was rejected as well as what was accepted and why the choice was made.

Users predict, from constructs formed through prior experience, what will be useful and expedient in information seeking. Their predictions determine the sources used, the sequence in which they are used, and the information that is gleaned from the sources. Conversely, user predictions determine information, sources, and even ideas that are not useful and are discarded. This is a highly individual process based on one's existing constructs at the time.

Predictions are made about topics and information related to topics, but predictions are also made about process. Expectations are formed through the holistic experience of information seeking. Therefore, personal constructs relate not only to the cognitive aspects of the process but also to the affective experience in the search process. Feelings of anxiety at the beginning of a search affect the choices that one makes, as do feelings of confidence in later stages. Predictions of outcome vary depending on where the user is in the process.

The four criteria for choices discussed previously shed some light on how a person's expectations affect decisions made in the process of information seeking. The studies discussed in previous chapters identify the criteria of personal interest, assignment requirements, information available, and time allotted as important concerns in making choices during a search. In the selection stage, people weigh potential topics against these criteria, predict outcomes of possible choices, and choose a topic with potential for success. In the formulation stage users predict outcome using the same four criteria, but at this point they use the criteria to form a focus for completing the search task.

Interest Corollary

Interest is not always maintained at the same level throughout the search process. Interest was found to increase as the exploratory inquiry led to formulation in the information search process. Motivation and intellectual engagement intensified along with construction. Therefore, personal interest may be expected to increase as uncertainty decreases.

Although an invitational mood seems to match the early stages in the search process and an indicative mood matches the later stages, there is another element of the information-seeking experience closely related to mood. Interest is an important factor throughout the search process in these studies. Individual interest was reported to increase after the formulation of a focus. When construction was well underway and the topic was personally understood, users responded that they had become more interested in the topic or problem. This finding indicates that motivation resulting from personal interest is more pronounced after the midpoint of the search than at the beginning. It takes some time to become intellectually engaged in the topic of a search. The image of "hitting the ground running" may not be descriptive of the search process from the user's perspective. Rather, the image of a gradual exploratory inquiry leading to discovery is a more accurate depiction, with interest increasing along with construction.

Dewey (1934) explains the influence of interest in learning by differentiating between the quality of a whole experience and that of an incomplete experience. A whole experience is an interaction of emotions and ideas in which conscious intent emerges. All experience is not consistently satisfying, however. Sometimes there are

---

distractions and dispersion; what we observe and what we think, what we desire and what we get, are at odds with each other. We put our hands to the plow and turn back; we start and then we stop, not because the experience has reached the end for the sake of which it was initiated but because of extraneous interruptions or of inner lethargy. In contrast with such experience, we have an experience when the material experienced runs its course to fulfillment. Then and only then is it integrated within and demarcated in the general stream of experience from other experiences. A piece of work is finished in a way that is satisfactory; a problem receives its solution; . . . a situation . . . is so rounded out that its close is a consummation and not a cessation. Such an experience is a whole and carries with it its own individualizing quality and self-sufficiency. (p. 35)

A whole experience is one in which intrinsic motivation directs the individual's action toward a satisfying conclusion.

Another factor in influencing interest in information seeking is the notion of fun and play. All creative pursuits have an element of fun, enjoyment, and pleasure. Work and play merge in a fully satisfying, creative experience. Some users profess an enjoyment in searching, but in general aspects of drudgery and boredom are also evident. Bates (1986) asserts that information retrieval systems should be fun. The creative process of learning from information should be pleasurable. We overlook an essential human element by not investigating the play aspect of information seeking.

A number of researchers have studied motivation, investigating the explanations underlying the Yerkes-Dodson Law, which reveals the relation between intensity of motivation and level of learning (Biggs, 1976; Entwistle, 1981; Marton and Saljo, 1976; Pask, 1976). Under the direction of Marton, a group of researchers at the Institute of Education at the University of Gothenberg, Sweden, have made some important findings in this area. Frannson (1984), in an extensive series of studies on intrinsic and extrinsic motivation, found that interest plays a significant part in determining whether a person adopts a surface learning strategy or a deep learning strategy. Extrinsically motivated learners have higher levels of anxiety than do intrinsically motivated learners. According to Frannson:

The conclusion to be drawn for teaching is that if deep-level process-ing is valued, every effort must be made to avoid threatening condi-tions, which rely mainly on extrinsic motivation. This is especially important when the initial level of interest of the students in the learn-ing task is low. (p. 115)

Perhaps similar implications may be drawn for mediation in the informa-tion search process, particularly at initial points when level of interest in the task may be relatively low. This opens a fruitful area of research for investigating the relation of interest and anxiety in information-seeking situations.

Summary of the Uncertainty Principle and Corollaries

Uncertainty is a cognitive state that commonly causes affective symptoms of anxiety and lack of confidence. Uncertainty and anxiety can be expected in the early stages of the information search process. The affective symptoms of uncertainty, confusion, and frustration are associated with vague, unclear thoughts about a topic or question. As knowledge states shift to more clearly fo-cused thoughts, a parallel shift occurs in feelings of increased confidence. Un-certainty due to a lack of understanding, a gap in meaning, or a limited construct initiates the process of information seeking.

The central principle is supported and expanded by six corollaries, as shown in Table 6.1.

Table 6.1. Uncertainty Principle Corollaries

Uncertainty initiates the process of information seeking.

Corollary	Defininition
Process	Constructing meaning
Formulation	Forming a focused perspective
Redundancy	Encountering the expected and unexpected
Mood	Assuming a stance or attitude
Prediction	Making choices based on expectations
Interest	Increasing intellectual engagement

Process Corollary

The process of information seeking involves construction in which the user actively pursues understanding and meaning from the information encountered over a period of time. The process is commonly experienced in a series of thoughts and feelings that shift from vague and anxious to clear and confident, as the search progresses.

Formulation Corollary

Formulation is thinking, developing an understanding, and extending and defining a topic from the information encountered in a search. The formulation of a focus or a guiding idea is a critical, pivotal point in a search when a general topic becomes clearer and a particular perspective is formed as the user moves from uncertainty to understanding.

Redundancy Corollary

The interplay of seeking what is expected or redundant and encountering what is unexpected or unique results in an underlying tension of the search process. Redundant information fits into what we already know and is promptly recognized as being relevant or irrelevant. Unique information does not match our constructs and requires reconstruction to be recognized as useful. Redundancy may be expected to increase as uncertainty decreases. The lack of redundancy at the beginning of the search process may be an underlying cause of anxiety related to uncertainty.

Mood Corollary

Mood, a stance or attitude that the user assumes, opens or closes the range of possibilities in a search. An invitational mood leads to expansive actions, whereas an indicative mood leads to conclusive actions. The user's mood is likely to shift during the search process. An invitational mood may be more appropriate for the early stages of the search, and an indicative mood more appropriate for the latter stages.

Prediction Corollary

The search process may be thought of as a series of choices based on predictions of what will happen if a particular action is taken. Predictions are based on expectations derived from constructs build on past experience. Since each of us constructs our own unique personal worlds, the predictions and choices made in the search process may vary widely from user to user. Predictions may be expected to change during the search process as the user moves from uncertainty to understanding.

Interest Corollary

Interest increases as the exploratory inquiry leads to formulation in the information search process. Motivation and intellectual engagement intensify along with construction. Personal interest may be expected to increase as uncertainty decreases.

From Uncertainty to Understanding

The uncertainty principle and the six corollaries propose a theoretical view of users in their search for information to gain understanding. Figure 6.2 compares the transition from uncertainty to understanding on three levels of experience: thinking, feeling, and acting. Uncertainty, at the initiation of the information search process, is characterized by vague thoughts, anxious feelings, and exploratory actions. Understanding, later in the process, is characterized by clear thoughts, confident feelings, and documentary actions.

Uncertainty . . . . **Understanding**	
T vague	clear
F anxious	confident
A exploring	documenting

Figure 6.2. From Uncertainty to Understanding.

Mediation based on the bibliographic paradigm ignores the holistic view of information seeking as experienced by the user. Intervention is limited to actions for collecting and documenting. Mediation based on an uncertainty principle incorporates cognition, affect, and action from the user's perspective. Intervention encompasses actions for exploring and formulating. Although it may not be necessary to dwell on feelings in information-seeking situations, it is necessary to incorporate an awareness of affect into our professional construct of information seeking. Until the triad of thinking, feeling, and acting is fully accepted as the nature of information seeking, mediation is likely to be fragmented and limited. The uncertainty principle is proposed as a basis for mediation in the process of learning from access to information, thereby enabling users to move from uncertainty to understanding.

Roles of Mediators in the Process of Information Seeking

The uncertainty principle provides a basis for a process approach to intervening with users of libraries and information systems. Before exploring the ways that intervention might assist the search process, it is helpful to be aware of users' perceptions of the role of mediators, in general, and librarians, in particular. The studies of the search process revealed a role for both formal and informal mediators. The term *mediator*, rather than *intermediary*, is used for human intervention to assist information seeking and learning from information access and use. An intermediary intercedes between the information and the user, but this interchange need not involve any human interaction. A mediator, however, implies a person who assists, guides, enables, and otherwise intervenes in another person's information search process.

Users' Perception of the Role of Mediators

In each of the studies of the user's perspective of information seeking, data were collected on the participants' perception of the role of mediators during their information-seeking tasks. These studies identified two types of mediators, formal and informal. Formal mediators are professionals employed in the information system, such as librarians, and in the case of students, professors and teachers. Informal mediators are other people whom users talk to about their work, including family, friends, colleagues, and subject experts.

The findings of the studies reported in this book revealed a limited role for formal mediators, regardless of whether library users were in an academic, public, or school library. The longitudinal studies further verified a limited role for librarians as described by users. Librarians, in most cases, were considered primarily organizers of the sources and sometimes regarded as locators of sources.

The high school students in the initial study (Kuhlthau, 1983) did not consider librarians to be major contributors to the accomplishment of their information-seeking tasks. Constructs of the role of the librarian in their search process were very restricted. When asked if they needed the librarian's assistance when researching a topic, only three of the twenty-five students responded either "almost always" or "often." When asked if they requested help before choosing a topic, the students' responses indicated that this type of assistance was not considered to be the librarian's role. None of the students responded that they "almost always" or "often" asked the librarian for help before choosing a topic. Even after choosing a topic, most of the students did not "almost always" or even "often" seek a librarian's assistance. The students lacked constructs that would prompt them to request mediation from a librarian in even the more traditional tasks of topic selection and information collection. They regarded the library as a self-service operation with little provision for professional/client interaction.

The verification study (Kuhlthau, Turock, George, and Belvin, 1990) of three types of library users, which included 385 people, also revealed a limited use of librarians during information seeking. One of the items on a questionnaire, "Who have you talked to about your project?," sought to uncover those who were perceived as mediators during the search process. This question may not have revealed who actually was used as a mediator, but it did show participants' perceptions of who served that function for them. The following four categories were used: friend or family member, peer (one doing a similar task), expert (teacher, professor, or one who knows about the topic), or professional (librarian). Responses indicated that 39 percent of the respondents consulted experts, 25 percent conferred with librarians, 20 percent reported using friends and family, and 13 percent talked with peers. There was no significant change during the search process, nor was there a significant difference by type of library. Although librarians were a group with whom all of the participants in this study had direct contact, they were not identified in 75 percent of the responses. A wide range of experts was mentioned, however, drawing from the community and other contacts.

The case studies (Kuhlthau, 1988c) verified the limited role and disclosed a perception of the librarian as a "last resort" source locator. The librarian was described as a person to go to when one is "stuck." One person explained that when he is "totally stuck," he asks a librarian and expects to be directed to a specific source. Another student stated that the librarian helps with "obscure sources, like how to use law books." And another related that if "I can't find something, I guess I try to find the easy way out and ask the librarian." Seeking assistance from the librarian was seen as taking the "easy way out" and not as a legitimate approach to researching a topic or as an integral part of the search process.

The Role of Formal Mediators

Although the role of the librarian was considered to be quite narrow, the participants frequently turned to informal mediators, including parents, siblings, and friends. Many students considered talking about their topics an important strategy both during and after topic selection. In the original study, only five students replied that they "seldom" or "almost never" discussed their topic in the process of selection. After they have chosen their topic, even more students responded that they talked about it with another person or used an informal mediator. Only one responded "seldom," and none of the students stated that he or she "almost never" discussed the topic. Although many of the students felt a need to discuss their topic selection and the development of ideas with others, they did not consider talking about the development of their topics with the librarian. Most of the students revealed that they expected (or were expected) to proceed totally on their own without assistance from formal mediators. They perceived that librarians had little or no role in their search process.

The case study subjects further explained that they wanted to discuss their topics with another person and that they sought help in thinking through some of the ideas that they confronted in the search process. For this help they frequently turned to informal mediators. One related a way that his father assisted him in formulating a focus:

> I showed him what I was doing and he would be able t o guide me. He would actually help me to organize it. He'd take out a piece of paper and say "OK, these are the ways you are headed, now which one do you want." He would just lay it out for me, but he would try not to influence me.

The study revealed that students attributed a limited, source-oriented role to librarians while they frequently reported making use of a variety of informal mediators in the process of their library research. The case studies confirmed the view of the librarian's role as very limited and source-oriented. The librarian's role was described as directing them to sources that they had difficulty locating on their own. Some students warned that too much assistance might in some way spoil the project by making it less than their own work. Informal mediators assisted students by listening, offering encouragement, and sometimes recommending a strategy. Although the students were seeking guidance in formulation, they wanted the important decisions about the project to remain with them.

Call for Formal Mediators in the Process of Information Seeking

The students seemed to recognize their own need for help and sought process intervention from informal mediators. They frequently discussed thoughts that they were forming about their topic with informal mediators, but they seldom mentioned the specific sources that they were using. At the end of the study, the case study participants expressed a need for an expanded process-oriented role for the formal mediator, either the teacher or the librarian. They revealed some confusion between the role of the teacher and of the librarian as formal mediators. Each participant described a desire for guidance with the process of the search, as well as with the sources of information. The following are examples of the statements from case study subjects made in response to the question, "What further help could you have used?" One person said:

> Encouragement. Being able to go to the teacher and say, "This is my topic what do you think." I don't know if anyone did that. I did it with friends, but friends don't know what the possibilities are. . . . They don't know what information is available. You could say to the librarian, "This is my topic. Do you think I could find enough information? Where should I go?" That would help at the beginning.

This person's statement, although primarily source-oriented, first and foremost seeks encouragement. When asked how a mediator might be helpful, she responded without hesitation, "encouragement." Acknowledgment of the uncertainty and encouraging support are primary features of process-oriented mediation. Second, the statement reveals a need or at least an inclination to talk about the topic with someone. Conversation and dialogue facilitate formulation and are important elements in any constructive process. Third is the realization that informal mediators have a limited capacity to help and that formal mediators provide professional guidance. Another student's statement regarding further help reveals even more need for the introduction of intervention in the search process. As this participant explained:

> You have a research paper. It's due in four weeks. . . . It's all on your own; I guess, research papers are. . . . They could have done something in between; given us ideas. Teachers are so nonchalant about giving research papers. . . . They don't discuss it with you. . . . In the meantime, the teacher isn't really being there. I don't think they should say "Let me see your note cards." But they should say, "OK, tomorrow we'll talk about what you found, if you have any problems, or what

point you are at." Not pressure you, "Well if you haven't started just forget it." Sometimes you haven't started because you don't know what you're about. It would help to know if everyone else was lost, too.

Within this person's statement is a clear call for process intervention, the need for someone "being there" during the process. "Being there" is further described as including the following: intervention to address what you have found, any problems you may have, and the point you are at in the process.

Both of these people were groping for some formal intervention, beyond mere location of sources, in the process of their search. They indicated a need for more help at the beginning of the process. In the collection stage, after a problem has been well defined and formulated, the library system works fairly efficiently. After most of the uncertainty has been resolved the system functions effectively. But these people seemed to be calling out for help in the midst of the uncertainty and confusion of the earlier stages.

Process mediation would provide opportunities to "talk about" ideas as they emerge. A process approach would acknowledge common experience of uncertainty in the early stages of the process. There is a need for process mediation because such intervention does not increase anxiety by "pressuring you" into premature closure. Caution is recommended against overly indicative intervention, such as the traditional requirement of a thesis statement and outline before the exploration and formulation necessary for collection and closure. There is a call for more invitational intervention, such as dialogue for clarifying emerging ideas, which fosters exploration and formulation. It is in these early stages of the search process that traditional intervention is at its weakest.

Providing Information for the Process of Construction

Scrutiny of these statements of users reveals a need for intervention addressing two major aspects of information seeking, access to sources and guidance in process. Although the major concern of this work is the process of information seeking, that is not to suggest that help with sources of information is unnecessary. The two types of intervention are connected and interrelated in subtle ways. The tension experienced by users between physical access and intellectual access should be addressed in intervention.

Source and Process

The source versus process debate, which differentiates between help with physical access and help with intellectual access, needs further attention in light of the findings of the research into the information search process that reveal the two inseparably intertwined from the user's perspective. Source-related intervention assists with access to information. Process-related intervention assists with learning through the use of information. Uncertainty may underlie both source and process and is likely to be compounded in actual situations of information seeking. Although not the main focus of this research, physical access also factors into uncertainty.

Uncertainty can be caused by a lack of ability to find needed information or being overwhelmed by the quantity of information. Users' perceptions of quantity as well as their perceptions of ignorance seem to factor in their uncertainty. Studies by Mellon (1986) showed that anxiety is prevalent when students are required to use a library that is unfamiliar to them. Perceptions of quantity may relate to the sheer size of the facility, collection, and information available. Perceptions of ignorance relate to a sense of not knowing how to find information, of not knowing what sources are available, and of the expectation that everyone should know how to search for information. Information access through the Internet may intensify the problem of anxiety and uncertainty related to an overwhelming quantity of information.

The two aspects of intervention, one source-related, leading to access to information, and the other process-related, leading to construction and learning, are interrelated. There is a need to develop strategies for intervening with users that incorporate both informed access and enhanced process. The structure, sequence, format, and depth of information are critical considerations when access to sources is placed within the context of the information search process.

Structure and Sequence

Information does not serve the same function in all the phases of the information search process. It follows that for information to be most useful it should be presented in ways that match the user's cognitive and affective stage in the process of information seeking.

Bruner's (1973) three basic considerations for learning are the nature of the knowledge to be learned, the nature of the knower, and the nature of the knowledge-getting process. This book concentrates on the nature of the knowledge-getting process. In addition, the nature of the knowledge and the nature of the knower should be considered for providing intervention in the search process.

Structuring a discipline for learning is based on the idea that "any subject can be taught to any person at any age in some form that is honest" (Bruner, 1977, p. 33). To facilitate learning, information is sequenced to present ideas meaningfully for the learner. Thus, Bruner recommended a spiral curriculum, building on a concept introduced by Dewey some years before, which starts where the person is, uses the mode of thinking that he or she possesses, and makes information accessible to the person in the process of learning. This concept underlies the practice of recommending paths through a collection of information and suggesting a sequence for encountering and gathering the information.

Format and Depth

Bruner (1975) extends Piaget's stages of cognitive development to encompass all learners depending on their point in the learning process, their prior experience and knowledge, as well as their stage of cognitive development. Enactive, the earliest stage, is acting within a concrete experience and learning from that interaction. Iconic, one step removed from the actual concrete experience, is visualization within a vicarious experience. Symbolic, the third stage, is using verbal and written symbols to learn and think. Learning moves through the stages of enactive, iconic, and symbolic as the learner's knowledge and level of understanding deepen.

When these stages are placed within the context of the stages of the information search process, we begin to see patterns for information presentation. During initiation and selection, enactive information may increase understanding of the concrete aspects of the problem and provide a personal connection. During exploration, iconic information may provide vicarious experience on which to build abstract dimensions. During formulation and collection, symbolic information may extend abstract thinking grounded in a deep personal understanding.

Dale's (1969) cone of experience, which depicts where various types of media might fall within Bruner's three categories of experience, serves to illustrate how information may be sequenced by format. For example, enactive media would include exhibits, field trips, and demonstrations; iconic media would include video, film, recordings, and pictures; and abstract media would include all printed materials. Although Dale's analysis is somewhat dated, the underlying concept may be applied to advanced computer and information technologies.

Two aspects of the presentation of information must be recognized. One is the format of the information, the medium or the package in which the information is presented to the user. The other is the depth of the information in terms of subject matter content. The concrete to abstract continuum addresses both format of presentation and depth of presentation. Although we may be tempted to view the format/depth issue in a simplistic way, at closer scrutiny the complexity of the issue becomes obvious. All iconic presentations are not of equal depth. Some films are unquestionably more abstract than others. Of course, symbolic presentations vary in a similar way. There is no simple pattern for sequencing information into the search process of users. The challenge for information professionals is to consider the concrete to abstract continuum and connections between format and depth for interventions that sequence information in a meaningful way.

Different ways of knowing support different stages of knowing. The information-rich environment of our technological age offers constant access to diverse formats of information in our everyday lives. Understanding the interrelationship of different information media is a critical element in interacting with information users. Many of the more pervasive media are enactive and iconic. How does the library that is primarily symbolic connect with other ways of knowing? Intervention may enable people to make connections, to move from concrete to abstract, to recognize the need to know more, to dig deeper, and to gain greater understanding.

Reference and Instruction

Traditionally, libraries offer two areas of service to assist users: reference and instruction. As noted in Chapter 1, these two well-established services incorporate sophisticated techniques for intervening with users. However, physical access within a source orientation remains the primary objective of these services. Following is an examination of reference and instruction to identify where intellectual access within a process approach is being or may be incorporated within these services. Reference is examined on five levels of mediation, and instruction is depicted on five levels of education.

Levels of Mediation

From librarians' point of view, there are a variety of roles in relation to the user that may be thought of as different levels of service. Within reference, five levels of mediation have been identified: level 1, the organizer; level 2, the locator; level 3, the identifier; level 4, the advisor; and level 5, the counselor (see Figure 7.1). For each level, the type of intervention is described with underlying assumptions related to the bibliographic paradigm (source orientation) and/or the uncertainty principle (process approach). The level of mediation is discussed in terms of the complexity of the user's problem and the user's stage in the process. Interventions for each level of mediation are described.

Level 1: Organizer

At level 1, organizer, no direct intervention is provided. Many possible interventions do not include direct human contact. The system as intermediary encompasses everything from the arrangement of the facility, the signs and directions, accessibility of materials, the organization of indexes and catalogs, and all of these factors in relation to advanced technology. The collection of sources is made available through a system of classification and through catalogs and indexes. Little differentiation is made among sources, with the exception of subject classification and identification of format. Physical access is offered in house or from remote locations. In this case, the role of the librarian is to provide an organized collection of sources for independent access.

Table 7.1. Levels of Mediation

Level	Description
1 Organizer	No intervention Self-service search in an organized collection.
2 Locator	Ready-reference intervention Single fact or source search; query/answer
3 Identifier	Standard reference intervention Subject search; group of sources in no particular order; problem/interview/sources
4 Advisor	Pattern intervention Subject search; group of sources in recommended order; problem/negotiation/sequence
5 Counselor	Process intervention Constructive search; holistic experience; problem/dialogue/strategy/sources/sequence redefinition

The underlying assumption of level 1 is firmly grounded in the bibliographic paradigm and is based on a concept of certainty rather than uncertainty. The organizer's ultimate task is to collect and organize sources and to maintain the collection for efficient retrieval. Total attention is given to sources and technology. The individual user and the individual's problem are peripheral to the organizer's primary responsibility and concern.

Access to sources is through a self-service search that the user conducts, often without human intervention, through a system of classification. Access is available to the total collection, all at once, all the time. This is the most common use of libraries and databases. An individual comes to the collection with a topic or problem, with the intent of collecting relevant sources. The index gives rudimentary information on sources, such as format, citation, and classification. Little human intervention occurs, with the possible exception of the transaction at circulation. No mediation into the intellectual process of the user takes place. The effectiveness of this level depends on the user's proficiency in the search and on the complexity of the problem under investigation. Later stages in the search process are more suited to the organizer level than are the early stages.

The organizer's role, however, underlies all of the other levels of mediation. Without the organizer there would be no access to sources for learning or for any other purposes. The demands of the organizer's role, however, have tended to consume the librarian and to overshadow the importance of the other levels of mediation for improving access and guiding use.

Level 2: Locator

Level 2, locator, offers what is traditionally called ready-reference intervention, when the user has a clear, simple question. A single fact or item search is conducted and the answer or the source is provided. The principle underlying this type of mediation is that there is a right answer and a single right source that will match the user's question: "Tell me what you want and I can give it t o you." Information is treated as a thing that can be produced and provided.

The underlying assumptions of the locator level are that the system is certain, questions are simple, and there is one right answer. The concept of accuracy as a measure of outcome of service fits this level of mediation. Many of the accountability measures for reference service have been built on this concept. How many questions can be answered in an afternoon or evening at the reference desk? The more the better. "Quickly, tell me your question and I will locate the answer," is the synopsis of this reference approach: a single incident, a simple question, and a matched source.

Locator mediation may include a range of interventions, from a directive to use a specific tool for locating sources, such as a catalog or an index, to the location of a specific answer to a specific question. The user may be present at the reference desk or at a terminal, or the user may be at a remote location on the phone or computer, in an office down the hall, at home, or in another part of the world. The locator's responses may range from a direction to search for an item to giving an answer. In most instances, a source is located in response to a specific request.

The locator is effective for simple, straightforward, single-issue questions. Although the locator considers the user's query, intervention centers on locating the right source and not on the subjective complexities of the user's problem underlying the query. Mediation at level 2 is solidly source-oriented, and the process of the user is not considered. Locator-level intervention is effective with simple routine questions and in the later stages in the search process when a specific question can be articulated and a single source located relating to some particular aspect of a focused topic. The locator is of limited value when there is vagueness, ambiguity, or uncertainty.

Level 3: Identifier

The identifier, level 3, expects to see the user only once during the information-seeking process. This hypothetical user has a topic to investigate or a problem to solve more extensive than the single reference question. A group of sources are identified as related to the topic or subject. These are recommended as a group in no particular order, provided in no specific sequence. The sources may be from a variety of formats and depths. Typically, when the user comes to the collection with a general topic, seeking information from a number of sources, one comprehensive search is conducted and a "pile" of information is identified as relevant to the subject without consideration for the users' particular point of view, level of knowledge, or stage in the search process. The information is identified usually without any advice on approach or any suggestion of continuing dialogue with the mediator.

The underlying assumption in this level of mediation is the system's point of view and is firmly within the bibliographic paradigm. The system responds to the user's query but does little to accommodate the user's information need. Users' queries are addressed in the collection by identifying sources that match the topic. Information needs are addressed by identifying the sources that relate to the general subject under investigation. Users are assumed to approach problems from a uniform perspective, knowledge state, and stage of process. The identifier level addresses all users in the same way: "Tell me your subject and I will identify the sources that relate to the subject."

Identifiers mediate most effectively when a topic or problem is focused and information is being collected to define the focus. In the early more exploratory stages, Identifiers often overwhelm users with numerous sources and overload them with the sheer quantity of information. There is a compulsion to name every source that might be relevant. That completeness is necessary because there is only one point of contact with the user. Subject access to databases and search engines for the Internet are commonly based in the identifier level.

Identifiers do not address the complexity of the learning process that users commonly experience in extended searches. They often mislead users into thinking information seeking is merely identifying sources and not interpreting them. Users tend to think that they are the only ones experiencing confusion because the certainty of the system is predominant in the identifier's approach. Users are also misled into thinking that the search process does not require exploring and formulating or that the mere collection of sources on the general topic is sufficient for understanding and presenting. Unfortunately, many users encounter severe "writing blocks" when they attempt to prepare to present information gathered in this way. They have not formed new constructs during the search process and have not sought meaning from the information encountered as the search progressed. The "pile of sources" does not necessarily lead to understanding and learning.

Level 4: Advisor

Level 4, advisor, is a pattern approach to intervention. The advisor guides users through a sequence of sources on a particular topic or problem. The advisor responds to users who indicate that they have a problem that they intend to investigate in some depth over a period of time. The advisor not only identifies sources on a topic but also recommends a sequence for using the sources, usually from general to specific or concrete to abstract, with some consideration for the format and depth of the sources. The user asks a complex question or requests information on a topic, and the advisor recommends a way of navigating through the information by using source *a,* then source *b,* then source *c,* and so on. The advisor may suggest that the user return periodically during the search or, once the sequence has been recommended, may leave the user to follow the path independently.

The underlying assumption of the advisor is source-oriented and falls well within the bibliographic paradigm. The user's problem is addressed within the frame of reference of sources and within a prescribed sequence of use. Therein lies the limitation of the advisor's mediation. Heavy emphasis is placed on the sources of information, the tools to access the sources, and the appropriate sequence for use of sources. One sequence is recommended for all. The underlying assumption of the advisor level of mediation is that there is one sequence to use sources to address any topic for every user. Users' problems are expected to be static, with a specific end in sight. The underlying assumption is similar to those of "pathfinders," which are standardized descriptions of a generic search offered to those who have a similar topic to investigate.

Although advisors move along the continuum of mediation to accommodate a user's information-seeking process, the individual's creative learning process is not taken into account. No mention is made of the user's state of knowledge or stage in the process. The user's dynamic problem, as that person learns from information access and use, and his or her unique individual process are not addressed. Users are easily misled into thinking that there is one right search for all, no matter what their constructs as they enter the process and no matter what ideas they encounter along the way.

These four levels of mediation provide various forms of source intervention in the information seeking of users. Librarians and the systems they have designed have been quite helpful for source intervention in response to simple queries. Source intervention is also helpful in the later stages of the information search process after formulation has taken place. At that point in the process, users can articulate fairly clearly what they are looking for, and the information system can respond consistently and directly. The system has, in fact, been designed for just this sort of intervention. It is when we get into the more murky waters at the early stages that the system does not respond as well.

Level 5: Counselor

Level 5, the counselor, provides intervention into the process of the user. Although the concept of information counselor (Debons, 1975; Dosa, 1978) is not new, the role of the counselor should be expanded in response to research into the users' perspective on the search process. Dosa (1978) described information counseling as the interactive process by which an information intermediary (a) assesses the needs and constraints of an individual through in-depth interviewing; (b) determines the optimal ways available to meet such needs; (c) actively assists the client in finding, using, and if needed, applying information; (d) assures systematic follow-up to ascertain that the assistance enabled clients to achieve their goals; (e) develop systematic quality control and evaluation processes. (p. 16)

The underlying assumption is that the user is learning from information in a constructive process as the information search proceeds. There is no one right answer and no fixed sequence for all. The person's problem determines the intervention. The holistic experience is understood, acknowledged, and articulated as an important aspect of mediation. The user and the mediator enter into a dialogue regarding the user's problem over time.

The uncertainty principle underlies the counselor's intervention. Information seeking is viewed as a process of construction rather than a quest for right answers. The user is guided through the dynamic and fluid process of seeking meaning. The recommended sequence of sources of information emerges as the topic or problem evolves in a highly individual way. The depth and format of information is understood from the user's past experience and the constructs he or she holds. There are many meanings and many focuses within a general topic. The user forms a focus that is a personal perspective on the general topic under investigation. The counselor approaches information seeking as a creative, individual process that is dynamic and unique for each person.

In contrast, mediation in levels 1 through 4 is based on the principle of certainty. The sources are organized for accurate retrieval. Confusion increases when the mediator proposes a definite answer, but the user seeks to learn more about a vague topic or an unfocused problem. Mediation within the bibliographic paradigm may be appropriate for the collection stage or when a problem is clearly defined. But when a person is in an exploration stage seeking to formulate a focus, mediation from the bibliographic paradigm is not likely to match his or her information need.

The counselor establishes a dialogue that leads to a strategy incorporating depth, format, structure, and sequence for learning tailored to the user and her or his task. The mediator expects the user to return periodically to reestablish the dialogue based on his or her emerging constructs. The user redefines the problem with the counselor, determines a strategy, identifies appropriate sources, and determines a sequence for use. A variety of searches may be conducted with different purposes that match the user's experience at the different points in the process. Strategies are adapted during the process to meet the user's tasks at a particular stage. Sources are recommended in terms of the user's state of knowledge and constructs built from past experience. The relevance of sources is expected to change during the information search. The entire search process is considered highly individual, creative, and personal. There is no one perfect solution, but there are many approaches in response to the creative formulation of each individual.

Use of sources is matched to the stage of the process that the person is experiencing. The type of search conducted may be a preliminary search to get started, an exploratory search for the early stages before formulation, or a comprehensive search for the later stages in preparation for completion. Research indicates a number of innovative intervention strategies, such as search and idea tactics (Bates, 1979); neutral questioning (Dervin and Dewdney, 1986); and chaining, differentiating, and extracting (Ellis, 1989). Strategies appropriate to the stage of the process are recommended, including browsing, skimming and scanning, reflecting, listing ideas, discussing possible choices, and writing short explanations. Four basic strategies for seeking meaning may be applied: recall, summarize, paraphrase, and extend (Kuhlthau, 1981). Recall is to reflect on what is remembered, summarize is to describe in a concise form, paraphrase is to retell in one's own words, and extend is to connect to other ideas or to go beyond the information given. These basic abilities for using information are discussed in Chapter 8.

Levels of Education

Instruction is another well-established library service that may similarly be differentiated into five levels of education: level 1, the organizer; level 2, the lecturer; level 3, the instructor; level 4, the tutor; and level 5, the counselor. Levels of education are differentiated by the number of sessions, the content of instruction, and the type of user problem typically addressed. Education is categorized as being planned for one session, a variety of unconnected sessions, a sequence of related sessions, or holistic interaction over time.

The term *education,* implying the development of transferable knowledge and capabilities, is used rather than *instruction*, which refers to more immediate outcomes. Terms currently applied to formal teaching, such as bibliographic instruction, library instruction, and information skills instruction, are used interchangeably when referring to current practice across types of libraries. Education is applied as a generic term depicting any planned instruction related to the use of sources found in libraries as well as the use of information in a broader context of learning. Information literacy has become the overarching term for education programs from preschool to postgraduate.

Although education takes place in all types of libraries, it is given priority in those that are part of educational institutions. Although this discussion centers on school and academic libraries, where instructional sessions are frequently planned for groups of students, it also applies to education, perhaps less formal, given in public and special libraries. The concepts have direct implications and applications for education in all types of libraries.

An important consideration for education programs is whether instruction is integrated into the user's problem-solving situation. Much has been written about integrating library instruction with the curriculum of the school or university. Loertscher's (1982) taxonomy of integration of school library services conceptualizes a hierarchy of involvement and coordination. The user's perspective on the information search process offers a further dimension for defining levels of education. The relationship of instruction to the user's specific problem is defined at each level as well as the integration of instruction with the user's information-seeking process. Education below level 3 is not directed to a specific information need or problem. Levels 3 through 5 are offered within the context of the user's information problem. While levels 3 and 4 *may* be integrated with assignments from the subject areas of the curriculum, Level 5 *must* be integrated with the curriculum and educational objectives of the institution. As with the levels of mediation, the levels are heavily source and system oriented, with only the counselor at level 5 addressing the holistic experience of the user in the information search process.

In the following description of each of the five levels, the primary objectives, content of instruction, and some typical approaches are discussed (see Table 7.2).

Table 7.2. Levels of Education

Level	Description
1 Organizer	No instruction Self-service search in an organized collection
2 Lecturer	Orienting instruction Single session; overview of services, policies, and location of facility and collection; no specific problem
3 Instructor	Single-source instruction Variety of independent sessions; instruction on one type of source to address specific problem
4 Tutor	Strategy instruction Series of sessions; instruction on one type of source to address specific problem
5 Counselor	Process instruction Holistic interaction over time; instruction on identifying and interpreting information to address evolving problem

Level 1: Organizer

At level 1, the organizer gives no instruction. The responsibility of the organizer is to provide an organized collection of sources with access through a system of classification. The organizer's role underlies all of the other levels of education as it does all levels of mediation. Without an organized collection of sources and information classified for subject access, information seeking is severely hampered if not impossible. The library or information system is considered a self-service operation in which users are left to their own devices to learn how to locate and use sources.

The primary goal of library instruction, according to an American Library Association (1980) Council policy statement, is to develop "independent information retrieval," or what Tuckett and Stoffle (1984) refer to as "self-reliant library users." The underlying principle of traditional instruction is the concept that users can be taught to rely on the organizer level of intervention. Traditional source-oriented instruction has fallen woefully short of expectations for developing independence in using libraries and information systems. Library skills have not been found to transfer very well to other libraries, let alone to the broader spectrum of information need. We are beginning to understand the complexity of what users need to know to be self-reliant in their information use. Research into the information search process indicates that users benefit from knowledge of the process of constructing from information along with knowledge about the access to sources of information. Self-reliant users have skill in interpreting information and seeking meaning as well as skill in locating sources and seeking information. Self-reliant users also know when to proceed on their own and when to ask for mediation at a level beyond that of the organizer. Advances in information technology have promoted the objective of the self-reliant user and have fostered the development of extensive programs of information literacy to prepare users for independent access to and use of vast sources of information.

Level 2: Lecturer

At level 2, the lecturer conducts planned orientation in a single session for a large group. A typical orientation session takes place at the beginning of the semester for a group of incoming students. Orientation sessions are offered in all types of libraries for the full range of potential library users.

On the lecturer level, one session of instruction is offered with the objective of orienting users to the location of the library and to the sources within it. A map is frequently used to illustrate the location of the collections and services of the library. In addition, an overview of procedures and policies is given. Lecture methods are most common, accompanied by a tour of the facility. Multimedia productions, in the form of videos and computer presentations, are frequently used. The tendency to tell everything once and for all is often the objective of the lecturer, frequently overwhelming people with an abundance of new and unconnected facts and directions.

The lecturer level of education is not related to a specific assignment for immediate use but rather consists of a general orientation for future use. By not being integrated into a particular information problem, lecturer sessions tend to be superficial and isolated. They cannot be relied on for a substantial amount of recall and transference beyond awareness of general location and procedure.

Although education at this level serves to orient new users to general location and procedures, the expectation that they will be able to use the library and information systems effectively following such sessions is unlikely to be met. Much depends on the background and experience of the individual user. All too often instruction stops at this level, leaving the person with the feeling that he or she is the only one who does not know how to use the system independently. These sessions should be thought of as a beginning or an introduction for further education on other levels.

Level 3: Instructor

Level 3, the instructor, provides instruction on a single source usually related to a specific problem or assignment. A source is identified as being particularly useful for addressing the user's problem or the problem of a group of users. Instruction in how to locate information using a particular source or database is offered preferably at the time when the content is to be used. A typical example of a lesson at the instructor level is a demonstration of how to use an index to locate articles in journals and current periodicals. An understanding of underlying concepts, such as subject access, is important for transference of learning to other similar sources and systems.

The primary objective of the instructor is to identify appropriate, relevant sources and to teach about their use at the point when the person is ready to apply the learning. Teaching at the instructor level may consist of a variety of independent sessions, each concentrating on one type of source or technology. To be most effective, instruction is given at the time that the source is needed to address a problem, rather than in isolation for some future use. The key to motivation and retention is connecting the instruction to the actual information need of the individual user. Some printed instructions provided for the "typical user" may fall within the Instructor's level. One example is "point-of-use" instructions for using a source and the technology to access the source.

The instructor connects with the teacher or professor by identifying sources for learning. Some advanced planning is needed to schedule the instructional session, but at this level separate teaching responsibilities rather than team teaching require a minimum of joint planning. The Instructor level is primarily source-oriented and is unlikely to accommodate the experience of the user in the process of information seeking.

Level 4: Tutor

At level 4, the tutor provides instruction in a series of sessions in which advice is given on strategies for locating and using sources to address a specific problem or assignment. At this level, the primary objective of education is to teach a sequence for using sources and a search strategy, perhaps including some advice on depth and format of information in relation to the user's task or problem.

Tutors direct users on a path through the sources. The metaphor of "navigating" through the literature is commonly applied for describing a sequence of sources. Knapp's (1966) work on conceptual frameworks provides the foundation for the search strategy approach. The Knapp program was designed to teach students the library as a system of pathways: "Whoever would use the system must know the 'way' to use the system. Knowing the way means understanding the nature of the total system, knowing where to plug into it, knowing how to make it work" (p. 130).

Tutors help users to understand the relationship among sources of information. At this level, users may be led through a wide range of sources in the library as well as multiple sources in the larger information environment. Some printed materials may be provided on the tutor level. An example is pathfinders that chart a series of sources to use that are relevant to a general subject.

The full range of experiences and abilities in the process of learning from information access and use is not addressed at the tutor level. As on the instructor level, skill in the location of sources and the use of information technology is the primary emphasis. The reasoning process that underlies independent research is not developed. Most computer-assisted instruction in the form of tutorials to guide use of sources falls into this category of education.

Tutors plan with teachers and professors well in advance of the assignment to integrate library instruction into the course at significant points. The teacher provides the subject context and the learning objective, and the librarian offers the sources to meet the objective. In addition, the tutor has specific instructional objectives related to developing information literacy skills that are to be met within the series of instructional sessions. Tutors and teachers discuss objectives and sources and plan their shared teaching responsibilities.

Level 5: Counselor

At level 5, the counselor provides process intervention that accommodates the user's thoughts, actions, and feelings in each stage of the information search process. Emphasis is on the process of learning from a variety of sources of information. The primary objective is to prepare users for future situations of learning from information access and use through knowledge of and ability in the process of information seeking. Strategies for working through the stages of the search process are incorporated with strategies for locating sources of information. Encouragement and support are an important attribute of education at the counselor level.

The counselor's instruction is fully integrated with the user's problem. In school and academic settings, the counselor is an active participant in the instructional team with teachers, administrators, and curriculum planners. The counselor is involved in all phases of designing instruction, from setting goals and objectives, to designing methods and activities, to establishing the means for evaluation. The counselor is a partner in the implementation of the educational plan. The counselor level of education incorporates learning theory into teaching methodology and is based on individual construction and learning. The approach involves using, interpreting, and seeking meaning in information from an inquiry perspective. In educational institutions course assignments drive the information education program. Assignments that center on inquiry lead to higher-level thinking of analysis, synthesis, and presentation, with particular attention to the earliest stages of the information search process. Opportunities are provided for students to understand the search process by reflecting on their own efforts and learning ways that their process might be effective in future information use.

Educational programs are moving beyond a library orientation, single source, and simple navigation approach to the use of information for thinking and learning. The necessity for enabling students to learn the process of a search for information access and use as well as the sources of information has been recognized in elementary and secondary school library media programs (Irving, 1985; Stripling and Pitts, 1988; Eisenberg and Berkowitz, 1990) as well as in academic library programs for university students. Guiding students through the process involves recognition of the crucial early stages of a search when thoughts are being formulated and counseling students in strategies that allow thoughts to develop through the information encountered in located sources (Kuhlthau, 1985b). An inquiry-based learning approach to using school library media centers for learning is an important initiative in K–13 education, with comparable initiatives taking hold in university libraries as well.

The broader view of information education goes beyond location of sources to the interpretation and use of information for learning. Information education centers on thinking about the ideas in information sources. It emphasizes seeking to shape a topic rather than merely getting a right answer. It is concerned with seeking meaning and gaining understanding. The emerging theoretical base for information education, combining learning theory, research in information-seeking behavior, and a broader view of library and information skills, provides a framework for assessing existing instruction and developing the fifth level of education.

At the counselor level the two forms of intervention, mediation and education, merge into one interactive service of guidance. The counselor's challenge is to provide a new kind of intervention that is becoming essential in the technological information age. The vast increase in the amount of information calls for intervention into the process of information seeking that leads to meaning. The process of information seeking with the object of accomplishing a meaningful task need not require access to all of the information relevant to the topic but only to that which pertains to the particular focus the person has formulated. The focus formed in the early stages of the information search process enables choices of what is relevant, pertinent, and enough to accomplish the task in the later stages. The counselor guides and supports the user, offering encouragement, strategies, sequence, depth, format, and redefinition through exploration and formulation in preparation for collection and presentation.

Zones of Intervention in the Process of Information Seeking

8

It is clear from the research on the search process that the information seeker goes to others for help at various points in the process. It is also evident that people have a limited view of librarians as mediators, particularly in the intellectual process of using information during the process of information seeking. The analysis of reference and instruction on levels of mediation and education in Chapter 7 reveals that most intervention is based on a source orientation, with little attention to the user's process of construction. When a person confers with a librarian it is usually to ask for advice on how to locate or use a source. Although this is a legitimate use of the librarian's expertise, questions arise about the potential for professional intervention in the stages of the information search process. How do formal mediators become involved in the constructive process of another person? What is the role and function of process intervention in information seeking and use?

Intervention Based on an Uncertainty Principle

Schon's (1982) work on "reflection in practice" offers insight into how professionals diagnose and design intervention to meet an individual's problem situation. The novice practitioner depends on specific rules and procedures, but the expert relies on experience and theory. Other professions, such as law and medicine, have developed rules, procedures, and theories for intervention. The professional's expertise in diagnosing when a client needs assistance and what type of help is needed is an important element in successful professional practice. Librarianship has extensive rules, procedures, and theories related to the bibliographic paradigm that enable effective intervention in access to sources. Can the information professional's expertise and theory be extended to incorporate uncertainty and process within the user's information seeking and use?

Intervention based on a principle of certainty and order, that is intervention in the bibliographic paradigm, concentrates on matching a person's query with the organized collection. Intervention based on a principle of uncertainty encompasses the holistic process of seeking and using information from the perspective of the individual user. The uncertainty principle suggests new ways of thinking about intervention to accommodate the holistic experience of users in the information search process. Such intervention addresses evolving information needs within the dynamic stages of the information search process to accommodate initiating, selecting, exploring, formulating, collecting, and presenting. This is not to recommend that librarians be involved in every stage of the information search process of every person. On the contrary, it is necessary to determine when it is helpful to intervene and when intervention is unnecessary. The critical question is when is intervention needed and what intervention is helpful to an individual in his or her information seeking and use. Identifying when intervention is needed and determining what mediation and education are appropriate is the professional's art, the role of the reflective practitioner.

The Concept of a Zone of Intervention

Professional intervention calls for diagnosing the user's problem and identifying what intervention would be helpful. Intervention where the individual is experiencing difficulty is warranted. Intervention into the areas where the individual is self-sufficient is unnecessary, as well as intrusive and annoying. The concept of a zone of intervention offers the information professional a way to make decisions regarding interaction with users that is enabling and enriching. The concept enables the professional to analyze the user's task to determine the type of intervention that might be helpful and to tailor service to the user's specific task and information need. Using the framework of the model of the information search process and the underlying theory of uncertainty the professional can differentiate between routine tasks that may be addressed with source intervention and more complex tasks that engage the user in different stages of information seeking and may require process intervention.

The zone of intervention is a concept modeled on Vygotsky's (1978) notion of a zone of proximal development. Vygotsky, the Soviet psychologist whose work had a profound influence on learning theory, developed the concept of identifying an area or zone in which intervention would be most helpful to a learner. The zone of proximal development is the distance between the actual developmental level as determined by independent problem solving and the level of potential development as determined through problem solving under professional guidance or in collaboration with more capable peers (p. 131).

This concept provides a way of understanding intervention in the constructive process of another person.

The zone of intervention in information seeking may be thought of in a similar way. The zone of intervention is that area in which an information user can do with advice and assistance what he or she cannot do alone or can do only with difficulty (see Figure 8.1). Intervention within this zone enables users to progress in the accomplishment of their task. Intervention outside this zone is inefficient and unnecessary, experienced by users as intrusive on the one hand and as overwhelming on the other.

> # Zone of Intervention
>
> That area in which an information user can do with advice and assistance what he or she cannot do alone or can do only with great difficulty.

Figure 8.1. Zone of Intervention.

Zones of Intervention

People arrive at the library or information system with different types of information questions and problems and at different points in the information search process. Types of problems and stages of process require a range of interventions. Interventions may be thought of as occurring in five zones (Z1–Z5), as described in Figure 8.2 (p. 130).

In the first zone (Z1), the problem is self-diagnosed, the need for information self-determined, and a search self-conducted. In each of the other zones (Z2–Z5), the person consults the librarian, who diagnoses the zone of intervention from a query or a problem statement. Through an interview the background of the problem is elicited. That background information centers on four criteria identified in the studies of the search process: the requirements of the task, personal interest of the user, time allotted for completion, and availability of information.

The interview seeks to identify the nature of the overall task that prompted the information search, the particular stage of the search process the person is experiencing, aspects of the overall task that are of particular interest to the individual, information that is readily accessible, and the extent and depth of the information available. These interrelated considerations create the context for choices the individual is addressing.

Z1	Problem self-diagnosed
	Search self-conducted
Z2–Z5	Problem diagnosed through interview
	a. Problem statement or request
	b. Background—tasks, interest, time, availability
	c. Diagnosis using theory base: product or process
	d. Intervention negotiated

Product	Process
Z2 Right source	Z5
Z3 Relevant sources	a. Dialogue
Z4 Sequence of sources	b. Exploration
	c. Formulation
	d. Construction
	e. Learning
	f. Application

Figure 8.2. Five Zones of Intervention.

Using the expanded theoretical framework that incorporates the uncertainty principle with traditional bibliographic frameworks, the librarian determines the zone of intervention that is indicated. The person's situation is identified as a source problem or a process problem. A source problem may be addressed with a source or sources of information within the available collection or in the broader information environment. A process problem is more complex, placing the person in one of the stages of the constructive process of seeking meaning and indicating a need for more holistic, ongoing attention.

The first few minutes of the interview are crucial for determining the zone of intervention. Based on professional experience and theory, the librarian makes a diagnosis as to whether the problem is a source problem or process problem. When a problem is identified as a source problem the second through the fourth zones of intervention (Z2–Z4) are indicated. The second zone of intervention (Z2) requires the right source. The third zone of intervention (Z3) requires some relevant sources. The fourth zone of intervention (Z4) requires a sequence for using relevant sources. Interventions in Z2–Z4 are source-oriented and address simple problems that are expected to remain static and be easily solved.

When the user's problem is diagnosed as changing and evolving, the fifth zone of intervention (Z5) is indicated, with the application of a process approach to mediation and education. The librarian enters into a dialogue with the user, and the interaction extends over a period of time. The fifth zone of intervention (Z5) encompasses exploration, formulation, construction, learning, and application in the information search process. The anticipated outcome of the intervention in Z5 is application of the user's new construction to the problem at hand. In addition, increased self-awareness of the search process may be learned and applied to other new situations of information seeking.

The zones of intervention may be thought of as a continuum, with the state of the user's problem determining the entrance and exit points. The solution to the problem or accomplishment of the task that initiates the information seeking signals the end of intervention. A task or problem may be diagnosed as falling into any of the five zones of intervention. The professional's judgment is crucial to avoid either over or under intervening in the individual's information seeking and use.

Levels of Mediation and Education in the Zones of Intervention

The model of the information search process and the uncertainty principle are proposed as a frame of reference for matching the level of mediation and education to the user's zone of intervention. The information professional assesses the user's problem, determines what role best fits the user's need for intervention, and designs mediation and education to match the user's task. The user's need for sources and information is incorporated with the user's need for process intervention. The levels of mediation and education may be used as a basis for designing services that are directly responsive to the task of the user in a process of information seeking.

The levels of mediation and education, described in Chapter 7, parallel the five zones of intervention (see Table 8.1). The organizer corresponds to the first zone (Z1), which requires an organized collection but no direct intervention. The locator/lecturer responds to the second zone (Z2) by offering ready reference and single source or single session intervention. The identifier/instructor provides standard reference intervention, introducing a group of sources and a series of instructional sessions in the third zone (Z3). The advisor/tutor offers a sequence of sources and instructional sessions for using sources in a recommended sequence in the fourth zone (Z4). The counselor engages in process intervention in the fifth zone (Z5). Mediation and education at this level incorporate holistic interaction over time through guidance in identifying and interpreting information to address an evolving problem. The counselor merges the role of educator and mediator in ongoing process intervention.

Table 8.1. Intervention Diagnostic Chart

Zones of Intervention	Levels of Mediation	Levels of Education	Intervention
Z1	Organizer	Organizer	Self-service
Z2	Locator	Lecturer	Single source
Z3	Identifier	Instructor	Group of sources
Z4	Advisor	Tutor	Sequence of sources
Z5	Counselor	Counselor	Process intervention

Libraries have developed extensive services to respond to intervention in Z2 through Z4. Source intervention of the locator/lecturer, the identifier/instructor, and the advisor/tutor is well established and quite effective in many cases, although perhaps not articulated in this way. Although there is always room for improvement and innovation, librarians take pride in the substantial accomplishments of interventions in these zones.

Process intervention in Z5, however, is in need of development. Although the notion of an information counselor is not new, the identification of the counselor as the provider of intervention in the constructive process of information seeking is an innovative way of viewing library and information services. When existing reference services and instructional programs incorporate a process dimension into the established service, there is a clear delineation of a new direction and not just an alternative way of articulating the traditional approach. That new direction places emphasis on the process of information seeking and the ongoing dialogue that engages the counselor in the user's unfolding information problem or topic.

Studies Indicate a Need for Process Intervention

Longitudinal studies of undergraduates indicate a critical need for process intervention. One of the college graduates who had been exposed to the process approach in high school noted that he was better prepared for college research assignments than other students. He describes a need for Z5 intervention as follows:

I had more exposure to research papers than most high school students. By working with you I learned not to panic if it doesn't all fall in together the first day you walk into the library. I had a lot of friends in college who were panicked at doing a research paper. I'll welcome a research paper any day regardless of the subject. To tell the truth I haven't come across any of my peers who think like that, not a one. When my roommate's research paper was due last semester, I helped him with it. He doesn't even know what he is afraid of; maybe of not finding the one article that is going to make his paper. I'll worry about a paper because things don't fall into place but it's not the kind of thing I lose sleep over. I've learned to accept that this is the way it works. Tomorrow I'll read this over and some parts will fall into place and some still won't. If not I'll talk to the professor. The mind doesn't take everything and put it into order automatically and that's it. Understanding that is the biggest help.

These longitudinal case studies continued as these participants entered the workplace. Two of the participants were interviewed as early career professionals to investigate their perceptions of the search process in two different work environments and their view of a need for intervention. One participant was a securities analyst for an established brokerage firm on Wall Street and the other an attending physician at a rehabilitation hospital in Chicago. These two participants had been interviewed at four- to five-year intervals since they were high school students, and case studies developed from earlier interviews lay the groundwork for this segment of the study.

The physician identified four different types of library services that she has encountered. The first was "just a room with some journals." The second she described as "a person who has the job of sitting behind the desk and filing things". The third she explained was a "real library with a librarian who does searches for you." The fourth library service she described as quite apart from the others. She called the librarian by name and said that, "If I want to do a search now I have Sara do it for me." In describing the fourth service she explained a different approach in this way, " When I ask Sara to do it, I will give her some key works and she will say 'well what about this and what about that and let me see what I come up with' and she will play around with it and then she will get back to me. And that is a lot more helpful and interactive. That is something that is different about the service I have now than what I had before. I don't know what her degree is in. But it is helpful to have her right there and be able to interact."

The securities analyst also described an interest in a more interactive role for information providers. He explained that although locating information is no longer the biggest problem for him, he and other workers like him are not completely self-sufficient. They could use help with the interpretive aspects of information seeking, which he sees as essential for accomplishing the more important tasks of the workplace.

These studies of users' perceptions of information seeking and use indicate the need for library and information services that interact with users to enable the process of seeking meaning within the process of seeking information. Although these participants were from vastly different situations and information contexts, there were marked similarities in their call for assistance in the process of gaining meaning in their information seeking.

The Counselor in the Information Search Process

The counselor's role in Z5 intervention is firmly grounded in an uncertainty principle. Understanding that "the mind doesn't take everything and put it in order automatically" is instrumental in constructing meaning. An important aspect of the counselor's role is to create an information environment that facilitates gaining meaning

At the counselor level of intervention the concept of a zone of intervention may be applied within the stages of the information search process. It is in the early, uncertain stages of the search process that the counselor's services may be particularly enabling. An important zone of intervention is indicated in the exploration stage of the information search process. Studies of the user's perspective on the information search process reveal that uncertainty is more likely to increase in the stage of exploration and decrease after formulation. The counselor may help users acknowledge and tolerate feelings of uncertainty and anxiety by assuming an invitational mood. The counselor may enable the user to work though the tasks of exploring and formulating as integral to the early stages of information seeking.

The user's experience of uncertainty in the search process may indicate a zone of intervention for information professionals. Process intervention calls for diagnosing the user's stage in the information search process and identifying points when intervention is most likely to be helpful. A zone of intervention may be indicated in the user's perception of the complexity of the task, level of uncertainty, and stage in the information search process. Taken together these three describe the user's experience in information-seeking tasks that involve a process of construction with stages of increasing and decreasing uncertainty.

Innovative ways should be developed for guiding and assisting people through the stages of the information search process. Mediation and education can be built around a range of strategies indicated in the findings of the studies of the user's perspective on the process of seeking meaning.

Strategies for Intervening in the Information Search Process

The counselor's role is becoming a critical component of services in all types of libraries. There are some practical strategies for implementing a process approach to information counseling services. Process strategies can be adapted for a wide range of library users, from the youngest child in a school library to the most sophisticated patron of a research library, to the person in the information age workplace.

The most important first step in counseling users is to become keenly aware of different stages in the process of learning from information seeking and use. Begin to listen for clues of early stages of uncertainty in a person's vague descriptions of his or her problem or topic. Become aware of the undertones and the mood of comments and questions. Be alert to signs of confusion, frustration, and doubt. This undertone of uncertainty is not limited to education and work-related information needs but may be apparent in more leisure and personal pursuits as well. The constructive process of seeking meaning pervades every aspect of human endeavor. Ignorance of the process of seeking meaning frequently underlies the limited choices that people make.

Some of the research methods and instruments used to elicit the user's perspective on information seeking have been adapted as intervention strategies. Journal keeping has been a particularly useful tool for enabling students to track their process and document their own experiences in the information search process. Search logs have been applied to keep track of the source encountered and determinations of usefulness. Timelines and flowcharts have helped users visualize their process as a unified whole. Process surveys and short pieces of writing at three points in the process have been adapted to help users see changes in their thinking over the course of their information seeking.

Six main strategies for counseling indicated in the findings of the studies of the information search process are collaborating, continuing, choosing, charting, conversing, and composing (see Table 8.2). The strategies are not in any particular order and most likely would be applied simultaneously or in tandem.

Table 8.2. Strategies for Intervening in the Information Search Process (ISP)

Strategy	Definition
Collaborating	Working jointly with others
Continuing	Proceeding at more than one point in time
Choosing	Selecting what is interesting and pertinent
Charting	Visualizing ideas, issues, questions, and strategies
Conversing	Talking about ideas for clarity and further questions
Composing	Writing to identify what is formulated and what is missing

Collaborating

Collaborating addresses the sense of isolation in the information search process. The information search process need not be thought of as an isolated, competitive undertaking but rather may be considered a cooperative venture, with other people working with the user to enhance information seeking and use. When the counselor takes on a collaborative role as an interested participant in the project, process intervention is the natural result.

Other people frequently serve as collaborators in an individual's information search process. Students often find that consulting with peers, in pairs or in small groups, at various stages in the search process enables them to learn from each other. Students need not be working on the same project to benefit from peer learning; they may be involved in completely different topics or on different aspects of the same project. Collaboration diminishes the common experience of isolation in research projects and enables people to help one another in the process of learning. A team approach to library research more closely matches tasks outside the academic environment. Collaborative techniques such as brainstorming, delegating, networking, and integrating are productive activities for information seeking and develop abilities valued in the workplace. Interventions that promote collaboration in the process of information seeking build skills and understandings that transfer to other situations of information need.

Collaborating enables users to try out ideas and develop questions at various stages in the information search process. Collaboration, particularly in the early stages of the process, is a productive strategy for Z5 intervention. When librarians become collaborators they take on an active role of counselor in the process of information seeking and use.

Continuing

Continuing addresses evolving information problems rather than queries that can be answered in a single incident with one source. The process of information seeking involves construction in which the person actively pursues understanding and meaning from the information encountered over a period of time. The process is commonly experienced in a series of thoughts and feelings that shift from vague and anxious to clear and confident as the search progresses. Continuing intervention responds to an individual's complex, dynamic learning process in Z5.

Process intervention that continues throughout the full duration of the information search process not only guides people in one specific research project but also establishes transferable process approaches and skills. Students who are led to view information seeking as a continuing process learn that exploration and formulation are essential tasks for bringing order to uncertainty through personal understanding.

Continuing intervention also addresses the concept of enough. An important concept for addressing complex projects is the notion of what is enough information for closure and presentation. What is enough was a relatively simple notion when a person could gather all there was to know on a topic. The concept of enough is quite a different matter in the present-day information environment. "Enough" relates to seeking meaning in a quantity of information by determining what one needs to know and by formulating a perspective on which to center. The information search process treats the concepts of enough as what is enough to make meaning for oneself.

The concept of enough may be applied to each stage in the information search process. Continuing intervention helps users to decide what is enough to recognize an information need, to explore a general topic, to formulate a specific focus, to gather information pertaining to the specific focus, to prepare to share what has been learned, and to accomplish the task that initiated the process.

Continuing intervention supports people throughout the information search process and guides them in using information for learning and constructing in each stage of the process. Continuing involves understanding that constructing a personal understanding is a process that requires time. When people become aware of the stages in their search process, they begin to see that inquiry involves more than selecting a topic, collecting information, and reporting. Learning through inquiry involves not only gathering information but also reading, reflecting, raising new questions, and exploring over an extended period of time to construct a new understanding.

Librarians as counselors who implement continuing intervention can help people to think about where they are in the information search process and offer suggestions for proceeding with the particular task they are confronting. Continuing is an important concept for seeking meaning in information-rich environments and is a basic strategy for counselors intervening in Z5.

Choosing

The information search process involves active engagement in making choices: choosing a topic, choosing questions and ideas within the topic, choosing sources, choosing information within those sources, choosing what to pursue, choosing what to leave out, and choosing what is enough. These decisions in each stage of the information search process are essential for moving along to culmination. Choosing as a strategy gives people a sense of control over their own search process. In the active process of making choices for themselves, rather than reproducing texts that reflect other people's choices, users construct their own perspectives and understandings within the information search process.

The four criteria of time, task, interest, and availability form the basis for making choices throughout the process. Choices are made to accomplish the task within the allotted time that are of interest and make use of the information available. These criteria are particularly useful in making choices that lead to the critical decisions of selecting a topic and formulating a focus. The formulation of a focus is the turning point of the information search process that marks the transition from choices that reflect general relevance to choices that reflect personal pertinence. Choices of relevance to the general topic are made at the beginning of the search, and choices of pertinence to the personal perspective are made after focus.

Counselors can help people to see their range of choices in each stage of the information search process. The choices one makes in process of a search are individual and unique for each person and lead to innovation and creativity. In personal construct theory, George Kelly explains that choices that are instrumental in moving the constructive process along are "elaborative" choices. Some choices are more important than others for shaping construction and determining the direction of the search. Choices that lead to formulating a focus are essential for establishing the parameters of the search. Once a focus has been formed, the user has a frame of reference for making choices about what is most useful, somewhat useful, and not useful. Counselors need to respect users' choices and anticipate individuality in the choices made in the search process. There is not one choice for all but many possible choices, determined by the individual's intention.

Charting

Charting intervention is effective for visually presenting a large amount of information in a compact way. Charting enables the user to visualize the total search process from initiation to closure and to anticipate what to expect in each stage of the process.

One particular charting intervention has been consistently effective for making users aware of the stages in the information search process and for helping them to understand what to expect in each stage. A chart of the model of the search process is used to illustrate the tasks, feelings, thoughts, and actions that are commonly experienced in each of the six stages. The model developed in the research described in this book (see Figure 5.1) may be adopted as an instrument for illustrating the process to library users. The diagram enables users to visualize a sequence of stages in information seeking.

The counselor also may use this chart as a basis for determining the stage that the user is experiencing and to describe the overall process to the user. The model may be prepared as a formal handout or can be simply drawn on a piece of paper. The objective is for users to reflect on the process and to analyze and decide at what stage they would place themselves in the sequence.

For most people a critical zone of intervention is the stage of exploration, after a general area or topic has been selected but before a personal perspective has been formed. By using the chart of the six stages of the information search process, the counselor may help to identify the person's stage in the process, acknowledge his or her feelings, clarify the task before him or her, and recommend appropriate strategies. For example, people in the exploration stage may find reading for general themes and listing interesting ideas to be most helpful, whereas people in the collection stage would be advised to read for details and to take comprehensive notes.

Conceptual mapping techniques may be applied to charting information and to visualizing emerging ideas. Conceptual maps organize ideas and show connections between disparate concepts in a manner similar to outlining, but with more visual elements. A simple conceptual map begins with a circle or box containing the general topic or main idea. Surrounding circles or boxes are added as related concepts, with lines and arrows connecting the elements in a meaningful display. The visual, nonlinear aspect of conceptual mapping fosters the creative process of connecting ideas and organizing information as a search progresses.

Timeline and flowchart techniques described in Chapter 3 may be adapted for counseling users in charting their own searches. These instruments are most effective for reviewing a recently completed search with a user and reflecting on what went well and what might be improved. However, they may be adapted as planning instruments as well. The timeline and flowchart reveal different aspects of the search process. The timeline is useful for eliciting thoughts that evolve on a topic in the search process. The flowchart is useful for revealing a sequence of sources encountered and used in the progression of a search. Together they offer two views of this complex, integrated process and enable users to understand their own experience in information seeking.

Surveys conducted at intervals, also, provide a way for users to chart their own search and to track changes in their understanding of both their topic and their search process. The process surveys described in Chapter 4 may be used to record users' responses at three points in the search process: initiation, midpoint, and closure. Users may compare the responses that they made at the various points to gain a sense of changes in their thoughts, actions, and feelings as the search progressed.

Charting intervention is a creative way to demonstrate common patterns in the information search process, to foster formulation, and to organize ideas for presentation.

Conversing

Conversations encourage users to discuss the search process from their own particular perspective. Counselors may encourage dialogue by drawing out the user's dynamic process through invitational, exploratory questioning, such as: What ideas seem particularly important to you? What particular questions do you have, and what problems are emerging? What is the focus of your thinking, and what are the guiding ideas for your search? What are the gaps in your thinking, and what inconsistencies do you notice in the information you have encountered?

Charting and composing strategies are an excellent basis for conversing with users. The timeline of the information search process is particularly useful for initiating a conversation about the process that the user is experiencing or is likely to experience. The counselor can discuss the sequence of stages in the process with the user and come to some agreement about what stage the user is in. Conversation provides an opportunity for the counselor to acknowledge feelings commonly associated with the particular stage that the user is experiencing. For example, if a selection or exploration stage is identified the counselor would say something like "you are probably feeling somewhat uncertain and a bit anxious at this point; most people do." If a collection stage is identified the counselor's comments would be directed toward the user's personal perspective and particular area of interest.

A counselor should use caution when discussing the stages of the search process and be careful not to belabor the issue beyond the point of being helpful to the user. Merely acknowledging the presence of confusion and uncertainty at the beginning and recommending strategies for proceeding is usually sufficient to get a person started. It is important, however, to suggest that some ongoing assistance may be helpful and to offer an invitation to schedule sessions or meetings for counseling throughout the process.

Conversation gives the counselor an opportunity to listen to the user and to recommend appropriate strategies for working through the particular stage in the process that the user is experiencing. Diagnosis of the user's stage is important since formulation of a focused perspective is the turning point in the search. The counselor recommends different strategies before and after the formulation of a focus. Prior to formulation a more invitational approach to searching is recommended; there might be exploratory reading and reflecting to better understand the problem. Following formulation a more focused approach of documenting and organizing to solve the problem is recommended.

In the early stages, counselors guide users away from overly indicative strategies that narrow the inquiry without exploring the broader prospects. After a focused perspective has been formed, counselors guard against overly invitational strategies that continue gathering general information rather than limiting the search to information pertinent to the focused perspective. Counseling in the stages of the search process guide users through the entire sequence of starting, exploring, focusing, gathering, and closing.

Composing

Composing and conversation go hand in hand to enable the user to focus or formulate a point of view. They comprise a means of documenting and organizing for presentation and application. Conversing enables the user to articulate thoughts, identify gaps, and clarify inconsistencies in the process of the search.

Composing promotes thinking, and journal writing is an excellent technique for advancing formulation in the search process. Counselors may recommend that users keep a research journal in which they record ideas, questions, and connections as they progress through their search. Writing in a research journal is much more comprehensive than jotting down notes on cards or in a notebook. The journal is started when the project is first initiated, but the purpose changes as the search progresses. Users are instructed to set aside ten or fifteen minutes each day or every few days to write about their problem or topic. Instructions might be stated in the following manner:

In the early stages, when you are deciding on what topic to choose, write to clarify or define possible choices. Write about conversations you have about your topic. As you proceed in the process, write your reactions to your readings as well as your thoughts and questions about your topic. Be sure to record all incidents where you made an important decision or discovery. Include the development of a central theme, a point of view, or focus in your thinking. Record any dead end of a path or change in the problem or topic that prompted a new approach.

Users may find it helpful to share their journals with the counselor, or they may want to keep their writings exclusively for their own reflective use. The main objective of the journal is to serve as a tool for formulating thoughts and developing constructs. Counselors may also recommend free writing as a means of assisting formulation. Users are encouraged to write about the focus of their topic or problem at several different points in the search process. These pieces of writing promote private reflection that can help users to make connections in and inferences about the information they have encountered and to see gaps that need further investigation. When the writings are shared with the counselor, they can form a basis for deeper understanding of the user's evolving information need.

Composing is commonly the outcome or product of the information search process. Composing interventions, however, apply to writing throughout the process as a means for fostering formulation of ideas on an evolving problem from the information encountered in an extensive search process.

Recalling, Summarizing, Paraphrasing, and Extending

Counselors can encourage people to collaborate, continue, choose, chart, converse, and compose to formulate the ideas that they find important in the information they have encountered. In addition, users may be counseled to use four basic abilities that underlie information literacy: recalling, summarizing, paraphrasing, and extending (see Table 8.3).

Table 8.3. Four Basic Information Literacy Abilities

Ability	Definition
Recall	Remember ideas from what has been gathered
Summarize	Organize ideas in capsulized form and place in meaningful sequence
Paraphrase	Retell in one's own words
Extend	Fit ideas into what one already knows to form new understandings

Recalling is thinking and remembering certain features of what has been gathered and read. Memory plays a critical function in the process of using information. With our limited capacity for recall, we remember selectively rather than recalling everything. Recall is based on our former constructs (worldview), which form a frame of reference for selective remembering. What is recalled is a selective process that may differ from person to person. Eliciting personal histories and narratives that relate to the problem is important for counseling users in selecting that which has some personal meaning. Counselors may guide users to make connections with what they already know and to note what fits or contradicts their view.

Summarizing is organizing ideas in capsulized form and placing the ideas in a meaningful sequence. Summarizing orders ideas and events, pulling out salient points or main themes. Not telling all, only what is important, requires an ability to decide what is relevant or pertinent from an individual point of view. Like recalling, summarizing involves selective attention and is based on the person's former constructs. What will be left out is as important a decision as what will be retained. For insight into the complexity of this ability, note how small children want to tell all and have great difficulty choosing parts of a story or event. The decision about what is enough to convey meaning is the difficult conceptual task of formulation. Summarizing involves mentally organizing the information encountered. Our constructs lead us to consider certain ideas as significant and others as less so. There is no one right way to summarize texts. As revealed in the transactional theory of reading, one reader's summary of a text may not match that of an author's. In addition, one reader is likely to summarize quite differently from another. The main objective of summarizing is to organize the information in an abbreviated form by determining ideas that convey meaning. Summarizing prepares information for use by enabling the person to formulate ideas from the information. The task of summarizing is to choose, not everything but enough to convey meaning, and not anything but only that which is important, pertinent, significant, and salient to the individual's formulation.

Paraphrasing is retelling in one's own words the information encountered in the search process. The use of language fosters formulation and prepares information for application. Paraphrasing may be used in enabling recall. Conversing or writing about information gathered may jog memory. One point cues another as the telling occurs. In a similar way paraphrasing may also enable summarizing. The story unfolds within the act of telling. The concept behind paraphrasing is that the reader's words are as acceptable as the author's and more appropriate under certain circumstances. The person is encouraged to break away from the text and to tell the story in his or her own way. When paraphrasing is not valued, copying and plagiarism frequently result. From the earliest age, children's retelling and paraphrasing should be valued and encouraged. Assignments should arise from a problem to be solved that requires paraphrasing ideas rather than a contrived directive that prompts copying word for word from a text. In a similar way, counselors for all types of users should encourage paraphrasing information as a means of understanding and guide users to value their own telling as well as that of others. Paraphrasing, however, may lead to assuming an author's ideas as one's own. It is essential that the origin of the idea be credited and documented. Counselors guide users in determinations of when to quote and how to document sources and in the use of paraphrasing as a powerful ability for formulating within the search process.

Extending is taking ideas from information as our own by fitting them in with what is already known. Extending also involves making connections between the ideas within the information and with information from other sources encountered. In this way, thinking about a topic or problem is extended. Extending also encompasses interpreting information and applying it to the problem in the creative process of using information. Extending occurs throughout the search process, not merely toward the end of that process. In fact, all four abilities should be thought of as interwoven in all of the stages in the active process of understanding, rather than as occurring in a sequence. Extending leads from one stage of the process to the next. As new questions arise, further information is needed. In this recursive process the connections lead to formulation of a focused perspective. The counselor develops strategies and techniques for enabling the user to apply recalling, summarizing, paraphrasing, and extending for working through the stages in the information search process.

Process-Oriented Library and Information Services

Library and information services comprise two basic forms of intervention with users—reference and instruction—which have been redefined here as mediation and education. The information search process and the uncertainty principle have implications for diagnosing the users' zone of intervention in each of these services. Traditionally, reference services have been based on sources rather than process. Heavy emphasis on locating the right source and the goal of accuracy detract attention from the more dynamic aspects of information seeking and use. Mediation in the information search process requires expanding the more traditional roles of the librarian from locator, identifier, and advisor for physical access to counselor for intellectual access through process. Awareness of the process in which the user is learning from information seeking and use by exploring and formulating during a search broadens the mediator's scope from concentration on sources to consideration of use.

What is the role of the information professional in an environment where information systems provide direct access to the end user? The user's perspective on complexity, uncertainty, and process indicate a zone of intervention in which the information professional may play an important role in helping with the evolving information need in the process of construction in a complex task. Within an information-rich environment a greater number of users' problems are within the fifth zone of intervention. Library and information professionals should be prepared to meet the rising demand for process services on the Counselor's level to address seeking meaning in an increasingly abundant information environment.

The zone of intervention varies according to the user's task and state of knowledge. In a similar way instruction has been based on learning the sources in an organized collection rather than on understanding the process of learning from information access and use. The very term *bibliographic instruction* connotes teaching sources without attention to use, interpretation, or meaning. Problems with transference of skills have been recognized as pervasive and have been widely criticized. By centering exclusively on the sources and the product of a search, the dynamic process of using information has been neglected. Process strategies for exploring and formulating enable students to learn how to learn. Educational programs that offer users an understanding of their search task are better aligned with the natural progression of their thoughts and feelings. Education programs that teach students to become aware of their own process of learning from information prepare them for the process of using information in other situations of an information need. By identifying the zone of intervention the mediator instructs in those areas where the user can learn.

Classification systems are based on the prototype of a generic search rather than an individual process of construction. The organizer's task of providing all there is, all of the time, in every instance falls within the traditional approach to library and information system design. Information overload and information anxiety are problems resulting from this approach. Designers of online catalogs, end-user bibliographic databases, and searcher training programs should address the question of how the user's process can be accommodated in interfaces between information systems and users. In this way, the system may be made to accommodate the zone of intervention.

The counselor level of intervention addresses the full range of experience in the constructive process of seeking meaning within the information environment. The counselor is an essential role for librarians and information professionals in the information age. The counselor level is emerging and developing in response to the demands of the information environment. The changing information environment has prompted a reassessment of traditional library and information services and requires information professionals to assume new roles to support users.

The process approach does not advocate throwing out all traditional practices. Rather, it proposes building on existing programs of service to incorporate sensitivity to process to better meet users' needs in an information-rich environment. The librarian, with a clear understanding of the user's zone of intervention within a dynamic process, is prepared to expand and change current common practice.

Implementing the Process
Approach

9

The Information Search Process model was initially developed in a study of high school students engaged in an assigned research paper. Over the past fifteen years a process approach has been adopted and implemented in a number of elementary and secondary school library programs. This chapter discusses two studies that investigated the implementation of the process approach to library and information services in educational contexts. Findings from these studies reveal some enablers and inhibitors to process-oriented library and information services that have implications for implementing a process approach in other settings.

Information Search Process in Education

The challenge for the information age school is to educate children for living and working in an information-rich technological world. The three basic charges of education in a free society are to prepare students for the workplace, citizenship, and daily living. To prepare students for the workplace, consideration must be given to the ways that information technology changes the nature of work and raises new questions about how we contribute to and innovate productively in the global economy. To prepare students for citizenship, consideration must be given to the ways that information technology changes our sense of community and raises pressing questions about how we participate as an informed electorate in a democratic society. To prepare students for daily living, consideration must be given to the ways that information technology increases the complexity of everyday life and raises troubling questions about how we gain a sense of self in relation to others and experience creativity and joy in our personal lives. Basic to meeting these three charges is developing student competence in learning in information-laden environments and in finding meaning in a variety of sources of information. All three charges involve a process approach to information seeking and information use that underlies information literacy.

Library Media Programs Based on the Process Approach

The process approach is a perspective on learning rather than a formula for teaching. There are some general guidelines, however, for guiding students in the development of skills in seeking and using information in each stage of the information search process. First and foremost, the process approach is initiated by treating issues, questions, and problems as open-ended ones that must be addressed by using a number of sources over a period of time. These open-ended topics arise directly from the curriculum to initiate inquiry-based research rather than artificially imposed research assignments that only peripherally relate to the context, content, and objectives of the course of study.

During initiation, an invitation to research is extended to students to prepare them for the creative process ahead. Some basic groundwork is laid to prepare students for the research process. An introduction, such as a particularly gripping work of fiction, a vivid film or video portrayal, or an engaging speaker, can capture the attention of students and enable them to form some basic constructs upon which to build. During this initial stage the students become aware of ideas, issues, and questions worthy of further investigation and identify those that are of particular personal interest to them.

In the early stages brainstorming draws out what students know and provides opportunities for generating, clarifying, and sharing ideas. Raising questions about their existing knowledge provides motivation for proceeding to find out more. An audience for their work beyond the teacher should be established at the start. Brainstorming encourages collaborative learning at the very beginning of the process.

In the early stages, students concentrate on topics, ideas, and questions that need further investigation rather than getting enmeshed in the mechanics of the project. Mechanics are stated directly but in no way overshadow the central task of gaining a deeper understanding of a particular problem, issue, or topic. Keeping a journal is a useful strategy throughout the process and can serve a variety of purposes at different points. For example, at one point students use their journals to record thoughts on possible topics, plans for addressing the project, and prospective problems. Later in the process they use their journals for detailed note taking.

At the beginning students are introduced to the concept of stages in the search process and become aware of what to expect in the ensuing project. The model of the information search process is used to illustrate the sequence of tasks, thoughts, actions, and feelings that are commonly experienced in each stage of the process. Students may refer to the model from time to time to determine where they are in the process.

After students have selected a topic or area for research, they are carefully guided and coached through the exploration stage. This is frequently the most difficult stage. Uncertainty prevails as students encounter information that is inconsistent and incompatible and does not match what they already know. Reading and reflecting in a receptive mood and in an unhurried environment are conducive to formulating new understandings. Opportunities for discussing newly formulated constructs are offered through one-on-one conferences, small group interaction, and large group discussions. Journals are helpful for recording interesting ideas, connecting themes, and emerging questions developed from a number of sources instead of extensive copious notes from one source. This activity also deters students from the tendency to copy word for word or to plagiarize when presenting.

Students gain a clear understanding that their task during this time is to form a focused perspective on their topics. A focused perspective provides direction for collecting information and is the turning point of the information search process. Once a focus is formed, the search takes on a central theme or guiding idea that provides the basis for making judgments about what information to collect and what to disregard. Note-taking strategies shift at this point to recording detailed notes on information related to the focused perspective on the topic.

The final stage is organizing ideas for presentation. Students are guided in determining what will be paraphrased, summarized, and quoted and how to document the origin of the information used. Connections are made between and among the ideas, and extensions of meaning are identified and explained. Presentations take many forms and are addressed to the collaborative learning group, not solely to the teacher.

An essential part of the process approach to information skills is assessing the process as well as the product at the end of the project. An opportunity to look back and take account of the entire process enables students to recognize that their experience has not been isolated to this one incident but is generally applicable to a wide range of situations. Journals provide an excellent means for students to review their process. By reflecting on their use of time, use of sources, and evidence of a focus in their presentations, they develop an awareness of their own information search process. Process folios of student work representing the various stages of the project provide an excellent way to assess the process of learning.

Implementing the Information Search Process in Schools

This chapter discusses two studies that investigated the implementation of a process approach in school settings. The first was a follow-up study of school library media specialists who had participated in a residential institute on the information search process. The second study was part of a large-scale evaluation of a national project to improve schools through school libraries.

Information Search Process Institutes

The first study investigated problems and successes in implementing a process approach in library media programs. The main question under investigation was: When a process approach is implemented in a library media program, what are the major problems library media specialists and teachers encounter, and what are the identifiable elements of success? Problems were identified as "inhibitors" and elements of success as "enablers."

The first step in implementation was to present the process approach to library media specialists. Without awareness training the process approach often is not self-evident even to experienced librarians. A training institute was developed to provide an opportunity for library media specialists to experience the information search process firsthand, reflect on the process they had experienced, and discover ways to guide students through the process. The institutes took place in or near a library where participants could research a topic of their choice. During the library research, they were called upon to reflect on the process in which they were involved through small group discussion, journal writing, and debriefing sessions. This intensive firsthand experience with the information search process formed a basis for developing process-oriented library media programs for students. With this new process perspective, the library media specialists worked together to design activities for students to develop skill in using information for gaining a deeper understanding of a topic. Information search process institutes were held at Rutgers University as well as in other locations across the United States, Canada, and Sweden. Although the length of the institutes ranged from one day to one week, each consisted of three essential components: firsthand experience in researching a topic, reflection on the process being experienced, and discussion with colleagues on ways to guide students in the process. Surveys of participants at the close of the institutes revealed considerable change in perception of the mission of library media programs, understanding of the information search process, and commitment to adopt a process approach to information skills instruction and information literacy.

Implementation Study

Participants in the institutes were invited to join in a study of implementation of the process approach in their school (Kuhlthau, 1993). Those who volunteered completed questionnaires identifying the subject, the instructional team, and the students targeted for integration of the information search process. In addition, participants identified and described process aspects in their present program and gave an overview of plans for implementing an extensive process approach.

Six months later, participants were sent questionnaires requesting their assessment of implementation progress. Library media specialists and teachers with whom they had teamed were asked to respond to the following questions: What worked well? What problems did you have? What advice do you have for people starting a process approach? What are your future plans for the process approach in your library media program? After two years of collecting responses certain patterns began to emerge.

Primary Inhibitors

Some programs seemed to be stalled, while others achieved considerable success. Participants in the stalled programs cited three primary inhibitors: lack of time, confusion of roles, and poorly designed assignments:

- Lack of time
- Confusion of roles
- Poorly designed assignments

Lack of Time

Lack of time became evident in two different ways. One was lack of student time on the task. Rarely was there enough time for students to work through the process under the guidance of the teacher and library media specialist. A common pattern was to have the class come into the library media center for one or two class periods at the beginning of the project, usually early in the exploration stage, and then leave the students to their own devices throughout the rest of the information search process. In such cases, the library media specialist continued to guide those students who came into the library media center on their own but did not see the final project and had no sense of how the students had fared in the process.

A second aspect of lack of time was insufficient planning time for development of team guidance and instruction. Teachers and library media specialists had no time set aside for working on activities and little time to develop the joint aspects of their teaming efforts. Essentially they assumed traditional roles because they lacked time to be more inventive and explore ways that they might work together to help students develop skills for seeking and using information within a subject area.

Confusion of Roles

The lack of time for planning may have contributed to another problem, a basic confusion over roles. No clear notion of who was responsible for what was developed beyond the traditional roles of the library media specialist as resource gatherer and the teacher as assignment giver. There simply was not sufficient time to identify new roles. There was also no recognized or articulated role for administrators to play. In fact, most administrators were not involved in any way.

Poorly Designed Assignments

The third problem that became evident in the stalled programs was assignments that did not encourage a process approach. In fact, some assignments actually seemed to impede learning. Assignments were primarily designed by the teacher, with the library media specialist joining in some time after initiation and frequently much later in the process. Many assignments were "added on," rather than being an essential component of the course of study and directly integrated into the subject area curriculum. To make matters worse, the assignments were sometimes given at the most inconvenient time in the school year, such as the week before winter break or after the marking period in the spring. Even the most enlightened teachers seemed to regard library assignments as enrichment activities rather than as ways of learning essential concepts and for developing the basic skills of information literacy for addressing emerging questions.

In summary, lack of time, role confusion, and poor assignments were the main problems participants identified as preventing successful implementation of a process approach in library media programs.

Investigation of Successful Implementation

It was more difficult to identify the underlying characteristics of programs that were judged to be successful. A number of positive responses described projects that students were involved in and plans for teaming in the future. In addition, there was noticeable evidence of excitement and enthusiasm among these respondents. Particularly interesting were the responses to the question, "What problems did you have?" Responses indicated a fundamental difference between successful programs and struggling programs. Respondents from successful programs stressed learning problems of their students, whereas responses from struggling programs dwelt on logistical problems of getting the program established. For example, respondents from successful programs described the need to develop new ways to help students form a focused perspective as they gathered information. Conversely, a respondent from a struggling program typically described the lack of time to work with students and teachers.

To investigate and identify basic elements underlying successful implementation, a longitudinal case study of one program was conducted over a period of four years. The school was a middle/junior high school with a long-standing reputation for quality education. The school was chosen as an example of successful implementation from survey responses, which indicated that the process approach was developing into an established program.

Three site visits and five phone interviews took place during the study over four years. Focus interviews during the site visits were the primary method for investigating the participants' perceptions of what was taking place. The researcher did not observe the actual program in practice but reviewed the observations, recollections, and assessment of each member of the instructional team. The focus interviews gave each member of the team an opportunity to respond to the questions and to hear the responses of other team members. Qualitative methods were used to collect data to provide insight into what was happening in this program. Multiple methods produced overlapping data from questionnaires, interviews, materials developed by the instructional team, and student projects.

The first focus interview was conducted with the instructional team in year 1. Participants included the principal, the assistant principal, the language arts coordinator, two language arts teachers, the reading/study skills specialist, and the library media specialist (two social studies teachers who were part of the instructional team were not available for the interview). In year 2, a questionnaire with similar questions to the focus interview prompts was administered to each team member. In addition, the library media specialist was interviewed by telephone. A focus interview was conducted with the library media specialist and teachers in year 3 and again in year 4. Each interview was conducted by this researcher and taped. In the focus interviews each participant was asked to respond to the following prompts:

- Describe your program and how it is different from what you have done before.
- What worked well?
- What problems have you encountered?
- What role did you play in the program?
- Tell an anecdote of process learning that you observed.
- What are your plans for the future of this program?

The series of focus interviews, questionnaires, phone interview, and other materials provided substantial data for case study.

Basic Enablers

Participants in the implementation study revealed four basic enablers of successful implementation: A mutually held constructivist view of learning, a team teaching approach, competence in designing process assignments, and a commitment to developing information literacy (see Table 9.2, p. 159).

- Constructivist view of learning

- Team approach to teaching

- Competence in designing process assignments

- Commitment to developing information literacy

Constructivist View of Learning

A mutually held constructivist view of learning compatible with the process approach that provided the foundation for actively engaging students in inquiry was an important element of success. The constructivist view of learning provided a solid theoretical foundation upon which to build the library media program. Constructivist learning was clearly articulated and readily understood by each member of the instructional team. They agreed that students come to a learning situation not as "empty vessels" or "blank slates" but with a range of personal constructs formed from prior experience and that learning takes place by building on what they already know. The team had a mutually accepted philosophical base from which to work.

The members of the instructional team were open and receptive to the process approach because it fit into their way of teaching and the way they viewed learning. Other process programs, such as the writing process and whole language, were established and common practice and formed the basis for building the process approach to information use. One of the school goals was to develop higher level thinking, and the information search process was recognized as a way to achieve this goal.

Team Approach to Teaching

A team approach to teaching, with administrators, teachers, and library media specialists playing essential roles on the instructional team, was identified as an important element of success. First and foremost, a process approach was revealed as a team effort. The faculty of the school was found to have extensive experience in team instruction. The administrators were an integral part of the instructional team. Each member of the team had a clearly defined role to play in the process approach. Genuine mutual respect and appreciation for each other as contributing members of the instructional team was evident.

The subject area coordinator articulated the goals and set the philosophical framework for the process approach. He explained to the instructional team how the approach fit into the curriculum and was tied to the school's goals and objectives. One school goal was to develop higher level thinking, and the coordinator explained that the "information search process is our way to achieve this goal." The coordinator articulated the constructivist view of learning and was able to describe how the process approach was compatible with this view. The writing process approach had been in place for a number of years, and he was able to describe how the process approach to information use was an extension and enhancement of the writing process.

The principal showed considerable interest in the project. He valued the process approach as integrating the library media program across the curriculum because of the impact he observed on student learning. He was particularly impressed by the collaborative work of the students. He observed that everyone was on task and that students were giving each other advice. The principal saw merit in the process approach and advocated its adoption.

The assistant principal of the school, who was responsible for scheduling, provided the environment for teaming and the opportunity for team planning. As he stated it, he "helped with the logistics." By arranging the schedule to allow for the teachers and library media specialist to have preparation periods at the same time, he provided the time for planning and working together during the school day.

As an administrator he gave the project credence. He conducted required formal observations of teachers and library media specialists as they worked with students in the library media center. He showed the students the importance of the project by talking to them about their work as he met them in the course of the school day. In something of an understatement, he said his role was to "show a little bit of interest." The administrator provided the climate for teaming and the time for planning, and promoted, recognized, and rewarded those involved in the process approach.

The teachers provided the context and content. They worked in conjunction with the library media specialist to design the assignment around the information search process. They were particularly pleased with student engagement and achievement. One veteran teacher related that this was one of the best experiences in her eighteen years of teaching. Teachers concentrated on identifying problems, designing instructional strategies to aid students, and assessing learning.

The reading and study skills specialist guided students in using information, which was found to take more time and energy than anticipated. She served as an additional professional for coaching students in reading, note taking, and writing about emerging ideas. She was dedicated to the team approach and enthusiastically described the outcome of cooperation: "Everyone was doing the part he or she can do best. No one of us could do this alone." Her expertise in helping students develop the skills needed to understand information once it had been located made an important contribution to the instructional team.

Last, but certainly not least, the library media specialist provided the resources, defined the information search process, and was the unifying force in directing the program. The principal described her as, "The person who gets it going and keeps it on track." She initially explained the process approach to administrators, coordinator, and teachers and then spent a full year laying the groundwork for implementation. In addition, she provided a creative climate in the library media center. As one of the teachers said, "She wants the library used and loves it when the place is crowded." The library media specialist initiated and facilitated the information search process approach, keeping student learning the focus of concern.

Competence in Designing Process Assignments

Competence in designing process assignments and in guiding student learning through those assignments was found to be another element of success. The instructional team was committed to improving learning. They were ready to experiment with method rather than expecting to be handed a packaged formula to follow. They used their competence and expertise to design, assess, and redesign the process program.

They were open to innovation and ready to assume professional responsibility for designing interventions and instruction to improve student learning. They were willing to let go of old ways of doing things to take the risk of trying something new and to accept the extra work involved.

Although the process approach was built on a library media program already in place, there was a clear notion that this was a different approach. This is a critical point, as one member of the team explained, "We had to rethink the way we had been doing it." This rethinking to identify features of the assignment, method, and strategies that inhibit or enable the process was an essential element in the successful program. In this case, their concept of process changed from considering process as moving from source to source in a library media center to the creative process of evolving ideas and thoughts during information seeking.

They focused on student learning and created interventions that helped along the way. They assumed the roles of coaches and guides rather than lecturers. They found that mini-lessons emerging from the stages in the process were more effective than "artificial lessons," which told too much at the wrong time. All agreed that while the process approach involved more work than a more prescriptive, transmission approach, it was well worth the effort when the impact on student motivation and learning was considered.

Commitment to Developing Information Literacy

A shared commitment to developing information literacy and for motivating students to take responsibility for their own learning was identified as another element of success. The team was not preoccupied with "teaching for the test." They had a clear understanding that they were preparing students for higher level thinking and problem solving needed in the information age. They were concerned with developing skills for locating and using information for lifelong learning as well as with teaching subject content and concepts.

Student engagement in learning was clearly evident. The team described students as having an emotional attachment to the problem they were investigating. The team was concerned with creating an environment where students would be motivated and totally involved. The instructional team worked together to create a collaborative learning environment in which students of all abilities worked together and learned from each other.

The identification of inhibitors and enablers provided insight into the problems of implementation. A constructivist view of learning was found to underlie successful implementation of a process approach. The library media specialist was the catalyst for "getting it going and keeping it on track." Thus the library media specialist's view of learning was a key factor in implementing a process approach in the library media program.

Large-Scale Study of Implementation of a Process Approach

The second study provided an opportunity to further investigate problems of implementation in a large number of library media programs. This study was based on assumptions drawn from the first study of implementation. The first assumption was that the library media specialist plays an important role in implementing a process approach to student learning from a variety of sources. The second assumption was that the vision, objectives, and emphasis of the library media program are dependent on the library media specialist's perception of learning. Based on these assumptions, the library media specialists' perceptions of learning were considered of utmost importance for studying implementation of a process approach to library media programs.

Library media specialists' descriptions of student learning within a national school improvement program provided an opportunity to gain insight into problems of implementing a process approach to learning in library media centers. The National Library Power Program, funded by the DeWitt-Wallace Reader's Digest fund, sought to improve opportunities for student learning by upgrading school libraries in nineteen communities across the United States. The program provided grants to approximately 700 public elementary and middle schools over a three-year period to improve teaching and learning through better and innovative uses of enhanced, up-to-date libraries. Total investment of the program exceeded $45 million and was the largest nongovernmental funding of school library services in the United States in over thirty years. Grants from the Fund, totaling $1.2 million over three years to each of the participating Library Power communities, were used to renovate library space; purchase new books and upgrade print and electronic collections; and provide professional development to library media specialists, teachers, and principals to learn how to work together to make the best use of their new libraries. In return, each school had to commit to hiring and paying the salaries of full-time library media specialists; keeping the library media center open and accessible to everyone throughout the school day; and increasing spending for books, software, and educational materials (Hopkins and Zweizig, 1999). The program was initiated in 1988, with the evaluation phase taking place from the fall of 1994 through June 1997.

A three-year study of librarians' perceptions of student learning was conducted within the national school improvement project. Data were collected from two sources: surveys of approximately 500 participating library media specialists and in-depth case studies of three sites. Findings indicate that over time providing up-to-date library media centers and programs stressing information seeking influenced students' opportunities to learn from a variety of sources. By the end of the study, many of the participating library media specialists' descriptions of student learning had changed to emphasize using information to achieve the overall learning goals of the school context. However, case studies reveal a difference among the schools related to an understanding of the research process and how to facilitate learning within the process of information seeking and use.

The study addressed two research questions. What are the library media specialists' perceptions of student learning? How do the library media specialists' perceptions influence learning opportunities for students, particularly in facilitating the process of learning from a variety of sources? One of the items on the annual Library Power evaluation survey of participating library media specialists was designed to elicit perceptions of student learning. In each of the three years that the survey was administered, the library media specialists were asked to respond to the following prompt. "Think back over your Library Power Program to when a student or students had a meaningful learning experience in the library media center. How did you know something new was learned? What stands out in your mind that made it a good learning experience?" The library media specialists' responses to the survey item provided critical insights that were considered to typify what first comes to mind when a library media specialist is asked to describe students' learning. These initial responses or reactions were treated as an indication of what librarians considered important to emphasize when asked to describe a situation of learning in the library media center. The examples of learning were then coded and compared for changes in the aggregate responses over the three-year period of the study.

A coding scale was designed to categorize the critical incidents by what was emphasized in each library media specialist's response. The coding scheme was used to identify the library media specialist's perception of learning as an indication of the vision and objectives of the library media program at that point in time. Was the library media specialist emphasizing more materials and technology, increased library media center use, improvement in attitude, better library and information skills, or use of resources for content learning? Although this analysis did not directly measure student learning, it revealed the assessment of learning by the person directly responsible for the students' information seeking and use in the library media center.

In the spring of the first year of the study, through content analysis of a sample of thirty responses, a 5-point coding scale was developed, which was intended to represent levels of perceptions of learning, with 1 representing the lowest and 5 the highest, as shown in Table 9.3. Responses identified as category 1 emphasized the library media specialist's actions and not what students did, such as adding to the collection or describing a lesson taught. Category 1 responses were coded as *input*. Responses identified as category 2 emphasized quantitative measures of student use, such as a greater number of materials circulated, more class visits, or increased technology use. Category 2 responses were coded as *output*. Responses identified as category 3 emphasized a change in student attitude, such as increased interest and enthusiasm. Category 3 responses were coded as *attitude*. Responses identified as category 4 emphasized library and information skills, such as ability to locate materials through a catalog or ability to use an encyclopedia on CD ROM. Category 4 responses were coded as *skills*. Responses identified as category 5 emphasized content learning, such as using resources to learn about a subject. Category 5 responses were coded as *utilization*. Surveys with no response or a response that did not answer the question were coded 0. Survey responses were coded over the three years by two researchers from the School of Communication, Information and Library Studies at Rutgers University.

Table 9.1. Coding Scale for Library Media Specialists' Responses

Category 1:	Input—emphasis on resources and instruction, not on student learning.
Category 2:	Output—emphasis on quantitive measure of student use.
Category 3:	Attitude—emphasis on change in student attitude.
Category 4:	Skills—emphasis on information seeking.
Category 5:	Utilization—emphasis on information use for content learning.

The survey responses were treated as critical incidents for evidence of the library media specialists' perception of learning over three years of involvement in the initiative. In the first year, the highest number of responses, 105 or 31.7 percent, were coded in category 3, emphasizing a change in attitude toward the library media center and its resources. Approximately one-third of the library media specialists noted that they saw a positive change in attitude in their students as a result of Library Power. The second highest number of responses, 95 or 28.7 percent were coded in category 4, emphasizing library and information skills. These responses gave examples of students using information-seeking skills to locate materials or some of the new technology provided by Library Power. The third highest number of responses, 89 or 26.9 percent were coded in category 5, emphasizing utilization of information sources for content learning. These responses gave examples of students using resources to learn about something they were curious about or that related to a personal interest. Taken together the three categories represent 86 percent of the responses.

In the second year the highest number of responses, 155 or 38 percent, were coded in category 4, emphasizing library and information-seeking skills. The library media specialists noted that they saw evidence of influence of Library Power on students' ability to locate information sources and to use technology. The second highest number of responses, 97 or 24 percent, were coded at category 3, emphasizing a change in attitude of the students. Change in attitude continues to be a strong indicator of student learning in the library media specialists' responses. The third highest number of responses, 94 or 23 percent, were coded at category 5, emphasizing students' use of information for learning in connection with a subject in the curriculum or related to a personal interest. Taken together these three categories represented 85 percent of the responses of the library media specialists.

In the third year the highest number of responses, 185 or 37.4 percent, were coded in category 5, emphasizing utilization of information for learning. Library media specialists' responses gave examples of students learning through collaborative research projects throughout the curriculum. The second highest number of responses, 122 or 24.6 percent, were coded in category 4, emphasizing library and information-seeking skills. The third highest number of responses, 113 or 22.8 percent, were coded in category 3, emphasizing a change in attitude regarding the library media center and its resources. Taken together these three categories represented 85 percent of the responses.

In each of the three years the combined levels of attitude, skills, and utilization represented approximately 85 percent of what the library media specialists emphasized in their responses. However, comparison of the library media specialists' responses in each of the three years showed important changes, as shown in Table 9.2. In the first year, the highest number of responses emphasized a change in attitude. In the second year, the highest number of responses emphasized increased competence in information-seeking skills. In the third year, the highest number of responses emphasized utilization of information for learning. Over the course of the Library Power initiative, many library media specialists had changed their emphasis on what they considered important to describe about student learning. Early in the initiative they noted a change in attitude. Next they stressed competence in locating information and using technology. In the third year many had turned their attention to using information for learning in the content areas. This progression would seem to indicate that, over time, fully functioning library media centers were influencing students' opportunities to learn, at least from the library media specialists' perspective. By the end of the three-year study, many of the participating library media specialists' descriptions of student learning emphasized using information to achieve the overall objectives of the school.

**Table 9.2. Summary Chart of School Library
Media Specialists' Responses on Learning**

	Year 1 n = 331	Year 2 n = 405	Year 3 n = 495
No response	12 (3.6%)	27 (6.7%)	44 (8.9%)
Input	10 (3.6%)	16 (4.0%)	20 (4.0%)
Output	20 (6.0%)	16 (4.0%)	11 (2.2%)
Attitude	105 (31.7%)	97 (24.0%)	113 (22.8%)
Skills	95 (28.7%)	155 (38.8%)	122 (24.6%)
Utilization	89 (26.9%)	94 (23.0%)	185 (37.4%)

A Closer Look at Three Schools

Three case studies addressed the question of how library media specialists' perceptions of learning influenced learning opportunities for students. The purpose of the case studies was to gain detailed information on how the contributions of Library Power may have enhanced opportunities for student learning and to identify and examine any differences between the library media programs offered in the schools. The case studies took a closer look at three schools coded in the utilization category to gain a better sense of the factors influencing opportunities for students to learn from a variety of sources and implications for the implementation of a process approach. This study of a small subset of Library Power schools, although not necessarily representative of the entire set, shed some light on the potential of library media centers to influence student learning and the problems of implementing a process approach in library media programs.

Case study researchers spent two separate weeks at each of the three schools. The second visit provided an opportunity to follow up on observations made in the first visit. The case study researchers used three methods for studying student learning to provide triangulation in the data collection: observations, conversations, and products. Each case study was submitted in a detailed written report that was analyzed for evidence of opportunities for student learning based on five categories along the same lines as the coding scale developed for analysis of the survey critical incidents. The framework for analysis of the case studies was:

- **Input:** What were the contributions of Library Power? (Contributions were identified in ten areas: funding, collection, renovation, technology, staffing, administrative support, flexible scheduling, professional development, collaborative planning, and prior reform efforts.)

- **Output:** What was the quantitative evidence of increased opportunity for student learning? (counts of student use)

- **Attitude:** What were the attitudinal changes? (observations of student interest)

- **Skills:** What development of skill in location of materials and use of technology were evident? (evidence of information seeking)

- **Utilization:** What opportunities for student learning through the use of a variety of sources were evident in the library media program? (evidence of information use)

These five categories provided a framework for making judgments about students' experiences in the learning process within the case studies of the three schools. Although a complete description of baseline data was not given in any of the three case studies, introductory background information revealed much about the schools prior to Library Power on which to base indications of change during the initiative. An analysis was made of each case study school and comparisons were made of the three sites:

- **Input:** All three schools had similar *input* from Library Power with contributions of funding to support collection development, renovation, technology, and staffing. Administrative support, flexible scheduling, professional development, and collaborative planning were required and facilitated by Library Power. Prior reform efforts differed substantially. Although the case studies revealed that Library Power clearly had influenced student learning in each of these schools, important basic differences were noted. Although all three of the schools had similar contributions from Library Power, the differences related to a mutually held philosophy of learning fostered in prior reform efforts and professional development that had laid the groundwork for the Library Power initiative. School 1 was involved in a major reform initiative stressing a team approach to inquiry-based learning, with intensive onsite professional development in place providing a foundation on which the library media program could build. School 2 also had some prior reform efforts that were compatible with Library Power objectives and offered a series of professional development sessions although not as intensive as school 1. In an ongoing professional development effort, the teachers and librarian at school 2 had identified the research process as a central element for providing opportunities for student learning and had requested further training in this area. At school 3, however, where prior reform efforts were scattered over a wide range of approaches, the concept of learning through research had not taken hold. Although professional development was provided, efforts did not specifically address the research process, and prior reform efforts were not aimed at an inquiry approach to learning across the curriculum.

- **Output:** Increased use of the library media center and its resources, coded as output, also revealed evidence of a difference in opportunities for student learning in the three schools. Although the case study at school 1 did not report specific numbers, a constant stream of classes were observed coming in for research as well as high individual use of the library. At school 2 circulation and library media center use had increased considerably, although some teachers were using the library media center for collaborative research projects more than others. At school 3 circulation and library media center use had increased in the first year but had gone down some in the second year. Even when considering the smaller student body due to a new school opening, it seemed a warning signal that changes in the school may have a negative effect on opportunities for students to learn in the library.

- **Attitude:** Attitude toward the library media center as a place for learning was evident in each of the schools. At school 1, where a process approach was established, the children were excited about and interested in what they were learning. Teachers at school 2 reported seeing a marked improvement in their students' attitude toward learning through the research process. At school 3 teachers and students were enthusiastic about the renovated facility and improved collection. For the most part, students also expressed increased interest in and enthusiasm about learning through a variety of sources, although some noted confusion and frustration about research projects when they felt rushed and when they thought they had received conflicting instructions from teachers involved.

- **Skills:** Library and information skills at school 1 and school 2 were integrated into content learning. In both of these schools, students who used the library media center for research were found to have the ability to apply their information-seeking skills to locating information and resources in other situations and in other libraries. Only at school 3 were isolated library and information-seeking skills lessons mentioned in the case study, and the library media specialist was described as orienting students in preparation for future research projects.

- **Utilization:** Utilization of information for learning was the most pertinent category of analysis for addressing the key questions under investigation. The other four categories provided the framework for interpreting the differences in utilization of information for learning when comparing the three schools. All three had been identified as places that were likely to have a high level of student learning. And indeed, each was found to be providing opportunities for students to learn through use of a wide range of information sources. The difference between the schools in the utilization of resources for learning seemed to relate to an understanding of the research process and how to facilitate learning within the process. The teachers and library media specialist at school 1 were most advanced in their understanding of the process approach and were providing numerous opportunities for students to learn through inquiry and research. At school 2 the teachers and library media specialist had reached a point in their provision of research opportunities for students where they had become aware of a need to know more about the research process and ways to guide students in learning in the process. Although the library media specialist and teachers at school 3 had gotten off to a good start with particularly good questions for problem-initiated research, their understanding of the underlying process of learning through research was not sufficient to sustain major changes in personnel at the school. They had difficulty identifying what was going wrong and how to remedy the situation.

In summary, the study addressed library media specialists' perceptions of learning as a key element in providing opportunities for students to learn through an inquiry process approach (Donham, Bishop, Kuhlthau, and Oberg, 2001). What the librarians emphasized when asked to describe student learning was coded in five categories and revealed that their perceptions changed over the three-year period of the study. In the first year most library media specialists emphasized improved student attitude, in the second year most emphasized improved information seeking skills, and in the third year most emphasized improved information use for content learning. This change suggests that over time the utilization of information for learning became more important than merely locating and gathering information. The case studies offered insight into underlying differences in implementing a process approach in three schools that on the surface appeared to be similar. The differences between the schools were found to relate to the library media specialist and teachers understanding the research process and how to facilitate learning within the process.

The difference in the schools in the case study related to the underlying philosophy of learning held by the personnel of the school. An understanding of the inquiry process and how to facilitate learning in the process contributed to a sustained, integrated program of using the library media center for learning across the curriculum. Within inquiry learning the primary goal of information seeking and use was student learning in the context of various subject areas. The concept of inquiry as a way to learn, when held by administrators and teachers as well as librarians, provided a rationale for utilizing the library in the content areas of the curriculum. The case studies also indicated that continuity in professional development that built a mutually held constructivist view of learning, specifically based on a process approach, was an important component for developing and sustaining library media center use that promotes student learning in the content areas of the curriculum.

A Process Approach for the Information Age School

Information age schools should be structured around a process approach to learning rather than a transmission approach to teaching. Students should be actively involved in the process of constructing meaning in an information-rich environment. Students should engage in issues and projects that involve them in raising questions, seeking information from a wide variety of resources, changing their questions as they learn, identifying what they need to know more about, demonstrating what they have learned, and sharing their new understandings with a community of learners. Students should be involved in creating what Bruner (1990) calls "products of mind." This is a far cry from the "reproducing texts" and "repackaging information" that have been the focus of schools in too many cases.

The library media center is an essential component of the information age school that has been consistently overlooked by the major school reform initiatives. Library media programs based on a process approach to learning across the curriculum should be developed by the whole school community around the four enablers: a constructivist view of learning, a team approach to teaching, competence in designing process assignments, and commitment to developing information literacy.

The primary objective of information seeking and use in the school context is to enhance student learning and to develop information literacy. Use of a variety of sources for learning prepares students for living and working in information-rich environments. Competence in information seeking and use are basic skills in the information age. Fundamental literacy in reading, writing, and calculating should be applied and adapted to information-rich environments and to new technologies. Teaching to the test, memorizing simple right answers, and reproducing texts are not enough to prepare students to lead fulfilled lives in the information age (Newmann, Secada, and Wehlage, 1995). Students need to develop the ability to learn in changing situations without becoming overwhelmed and discouraged. They need to develop the ability to go beyond finding facts to construct their own understanding at a deep level.

The information search process approach to information literacy is based on empirical evidence of how students learn from a variety of sources of information. Unfortunately, most information skills programs that recommend specific steps to research assignments and problem solving are not based on empirical studies of how students actually learn in the process of information seeking. There is a serious deficit in the advice given in many programs presently being used in schools. Information skills instruction that forms the basis of many information literacy programs frequently skips over the critical stages of reflecting, constructing, and internalizing to learn and understand for one's self. The studies of the information search process reveal the importance of forming a focused perspective from information gathered to gain a deep understanding of an issue or question. Programs that skip the critical stages of exploration and formulation and advise students to move directly from identifying a task to collecting information and solving a problem or completing an assignment give the false impression that the search process is simply finding and reproducing texts. The information search process approach gives students an understanding of their own process of learning from information that enables them to apply that knowledge in their own lives. The approach gives students a way to learn, and library media specialists and teachers a way to teach, the basic competency of the information age, the process of learning from a variety of sources of information.

An understanding of the process of learning from a variety of sources is one of the most important abilities for students to acquire to function and thrive in an information-rich environment. A sense of process enables student to draw on the wide range of skills and knowledge that they learn throughout their years of schooling for application in the workplace, citizenship, and everyday living. Without a sense of process, students have difficulty recognizing similarity in circumstances necessary for transferring skills from one situation to another. The central goal of information literacy is to instill in students a sense of the process of learning from a variety of sources of information and skills to construct their own understandings from that information. The library media program in the information age school is instrumental in developing these understandings.

Information Search
Process in the Workplace

10

The workplace is becoming increasingly information dependent, with workers seeking, gathering, and interpreting information to accomplish tasks critical to the function of an organization or a professional practice. The Information Search Process model presented in this book was developed from the findings of studies primarily within the context of educational settings. With the exception of a small sample of public library users, study participants have been students. An important next question is how people in the workplace experience the information search process. The six stages of the process may be summarized for more general application as follows:

- Initiation, when a person becomes aware of a lack of knowledge or understanding so that uncertainty and apprehension are common

- Selection, when a general area or topic is identified and initial uncertainty often gives way to a brief sense of optimism and a readiness to begin the search

- Exploration, when inconsistent, incompatible information is encountered and uncertainty, confusion, and doubt frequently increase

- Formulation, when a focused perspective on the problem is formed and uncertainty diminishes as confidence begins to increase

- Collection, when information pertinent to the focused problem is gathered and uncertainty subsides as interest and involvement in the project deepens

Portions of this chapter have been previously published in the *Journal of the American Society for Information Science* (Kuhlthau, 1999a) and in the *Journal of Documentation* (Kuhlthau and Tama, 2001).

- Presentation, when the search is completed, with a new understanding of the problem enabling the user to explain his or her learning to others

An additional seventh stage, assessment, occurs after the search is complete, when the person reflects on what has gone well and where there were problems.

This chapter addresses some of the issues related to how workers seek and use information for addressing problems, making judgments, and accomplishing tasks, and specifically how they experience the information search process. Does the Information Search Process model hold for work tasks as it does for educational tasks? Do workers experience the process of information seeking differently in different types of tasks? Do workers experience uncertainty as described in the Information Search Process model in some work tasks? Is the novice worker's experience of the process different from that of the experienced expert?

Studies of Information Use in the Workplace

Most studies of information use in the workplace have concentrated primarily on the sources of information used, not on the process of seeking and using information A few studies, however, do raise important questions related to the process of information seeking. One developing issue is the different approaches to information seeking related to different types of tasks (Aguilar, 1967; Choo and Auster, 1993; Auster and Choo, 1994). More complex tasks have been found not only to foster the use of more varied sources than routine tasks but also to lead to different approaches to information seeking (Hart and Rice, 1991; Pinelli et al., 1993; Bystrom and Jarvelin, 1995). More complex information-seeking tasks involving considerable interpretation and construction seem to be associated with increased uncertainty and anxiety (Bates, 1986; Whittemore and Yovits, 1973; Yovits and Foulk, 1985; Yovits and Kleyle, 1993). The number of years of experience of information workers, specifically securities analysts, also has been found to be an important factor in the effectiveness of information-seeking activities (Baldwin and Rice, 1997). Issues related to uncertainty, complexity, construction, and experience in the context of work environments raise some important questions for further investigation of the information search process. This chapter presents two studies that have explored the information search process in the information-intensive work contexts of securities analysts and lawyers. These studies sought to expand the process concept by investigating the process of information seeking of the worker who focuses on information. The basic problem was to understand the information worker's perception of the information search process, particularly regarding uncertainty, complexity of tasks, and construction of knowledge, as well as to gain insight into the difference that expertise makes in the information search process.

Information Search Process of a Securities Analyst: A Longitudinal Case Study

Securities analysts have been identified as a group of information workers in a highly volatile environment that functions almost entirely on information. Therefore, securities analysts were considered prime examples of information workers. Baldwin and Rice (1997) provide an extensive review of user studies related specifically to securities analysts, noting recent trends that are changing analysts' patterns of information seeking, such as sector specialization, globalization of markets, and new electronic systems, all of which increase the quantity of information and the speed of dissemination. In their study of securities analysts' information-seeking behavior, Baldwin and Rice found that the only individual characteristic to influence an analyst's effectiveness was the number of years working as an analyst. Experience had a direct influence on the outcomes of analysts' information activities.

An in-depth case study of one securities analyst was conducted by this researcher to investigate further how experience is related to the information search process. The work context of the case study subject was the investment industry on Wall Street, where he was employed as an analyst. A longitudinal case study method was used to explore the difference between novice and expert information seeking and use. This particular securities analyst was identified as an information worker appropriate for longitudinal investigation of changes in an early career employee's perceptions of information seeking over time. In eight years the subject had moved from an entry-level position to recognition as a ranked authority in the industry. The longitudinal study was initiated in 1983 when the participant was a secondary school student and has continued since at four- to five-year intervals (see Chapter 5). In a previous segment of this case study the analyst had revealed an understanding of the information search process and had integrated it into his approach to information seeking and use throughout his undergraduate years (Kuhlthau, 1988c). This five-year segment of the longitudinal project studied the subject from his entry into a career as a securities analyst shortly after college to his position as a recognized and ranked expert in the industry. In the latest interview in this series, he reported that he had been ranked third in his industry category by *Institutional Investment* two years prior to the interview and second the previous year, and he expected to be ranked first in the near future. This case study participant was identified as a competent information worker who had achieved sufficient success from entry level to be considered an expert (Kuhlthau, 1999b).

In-depth interviews conducted in 1990 and again in 1995 were taped, transcribed, and analyzed for evidence of uncertainty within the information search process in relation to perception of the complexity of the task and the difference experience made in these perceptions. The role of mediators in the process of information seeking was also analyzed. Interviews were approximately ninety minutes in length during, which time the participant responded to eight questions that served as prompts for discussion about his information seeking and use in the workplace from his perspective. At the end of the second interview the participant was asked to read the transcript from the earlier interview and comment on any changes he identified in his patterns of information seeking. Perceptions of the participant in the entry years of his career were compared with those five years later. For the purposes of this study, the operational definition of novice/expert was the number of years' experience in the field and recognition of expertise by an independent source. In this case, the participant was considered a novice when he had been employed as a securities analyst for a little over three years and an expert five years later when he was recognized as an authority in the field.

Evidence of Uncertainty in Information Seeking and Use

The participant described the presence of uncertainty in relation to some aspects of his work at both entry level and five years later. Uncertainty was manifested by heightened anxiety and a sense of being overwhelmed and was related to some tasks more than others.

As a novice the participant explained that he experienced uncertainty in preparing extensive reports that involved a dynamic change in his thinking. He referred to these tasks as "the really good ones that you lose sleep over." These projects took an extended period of time. "Those are the ones that are really time consuming because you are changing your entire thinking on an industry." He called this kind of learning "ramping up." He also noted that his uncertainty stemmed from a perceived need to be right. "You feel anxiety because you are changing your whole view of the world. . . . So you wonder is this right? Is this wrong? Is this going to work out? Is this not going to work out? Am I going against the grain here?"

As a novice, the participant acknowledged the need to tolerate the discomfort of experiencing uncertainty. He stated that he not only expects to be overwhelmed at the beginning but "wants to be overwhelmed." He described "becoming comfortable" with the industry as a signal to write the report. He also noted that he felt anxious at the end of a project regarding how his analysis would be received and if his conclusions were right. "The anxiety builds up in seeing how your scenario works out."

As an expert he stated that he found it took about four years to feel confident in his area of specialization. However, he continued to experience a sense of uncertainty related to major new projects. He expressed less tolerance for this experience of uncertainty because it signaled an extensive information-gathering task ahead. He stated that, "I don't want to be overwhelmed anymore. If I am, it means I have to write a very major industry piece and I don't want to do that." He explained that some projects take him into "new territory" and that "it is very unsettling to have to move out of your element and ramp up on something entirely new again." At this point, although the participant expressed a preference for the confidence and comfort of more routine information-gathering tasks, he acknowledged the necessity to occasionally engage in tasks that cause uncertainty and apprehension. Although he expected to be uncertain in some tasks, his tolerance for uncertainty-related tasks seemed considerably less than when he was a novice.

Evidence of the Relation of Uncertainty to Complexity of Task

At both points in the participant's career he drew distinctions between routine tasks and complex tasks. Routine tasks were associated with low uncertainty and complex tasks or major projects were associated with high uncertainty. As might be expected, as a novice he considered more tasks to be complex than he did as an expert, when most of his tasks were considered routine and part of the normal course of his work. The perception of the complexity of a task rather than the actual, objective complexity itself seemed to be the critical factor in experiencing uncertainty.

As a novice the participant used the term "resurge" in his description of his overall task. "We would tell investors whether they should buy, sell, or hold the stock. So we would 'resurge' the company from a financial perspective. We would look at the market they were involved in and try to come up with conclusions on their future outlook and we would write research reports."

He described his work as involving two types of information tasks. One he called "maintenance" or "soft" research, where the basic framework was already there and the task involved updating that research. He described this as "very traditional Wall Street research" where he might be working on as many as twelve mini-reports at a time and would complete about sixty reports over three years. He explained that in these tasks, "You don't go through the entire research process. It is stuff you already know and you cut and paste a lot." These tasks were considered routine.

The second type of task, which he called "pure" research, occurred when "you are trying to get a sense of how an industry is structured." He explained that in these tasks he was trying "to understand what the industry is all about and where it has been and where it is going. It is something that I approached with zero knowledge and I didn't know where it would lead me." He estimated that he had worked on about six reports of this type and that these tasks were, "really time consuming because you have to change your entire thinking on an industry." These tasks were considered complex.

As an expert the participant described the overall task of his work more clearly than he did as a novice, but he did not contradict his earlier explanation. "The overall task is to stay abreast of what is happening and to analyze trends. It takes a couple of years to fully understand the dynamics of the industry and what makes these companies move." Using the image of a "big chess board," he revealed extensive knowledge of the interaction within the industry. He again described his information seeking and use as involving a two-tiered task but this time in reverse order of his earlier description: first the complex task of "ramping up" on an industry and second the routine task of analyzing trends and writing reports on how the company addresses its competitive position relative to other companies in the industry. In the first task, called "a major industry piece to lay the groundwork for ongoing research," he described being, "out of my element" and "treading into new territory". He explained that, although he is not regularly involved in such complex tasks, occasionally he is required to address a new industry. The following remarks showed his strong reaction to this type of information-seeking task. "I hate complex tasks. I don't have time for complex tasks . . . to go through the whole process of having to add value to clients on a new industry." As an expert this participant was involved in about one complex project each year and was clear about the discomfort and uncertainty associated with a major project of this type.

Relation of Uncertainty and Complexity to Construction

The participant clearly described the need to interpret the information he gathered. At both the novice and the expert level he was not just reproducing texts or reporting gathered facts but involved in a thoughtful process of construction for presenting "new" information to clients. However, his emphasis was on a different objective at each point in his career. As a novice he emphasized being "right" in his conclusion. As an expert he emphasized "adding value to the client's knowledge."

The participant as a novice repeatedly described the need to expand his knowledge base, explaining that he was "getting a sense of what this industry is all about." The following comments pulled from various points in the interview emphasize this theme: "trying to get a sense of how the industry itself was structured"; "trying to get a sense of what earning they would derive in the future"; " I try to get a sense of what the market is within each of these segments"; "try to understand the industry and what it is all about and where it has been and where it is going"; and "getting a sense of how these people are reacting to change in the environment and how they are positioning themselves." These comments reveal a desire to understand, interpret, and learn rather than just gather and report facts.

The six projects that he identified as more complex than the others involved learning or "ramping up" and constructing a "story" to present. He explained that these major projects involved getting "a sense if there is an interesting story that I want to pitch. How has this been pitched before and do I have any new angles that I want to pitch." He explained that the need to present new information caused anxiety. "You always have to have a fresh angle on things to market. You have to be able to be constructive, and that is where the anxiety comes in. You have to have something to say. You have to have an overall perception." He explained that he constructs his point of view in the process of information seeking. "I build conclusions from day one. I just keep changing them as the information rolls in." As a novice he acknowledged experiencing considerable uncertainty and anxiety associated with extensive construction in the process of information seeking.

A further element that contributed to his experience of anxiety was his perception of the necessity for "being right." Coming up with the "right" answer was an important concern for the novice. In addition, as a novice the participant was concerned about being misled by "wrong" information. He explained that, "I don't think there is such a thing as too much information but I do think there is right information and wrong information. Right information is accurate and proves itself right over time. Wrong information is misleading."

The participant described his interpretation of the information he had gathered as his story and explained that he considered his audience's information-seeking process in his reports. "I simplify my story and provide options for the client, either the general conclusions and general story line or every little point. . . . My audience is a client who does not want to be overwhelmed with a complicated story. My job was to simplify it for him as much as possible." He explained how he provided options for the client so that his report would be accessible on a variety of levels. "The cover page of my report has bullet points. Here's what I found out, three or four highlights. The rest of the report is expanding on those bullet points."

The participant explained that after he has formulated his view of an industry or company through an extensive process of information seeking and construction he does not change it readily. "It is not easy to sway me on my conclusions on a perception of an industry once I have been working on an idea for a while. My conclusion is not based on one company but relative to everything else that is out there." Once he had constructed a point of view he seemed fairly resistant to changing his opinion.

As an expert the participant noted the difference between simply gathering and reporting on facts and interpreting information to provide new insights. He explained that, "we have gone from being data gathers to being data providers. My job is not to tell the client to buy or sell but to provide intelligent, insightful information to add value to his knowledge base." He described a change in his understanding of his work over the five-year period. He explained that he is no longer so concerned with being right or wrong or coming up with the right answer but with providing valuable information for the client. "The task has changed some from when I first started. It is not to buy or to sell but to add value. The best way I can help, particularly my more sophisticated client, is by adding value to their knowledge base. . . . The young analyst who is not confident in his industry worries about getting the story right. Now my attention is on adding value."

The participant as an expert went on to explain changes in his objective and approach from earlier in his career. "You learn to deal with the anxiety of 'will I be right' or 'will I be wrong' by making sure that whatever research you write, whether it is right or wrong, that it is adding value in the marketplace. Even if it is completely wrong at least it gets people thinking about an issue that they should be thinking about, and they may not agree with you but they may be thankful that you made them think about it and address that issue with other analysts on the street. I have learned to approach my job differently and to reduce that anxiety." Emphasis had shifted to adding valuable information and that had eased anxiety related to coming up with the right answer.

As an expert the participant explained that he, "used to write a lot more but it was a lot less insightful and less value added." He emphasized other pressures on his time that the younger analyst doesn't have but noted that when he was ready to write a report he set aside a block of time to concentrate on the task. He explained that, "I know I am ready to put out a report when I look at a company in a way that other people are not looking at it. When I know I have a piece of information that is critical to understanding this company that is not reflected in stock prices yet." The expert explained that the "trigger" for getting out a report is not merely the date it is due but the more conceptual "trigger" of having valuable new information.

As an expert the participant also had changed his view of "wrong information" from when he was a novice. He explained that, "I thrive on wrong information right now. I am living in markets where so many of my competitors put out wrong information or wrong interpretation based on incomplete information. . . . What I do love is having wrong information in the marketplace and then coming in saying that is wrong and explaining why. . . . It is easy for people to think they have right information when indeed it is not. . . . They should be looking at it from an entirely different perspective. So it is not just wrong information, a lot of the time, it is poor interpretation of right information." The importance of the interpretation of information, not just the gathering of information, was stressed, and confidence in being able to provide valuable interpretation was clearly expressed by the expert.

Role of Mediators

At each point in the participant's career when he was asked how an information professional could be of help, he responded that the biggest problem for an analyst is to produce clearly formulated research. As a novice he explained that, "The biggest qualm that directors of research on Wall Street have with research analysts is that they take too long. I have friends in the industry who can't bang out research reports. I have friends who have been tracking an industry for a year and have not written it up yet and have not picked up coverage of any companies." As an expert he stressed the same problem and identified a lack of understanding of the process of research as the basis of the problem. "Research directors complain that their analysts don't write enough. . . . One of the things I see on Wall Street in research departments and even in some of the corporate financial departments is the whole problem of being self conscious about the research process and getting a paper out and how to get rid of the anxiety that goes with writing a research paper. . . . For us it is really critical because we work under very tight time constraints. A lot of paper flow has to go out and in many cases there is a direct correlation between paper flow and transactions generated for a firm."

He suggested that one way to help might be to make research directors aware of the process of doing research. He particularly emphasized working with, " young analysts to make them conscious of what the research process is. . . . There are some very basic stumbling blocks that you should be aware of. . . . It is really not very complicated, but some people don't pay attention. A lot of people have a very hard time."

Another suggestion made by the participant was to teach the research process in business school. He explained, "If you go to business school you will find that this isn't taught. A lot of the focus in business school goes on learning to do team work so that you can get things out fast. But the fact is that when you go out in the marketplace, a lot of time we can't work in teams. A lot of the weight falls on your own shoulders. You have to do it yourself. How do you deal with that anxiety? How many courses on writing for business don't address the issue of the thought process and the emotional process that one goes through in getting out a research paper or getting out written material or getting out a report and how to deal with it?"

Summarizing the area in which information professionals might be of help, he stated that, "The best way to help us, I think, is to help us to get it on paper because a lot of good analysts understand the industry and have great insights into the industry but is just doesn't go on paper. Or by the time it goes out on paper it is not transaction oriented material. It is a day late and a dollar short. That's where I think people on my side of the business need the most help."

Discussion of the Securities Analyst's Information Search Process

The major research question addressed in this case study was: What is the early career information worker's perception of uncertainty, task complexity, and knowledge construction, and how do these perceptions change over time with more experience?

Uncertainty in Information Seeking and Use

Uncertainty was manifested by heightened anxiety and a sense of being overwhelmed. The participant described the presence of uncertainty in relation to particular aspects of his work both as a novice and as an expert. As a novice he showed considerable tolerance for uncertainty, stating that he actually "wanted to be overwhelmed" because he knew that he had much to learn about the industry. In many projects he was starting with little knowledge and uncertainty was associated with his lack of knowledge. In addition, he was anxious and uncertain about arriving at the right answer in his information seeking.

As an expert, he explained that he still felt unsettled over projects that took him into "new territory." He experienced uncertainty less often than as a novice but noted that uncertainty signaled a major project that would require an extensive amount of work. Although he expected to be uncertain in some tasks, his tolerance for uncertainty-related tasks seemed considerably less than when he was a novice. This may have been due to the pressure of additional responsibilities, as noted in Baldwin and Rice (1997), which left little time for the sustained work required in major projects.

Uncertainty in Complex Tasks

Complex tasks were associated with uncertainty by the participant at each point in his career. However, it was his perception of complexity that was associated with uncertainty, not the complexity of a task itself. As one would expect, as a novice he perceived more tasks to be complex. However, as an expert he continued to experience uncertainty in the early stages of the information search process in tasks that he perceived as complex. He was involved in at least one major project each year that he described as complex and was clear about the discomfort and uncertainty associated with such a project. At each point in the participant's career he drew distinctions between routine tasks and complex tasks. Routine tasks that involved monitoring and maintaining ongoing projects were associated with low uncertainty, whereas complex tasks that involved learning and constructing something entirely new were associated with high uncertainty. The perception of the complexity of a task, rather than the actual, objective complexity of the task, seemed to be the critical factor in experiencing uncertainty.

Learning, Interpreting, and Constructing Knowledge

The learning, called "ramping up," involved extensive construction within the information search process required in complex tasks. Both as a novice and as an expert, the participant was actively interpreting the information he was gathering. His comments reveal a desire to understand, interpret, and learn rather than just to gather facts. As a novice, he identified six projects as more complex than others that involved learning and constructing a "story" to present. Clearly he was not merely reporting facts or reproducing texts but constructing new information to present as a cohesive "story" or narrative. He explained that he constructed his point of view in the process of information seeking by building his conclusions from the very beginning and changing his view according to the information he collected.

However, his emphasis as a novice, was on being "right" in his conclusions and seeking the right answer. As an expert, his objective had changed significantly. Rather than seeking to be right, his aim was to add value to the client's knowledge. He explained that he understood that what seems to be wrong information is often the result of poor interpretation. As an expert, when he came across something that he considered wrong, he saw it as an opportunity to add value by presenting his own interpretation.

As an expert, he had developed two approaches to his work that aided him in learning and forming interpretations to present in his reports. He spent considerable time on gaining an understanding of the perspective of the market of the company he was analyzing. Rather than just forming his own view from the outside, he attempted to gain an insider's view from the company perspective. The other important factor was his overall understanding of the market, not just based on one company but incorporating what he calls "everything else out there." These two elements had evolved over time as fundamentals underlying his reports. He explained that he knew that he was ready to present a report when he had developed an interpretation about a company that was somewhat different from that of other analysts. He strove to construct an understanding of the company that had not been reported on and would be considered new information. His primary aim was to add value to the client's knowledge with some new information or new interpretation of existing information.

Role of the Information Professional

The information professional did not seem to have a role in the information seeking of this securities analyst. The logical area where a mediator might help would be in information provision for complex tasks. However, evidence that it was not necessarily the task itself but the user's perception of the task that determines complexity complicates the mediator's role. Ways to diagnose workers' perceptions of an information-seeking task may need to be developed as a first step in helping the information worker in complex tasks that involve uncertainty and construction.

When asked what would be helpful, the participant did not describe a traditional role for a mediator in the information seeking. He referred to the difficulty many analysts have in writing reports and suggested that it would be helpful for them to become aware of the process involved in research. He indicated that it is this process that these information workers need help with and that they are being tripped up by the process. New roles for information professionals may lie in developing ways to engage in the information search process of information workers. He suggested that one way to help might be to make research directors aware of the process of doing research. He also recommended that courses on writing in business schools should address the thought process and the emotional process that one goes through in getting out a research paper or getting out written material or a report, and how to deal with it.

Information Search Process of Lawyers: An Exploratory Study

The case study of the securities analyst as a novice and as an expert revealed that the model of the information search process was more applicable in complex tasks than it was in routine work tasks. Although the securities analyst clearly identified some tasks as complex, requiring considerable construction at each point in his career, as an expert he identified a different objective for the information seeking and use associated with these tasks than he had earlier in his career. As a novice, his emphasis was on getting the "right" conclusion. As an expert, he emphasized interpreting and constructing for the purpose of "adding value to the client's knowledge." This finding raised questions for further study about the information-seeking behavior of experts within the more complex tasks involved in their work. How do experts use information to accomplish complex tasks? How do experienced workers' perceptions of their information search process compare with the information search process model? What role do library and information services have in this process?

The underlying assumption, derived from the study of the securities analyst, was that information seeking within complex tasks encompasses a constructive process that goes beyond simply striving to reduce uncertainty and to find a right answer, and includes interpreting, learning, and creating to accomplish the task by adding value to an enterprise. This phase of the research concentrated on investigating experienced information workers' perceptions of the process of information seeking and use for accomplishing complex tasks.

Lawyers were chosen as a distinct type of information-intensive workers with professional tasks and goals. Although providing information for clients is the primary task of securities analysts and lawyers, the lawyers have a further role of acting on the information for the client. In an examination of information-seeking behavior of lawyers, Sutton (1994) found that relevance judgments shift along a knowledge continuum and that factors underlying these judgments are "complex, multidimensional, and knowable." A study of early career, experienced lawyers was conducted to gain a better understanding of changes in knowledge states within the variety of tasks in which they were involved and how they used information to accomplish these tasks. In addition, the study investigated the role mediators played in the process of information use of this group (Kuhlthau and Tama, 2001).

The study addressed the following research questions: Does this group of early career expert information workers differentiate between routine and complex tasks? Are tasks that are identified as complex related to the construction of new knowledge? Does this group of experts experience the information search process as depicted in the model in more complex work tasks? Is uncertainty related to more complex tasks? What are the roles of mediators in the process of information seeking and use of this group? What potential roles for mediators are identified by this group?

Structured interviews were conducted with eight practicing lawyers, four male and four female. The participants were identified as early career experts with six to ten years' experience in their area of practice. They were practicing in New Jersey in small to medium-sized law firms specializing in a variety of types of cases, including complex toxic tort, personal injury, contract disputes, criminal matters, environmental cases, real estate matters, and landlord-tenant disputes. One lawyer functioned in a dual role as an instructor/coordinator of a law school clinic representing homeless persons and welfare cases.

Each of the participants was interviewed in taped sessions of approximately one hour in length. The lawyers were interviewed individually, not as a group. The interviews were semi-structured, using the following questions and prompts to initiate discussion:

- Describe your work, specifically the tasks and goals in your work.

- How do you get and use information?

- Do you use a library, database, or other sources?

- Are some tasks more complex than others?

- How do you get and use information in different level tasks?

- Describe beginning, middle, and end stages of a task and your information use in each. What is most the difficult part? What is most the creative part?

- How do you know when you have enough information?

- What sources, systems, and services might be helpful to you?

Tapes of the interview sessions were analyzed according to the framework that had emerged in the longitudinal case study of the securities analyst conducted earlier. Evidence was sought for differentiating between routine and complex work tasks, perception of construction in relation to complex tasks, experience of uncertainty in relation to complex tasks, perceptions of information search process in accomplishing complex tasks, problems related to the information search process in complex task, and current and prospective roles of mediators.

Evidence of Differentiating Between Routine and Complex Tasks

This group of eight lawyers readily explained that their work comprised both routine and complex tasks. Tasks identified as complex involved preparing a case for trial. Complex tasks were described as being accomplished in stages "moving from fact gathering, to defining the theory of a case, to resolving the matter through trial." Matters that were settled out of court and did not require extensive pretrial or trial preparation or were otherwise resolved without full formal court proceedings were generally considered of a more routine nature.

Evidence of Construction in Complex Tasks

The lawyers described complex tasks as involving considerable thinking and formulation. They explained that these tasks need considerable construction of a new approach. These are tasks that are not readily apparent on the surface or at first glance but need to be worked out over time. They described a need for "figuring out a strategy for a complex case" or "looking at a tendency to decide what to do in a case." One lawyer described the task as "a puzzle to unravel." Another explained that the interesting part is when you "go to the next level." One of the lawyers further explained that, "The hardest part of the job is figuring out a strategy for a complex case and figuring out what path to take. . . . What you are trying to prove in order to succeed takes analytical skill. Trying to predict the future a bit. Trying to figure out how it is going to play before a jury. You should have in your mind what your closing statement is going to be before you start trying it." Some descriptions of a complex task were more in the "puzzle piece" mode, of filling a slot, but there was considerable indication of unspecified information need at the beginning of the process. A lawyer explained it this way: "You have an idea in your mind of what you are going to find out. You know there is a slot that needs to be filled and you know the name of that slot but you don't know what goes into it."

Complex tasks required formulating new approaches and creating different ways of looking at the evidence in a case. For example, one lawyer who practiced in an area that usually settled out of court described encountering a situation where a case would need to be tried and explained the different approach required in this way: "There are certain legal issues that we haven't even thought that much about because we really haven't gone that far into the case. Wow, when you sit down and think about how are you going to prove that, there is not only one answer. You are looking at it in a certain way. What is the strategy for this trial? It may sound unorthodox, but there is more than one way to do it. It's not black and white. You can be very creative in how your present your case."

When explaining more complex tasks, these lawyers described considerable construction related to accomplishing their objective. They emphasized that there is not just one way to develop a case but different ways to approach the information, facts, and evidence that are not readily apparent on the surface. Constructing a strategy entails considerable creativity and formulation on the part of the individual. Complex tasks involve developing one's own theory of a case and constructing a way to present the information as an interesting and persuasive argument.

Evidence of Uncertainty in Complex Tasks

This group of experts acknowledged a sense of uncertainty related to constructing new approaches to a case, as described in the Information Search Process model. As one lawyer noted, "At first you are unsure and worried and then you are confident." They exhibited affective experiences similar to the model of the information search process as moving from uncertainty to confidence.

However, these lawyers did not respond to uncertainty in the same way as participants in previous studies had. None of the lawyers expressed the feelings of anxiety and frustration related to uncertainty that the other participants had experienced. The lawyers expressed heightened interest and enthusiasm for more complex tasks that required considerable construction and creativity. To describe their feelings about the more challenging parts of their work, the lawyers used terms such as *interesting, imaginative, exciting,* and *fascinating,* with one noting that sometimes you "fall in love with your case." This kind of engagement with the more difficult, complex tasks was pervasive and consistent among these lawyers. As one stated, "That is the part that gets my adrenaline running and I feel really excited about it. The routine is just not as much fun." This finding indicates that these lawyers had learned from their past experience that uncertainty is to be expected in complex tasks where considerable construction is required.

Evidence of Stages of the Information Search Process in Complex Tasks

Evidence of stages in the process of information seeking of the lawyers was elicited from their descriptions of the beginning, middle, and end of their search process in preparation for a complex case for trial.

Initiation of the Search Process

At the beginning of the search process the lawyers were seeking background information to orient them to the issues surrounding the task. Several lawyers noted that more complex tasks occasionally require sources outside of the legal literature to gather background information about the context of the case, for example to address questions related to medical, environmental, or social issues. One lawyer described using such sources "to get general knowledge." Another explained that, "Every now and then something comes my way that is not directly in my zone of expertise. So I come to the university library and look up material not necessarily legal in nature."

At the start the lawyers were also seeking ideas about how to construct the case for trial. One of the lawyers described in detail the initiation of the process of constructing a case: "When I do my research for a motion or a brief. . . . I usually sit down and try to formulate what I think is the issue. After I totally understand what the facts are, I write down a couple of areas that I am interested in researching, that I think will answer the question I am trying to get to. I know that other people looking at the situation will come up with different areas. But I usually try to hit what I think is the key area and then I start to do my research. And, I do my research the old fashioned way. I go into the library and I pull out the index and I start reviewing the keywords and I find that it takes a long time." This lawyer expected to develop different ideas from someone else looking at the case and anticipated that it would take some time. Through experience, this lawyer had found that there is a pattern in his work, which at first seemed random. The consistency of initially finding information that he was not specifically looking for led to new understanding and formulation. As he explained, "I find that while I am looking for my issue I come across something else, apparently haphazardly. But it has happened so many times that it isn't haphazard and

I usually end up finding the case that way. I start looking for A, and while look-ing for A, I find B. Then A isn't the issue I am looking for. Now it's B. I have found something that really starts to formulate the issue I am looking for. It has happened so many times that I am convinced that there is something else going on there." This approach at initiation provided an entry to information relevant to the case with only limited specific knowledge about the case.

Another lawyer reflected on a similar experience in this way: "In every case that I have ever researched I have done this. I can sit here and visualize going through summary cases. [At first] I don't really see what I am looking for and then the next one after it catches my eye and I keep going. And finally, so far I have never missed, I find the seminal case that turns the key one way or another. I go in not knowing what the case is, but finding it. And once I get there, I do the research on it." This initial approach was a way to begin in preparation for ex-ploring to formulate a focus for the case.

Midpoint in the Search Process

At midpoint in their process, standard legal reference sources were used to construct a theory and develop a strategy for presenting the case for trial. A num-ber of other sources were used by lawyers in addition to the formal legal refer-ences. Three categories of other sources were identified in the study: internal office files, external electronic resources, and people both internal and external. Taken together these sources provided relevant factual and legal information that lawyers consulted and used in the course of their work and particularly when researching a complex case for trial.

All eight lawyers expressed a preference for print texts over computer data-bases for more complex tasks. Although there was the expectation that computer sources would or should make their work easier, and they considered themselves "old fashioned" for their preference for using books, the print sources seemed to support their work of constructing a complex case. "I like the book. I'm a little old fashioned that way. I like to see the hard book. I find that computer services aren't as user friendly. I can just look in one [supplement] and a short little blurb and the screen doesn't do that for me. I can't get an overview."

In the middle of the research they explained that they required sources that were structured in such a way as to enable extensive exploration. One lawyer de-scribed the difference between using printed texts and computer databases: "There is something about physically having those books and being able to look at it and to have a couple of them opened on your lap and to be able to kind of cross reference all at the same time. I need to do that. I need to physically see it. And when I put the queries into the computer, it seems like the right answers don't come back to me quick enough and I am very easily frustrated." This law-yer further explained how the text accommodated the constructive process as he progressed in his research: "You can have a bunch of digests open at the same time and you can rule out some things. It's almost like a doctor or a mechanic— you're looking at everything together. With the computer, I find that I almost have to remain isolated with my searches. It is very easy for me to lose track of my train of thought and I would have to go back to see where I was. Whereas, when I take the books out, albeit I can make a huge mess of the library, I can kind of see where I am and how I got there." This explanation of the use of texts stresses the active process of constructing from a variety of sources in the exploration, formulation, and collection stages of the information search process.

Close of the Search Process

Toward the close of the research process, these lawyers had a clear sense of when they had used sufficient sources to complete their task. In response to the question, when do you know you have enough information?, they consistently described a definite sense of closure. One lawyer stated that, "you have enough when you put yourself in place of the juror and figure out any real pitfalls and how to address them." Another described enough as "When I have answered all the questions to defeat their argument." Another added, "You can tell when you are formulating your argument what the strong points are and what the weak points are. Try to tie everything down and to anticipate other issues. I am done when I have responded to every issue that is relevant and there are no loose ends."

Determining when they had used enough information was related to their sense of having constructed a persuasive strategy. As one explained, "Is there sufficient information to meet the burden of proof? . . . You not only want to have the information but you want it to be persuasive."

The constructive process closed with preparing to present a case in court. At this point, the lawyers acknowledged that they were engaged in an intensely creative process. The use of sources supported this process. They commented that, "Putting it together is the most creative part." "Your own creative juices go into formulating those arguments."

Problems Encountered in the Information Search Process in Complex Tasks

The lawyers discussed some problems they had encountered in the process of constructing new understandings in a complex case. One lawyer explained that it was more difficult to initiate a complex task with current database systems available. "There is something I would miss if I did it the way [the system] would have you research, which is to plug in the phrase and have it pop up every case that says "George." Well, I can tell you, I have looked for "George" a lot of times and I have found "Kevin," and that's the key. I would never find it using the traditional search program they have now. So when I do research, I don't usually use [the system] now. In light of my experience, I go with the book. I go to the library and I sit down and I take some time. I peruse the digest summaries of cases under the keyword index. I read the case and I disregard and I Shepardize [update] and see if any cases fall in line that look interesting. And, ultimately, I find what I am looking for. But I do it in such a way that I would never get there using the computer. And that's why, even today, [the system] doesn't help me to get where I want to go."

Existing computer systems may have required these lawyers to be too specific at the beginning of their research, rather than opening up a broad range of options, and did not seem to allow them to look at enough variety of information at one time. As one explained, "I don't personally like using search programs. You have to be specific. You have to know the name of the defendant or the name of the case."

In many instances, the lawyers hoped or expected that computer systems would be developed that would assist them in their information seeking and use. These lawyers anticipated that systems would be developed in the future that could better accommodate their work. But at this point they expressed some disappointment and reservations about the application of current systems for meeting their information needs, particularly in more complex tasks. One lawyer described his reservations about using computer systems for legal research: "For my own personal work, I don't know. I am sure that at some point there has to be a way to make legal research easier as opposed to just punching in a keyword and having it spit out every case with that keyword. There has got to be a better way. I think the phraseology has to advance because you are looking for a particular phrase, and you don't get the phrase necessarily. You are just pulling the words out. There has got to be a better way to do research. If it ever got to that point, I would be more comfortable, but now I am not confident that I would get where I need to go the way it is set up." The difficulty that this lawyer was experiencing seemed to be the limitation surrounding keyword searching and the lack of confidence in the system's capacity to access the range of information needed for constructing cases in preparation for trial. This group of experts consider themselves to be "the generation between" print orientation and computer orientation. Although they were willing to use computers, they were impatient with the lack of flexibility in the existing computer systems and did not fully trust that they could construct within these systems.

Another significant problem expressed was related to organizing internal office files and the need for a classification system that would better serve the particular information needs of the lawyers' work. "I know what I would like to have happen. If you could have a system where somebody comes and looks at what we have and says, here is a uniform system of data entry that you will use from now on." However, the cost and difficulty of providing this type of assistance was recognized as a major concern: "The problem is that would be monumental because of what we use and what we do. It would be incredible and so cost prohibitive that we could never do it. But I don't know what resources are out there and who we can contact to come in to talk to us. And say, here's what we do. What can you do to make it easier for us?"

Role of Mediators

All of these lawyers used some type of assistance in information seeking and use to accomplish their work. Assistants were identified as secretaries and paralegals, one used a research assistant, and a few mentioned using a librarian. The assistance consisted of basic organization and access to information. However, they noted serious limitations in their current assistance and identified significant potential roles for mediators.

The role of librarians as mediators was very limited, although there seemed to be a call for a potential role in designing and mediating information systems and services directed specifically to the lawyers' work. Currently, the lawyers seem to be using librarians simply for locating a specific source. As one described, "I don't usually use a law librarian. The only time I go to a librarian is if I can't find the publication I am looking for." Even where a librarian was engaged on a more personal level, the role of locating sources prevailed: "There is one librarian who is very helpful to everyone but especially helpful to me. I used to be a clerk so I have extra status. I ask her for books on how to take depositions and if I need a particular case and the most up-to-date decisions. I use the library about twice a month."

Several lawyers called for a more central role for librarians that would organize, classify, and access information related to the lawyer's specific area of work and particularly for complex tasks. "I'll tell you that we could actually use a librarian. That's the solution! To have someone whose sole job is to make everything uniform and catalog it, so we all know where it is at any given time. Keep us ahead of the game, keeping up on the Internet so everyone can be trained. . . . If we had one person who would make sure everything was in order and our computer system was set up so we could find stuff and everything was uniform, it would be more efficient." A personalized information service was indicated that would meet the specific information needs of a lawyer's practice.

Although acknowledging the need for a personalized information service, another lawyer expressed a concern about the practicality of developing such a service: "I like to draw my sources from a wide variety of disciplines. . . . It would be good to have that information funneled to me. I don't know exactly what that way would be. . . . If there was some way that could be designed, . . . but that's so personal, so specific to what I do that I don't know if that's practical. It would really be setting up a system for me."

The potential role, as described by these lawyers, was a combination of information services and systems that would be tailored to the specific tasks they needed to accomplish in their work. The lawyers suggested that many aspects of their work would call for the competencies of a library information professional.

Discussion of Lawyers' Information Search Process

The major research question addressed in this study of lawyers as one group of information-intensive workers was whether the model of the information search process is applicable in the more complex tasks of this group of experts.

Construction and Uncertainty in Complex Tasks

Even in an area of work that would seem restrictive such as law, these lawyers clearly described the need to personally construct a creative way to present a case rather than simply gathering facts and finding "the right answer." As experts they agreed that people come up with different areas to emphasize when developing a case. In these instances, like the securities analyst in the earlier study, they were not looking for the one right answer or one specific case but were striving to develop a persuasive argument, similar to the analyst's goal of adding value to the client's knowledge about a stock. These lawyers concurred that this kind of work takes time and is characterized by uncertainty in the early stages. However, although they acknowledged experiencing uncertainty when they first initiated a complex task, they viewed uncertainty as a signal of important creative work ahead. These experts viewed the early stages of the information-seeking process of developing a case for trial not as looking for specific information but as more exploratory, seeking one thing and finding another. This seemingly haphazard process resulted in finding ideas and information that led to formulating an important issue in a case. They described a process similar to that of the Information Search Process model.

Stages in the Information Search Process in Complex Tasks

These lawyers used sources of information in different ways throughout the stages of constructing a complex case. Initially, sources provided an overview and background knowledge as well as ideas about how the case might be developed. At midpoint, sources enabled them to construct a theory or strategy in the case. Finally, they completed their work when they determined they had used sufficient information to create a persuasive presentation in court.

There was evidence of a sequence of stages in the search process of these lawyers comparable to the model of the information search process. Their description of the beginning, middle, and closure of their research revealed similar thoughts and actions as depicted in the model. Feelings of uncertainty of these experts, however, differed somewhat from those of the students in the earlier studies, as well as those of the securities analyst. For these experts uncertainty in the beginning indicated the challenge of constructing and creating that captured their interest. They described preparing for formulation from the very beginning of their research.

At the beginning of their research in complex cases they took time to think about the facts of the case and to write down key areas for research. They started searching with an openness for finding something other than what they were specifically looking for. This openness or invitational mood at the start enabled them to find information that was not initially known to them. In this way, they were able to gain access to new or unique information from known or redundant information. These beginning stages of research encompassed the initiation and selection stages of the Information Search Process model with transition into the exploration stage in preparation for formulation.

At the midpoint, they described strategies for constructing a complex case that required having a wide range of information available and in front of them at one time, "looking at everything together" so that they do not loose their train of thought. The construction was accomplished by choosing ideas from the cases they had located to formulate an argument. This creative process took time and concentration and went well beyond merely gathering information and facts. The midpoint stages of research encompassed the exploration, formulation, and collection stages of the Information Search Process model. Although the lawyers were working though these stages in a recursive rather than linear way, they described moving along in a progression toward completion in a sequence similar to that described in the model.

At the closure of the search they were thinking primarily of the presentation of the case for trial. This provided criteria for judging what was enough to close the search. Preparing the presentation was described as a creative process of formulating persuasive arguments from the information they had collected. They were seeking this formulation from the beginning of the research and were able to take time to construct their case gradually throughout the stages of the search process.

Role of the Information Professional

Although these lawyers may seem surprisingly bookish, they were fairly computer literate but had become impatient with information systems that did not allow them to explore information to facilitate their constructive process. They expressed a need for control in "knowing where they were" in the information sources. The print resources allowed them to look for "one thing and find another." These lawyers expressed serious reservations about the capacity of computerized systems to access the range of information they needed. Available databases worked well for routine tasks and specific inquiries but not so well for complex tasks and unspecified queries. Considerable rethinking is needed to design systems and services to provide a wider range of access that is more in line with the process of construction.

In addition, these lawyers were having great difficulty managing their internal office files. They had attempted to develop classification systems or had their assistants develop systems, but access to these files, which were considered critical to the success of their work, was not efficient or effective. Considerable rethinking is needed to adapt principles of classification to offer uniform, yet personalized, systems of organization with more predictable, yet flexible, access. More research is needed in line with Kwasnik's (1991) work on personal organization and classification systems. The potential for developing personalized services to improve the information seeking and use of these workers is indicated in this study. For the most part the computer systems currently available had been developed without sufficient research into how these users actually accomplish their work. The crux of the issue seems to center on routine versus complex tasks. This exploratory study indicates the need for further research into at least three aspects of information use related to accomplishing work tasks. The first is the way information is presented to the user. To develop a complex case, the lawyers called for an array of cases presented simultaneously rather than the sequence of single cases that the information system was providing. Simultaneous review of an array of information seemed to accommodate the constructive process in which the participants were engaged. Second is the limitation of keyword searching. The lawyers seemed to require the opportunity to locate information outside of the keyword range to spark an idea that enabled them to formulate the issues in a case. Keyword searching did not allow them to "find Kevin while looking for George." The capacity to present information outside of a traditional relevancy approach seemed to be needed to allow for individual creativity in developing a case. Third, these participants wanted a sense of control in doing legal research and seemed to become "lost" in the computerized information. A sense of where one is in a system seemed to be desired for having a sense of control in using information for developing a complex case.

The participants in this exploratory study indicated the need for "just for me" information systems and services. "Just for me" incorporates "just in time" and "just for you" concepts but goes beyond to provide personal information mediation. "Just for me" services and systems would be grounded in a clear understanding of an individual's work, the different types of information needed, and the range of access required to accomplish a variety of tasks. Although these lawyers expressed the usefulness of a service designed "just for me," they did not think such a service was practical or even possible. However, when we examine what they indicated would improve the information provision for their work, there are some basic needs that could be accommodated by applying a user-centered approach to the design of systems and provision of services specifically tailored to their information seeking and use. "Just for me" systems and services would enable information workers to accomplish complex tasks that require interpreting, learning, and creating.

Potential Roles for Librarians in the Information Search Process of Information Workers

Information workers consider information seeking as a necessary, but preliminary, activity to the more significant endeavor of using information to accomplish the tasks and goals that encompass their work. People who are proficient at this process are extremely beneficial to the success of an organization or an enterprise. Although the findings of these studies cannot be considered as describing information workers' process of information seeking in general or even of securities analysts and lawyers in particular, they contribute to our understanding of the information search process in the context of the workplace. We need to continue to gain insight into the variety of projects and tasks that involve information workers to meet different goals. An important insight revealed in this research is the difference between information seeking and use in routine work tasks and in those that are considered more complex. These studies show a relationship between task complexity and the stages of the information search process. These workers described a process similar to that of the Information Search Process model in more complex work tasks that require extensive construction of new knowledge (see Table 10.1).

Table 10.1. Evidence of Process in Work Tasks

Task Type	Routine Tasks	Complex Tasks
Uncertainty	Low	High
Construction	Low	High
Stages in the ISP	Low	High

These studies indicate the importance of understanding time considerations in different groups of information workers. There was a distinct difference between these types of workers' reactions to complex tasks that required extensive time. Both recognized uncertainty as related to a complex task, but each had a different reaction to this uncertainty. In one work context uncertainty at the beginning was dreaded as indicative of an extensive project ahead that would be difficult to accomplish in the volatile climate of the situation. In the other work context uncertainty at the beginning was welcomed as indicative of an extensive investigation that would involve creativity and challenge. The difference in reaction seemed to be related to adequate time for the task of construction or at least perceived sense of adequate time. Time constraints in information-intensive work tasks are an important factor to consider when planning library and information services.

The need for expanded library and information services is clearly indicated in these studies. All levels of mediation and education may be employed in the workplace to assist workers in their information seeking and use. The organizer's role is called upon to create new ways to classify and index for more effective access that build on traditional principles of librarianship. Within the organizer's level of service much needs to be done to enable better access to critical information, particularly for complex tasks. The lawyers stressed difficulty in using systems for constructing more complex tasks. Information systems currently available should be reevaluated from the user's perspective within the context of the task they are attempting to accomplish. Problems of these systems should be identified and addressed in response to users' specific work tasks. In addition a more active instructional role may enable these workers to make optimum use of the information systems in their fields. The securities analyst stressed the need for inclusion of the process of research in basic education programs. Vital new roles in user education were indicated in these studies to prepare information workers to provide the innovative use of information required in their jobs. Preparing information workers should be a major goal of the information age school, with vital new roles for library media specialists in collaboration with teachers.

There are many new ways that librarians can contribute to information seeking and use in the workplace that may not be considered within the realm of traditional services but are essential emerging services. These studies indicate a number of critical zones of intervention that may help information-intensive workers to accomplish their complex tasks. These are times when intervention may enable a worker to "do with advice and assistance what he or she cannot do alone or can do only with great difficulty." One such zone of intervention is providing critical background and idea-generating information at the initiation of a project that both the securities analyst and lawyers revealed as necessary for getting started in a complex task. Another area that was causing these workers difficulty was at midpoint, when librarians may be able to help in the selection and display of an array of sources to promote the construction necessary in a complex task. Another may be at closure, when assistance in determining what is enough to accomplish the task may be helpful. These areas of service highlight the important part the library can play in developing new projects and accomplishing more complex work tasks in new information environments.

Process-Oriented Library and Information Services

   Library and information services are in a vital period of redefinition and change. The traditional bibliographic paradigm, centering on the location of sources, is no longer adequate for accommodating the full range of users' problems in the information age. The traditional approach addresses locating sources and information but does not take into account interpreting, formulating, and learning in the process of information seeking. Increased access to vast amounts of information requires services that center on seeking meaning as well as locating sources. In an earlier industrial age, the bibliographic approach to services may have been adequate for addressing users' information needs. Advances in technology, however, have shifted the task of information seeking from locating to seeking meaning. Services must be redefined to respond to new fundamental tasks of information users.

   When the user's process of learning from information is recognized as an important element in information provision, we become aware of a critical gap in the theoretical foundations of library and information science. Although theory has been tentative and speculative for explaining users' experience in the process of seeking meaning from information, there is movement toward establishing a more extensive research base. However, the literature of the field reveals an underlying problem of overemphasis on source and underemphasis on process. The user's holistic experience in information seeking is not being adequately accommodated. Traditional emphasis on locating sources has detracted from the process of constructing meaning from information within sources. Users center not only on seeking sources of information but also on seeking meaning from sources. Seeking meaning incorporates an individual's cognitive, physical, and affective experiences. Library and information services that stop short of intervention into the meaning-making process fail to meet the full range of information needs of people in an information age.

Theory enables us to rise above the confusion of everyday life to see patterns, to understand principles, and to act purposefully and productively. To provide library and information services that purposefully and productively respond to a range of users' information problems and tasks, we need a theoretical framework with patterns and principles on which to build. Since theory in library and information science is presently inadequate for fully explaining the process of learning from information access and use, we have looked to the principles of learning in general for a borrowed theoretical explanation. A generic explanation of learning as a process of construction provides a conceptual premise for studying users' experience in information-seeking situations.

The theoretical premise that explains learning as a process of construction led to the conceptual assumption that information seeking is a process of construction. This premise derived from the borrowed theory was examined in a series of empirical studies of people in actual situations of information seeking. Five longitudinal studies were conducted; in the beginning, qualitative methods were used to investigate the assumption and derive a hypothesis. Next, case study and quantitative methods were used to test and verify the initial findings. In this way the borrowed theory was redefined into a grounded theory for library and information services. Further studies of implementation of a process approach were conducted in educational settings. In addition, small-scale exploratory studies initiated investigation of the information search process in the workplace.

Longitudinal Methods for Developing Conceptual Frameworks

Understanding the user's perspective on information seeking requires methodology that opens the holistic process for examination. Application of longitudinal methods is an effective way to study situations beyond a single incident and single point in time to observe people in the context of their lives. Longitudinal methods are applied at at least two points in time with the same participants or similar participants to study what has taken place during that period of time. These methods provide data over time to document change. They are useful for examining transition within study participants. A comparison of two or more points in time is provided by examining data collected at an earlier point with data collected at a later point.

The advantages of not being limited to one point in time, being able to document transition and change, and revealing evidence of process over time are well worth the effort and inconvenience of applying these methods to the study of information seeking and uses. The obvious disadvantage of this methodology is the requirement of extended periods of time, continuous organization and management, and a sustained cohort of participants. Longitudinal methods, however, offer opportunity to study questions of information seeking and use that are difficult to address at one point in time, such as: What use is made of the information that is retrieved? How does one source lead to another over the course of a search? What is the experience in the process of constructing from the information encountered in a search? How does experience affect the process of information seeking and use?

Longitudinal methods may be applied within a single study or across a series of connected studies and may adopt either quantitative or qualitative methods or some combination of the two. Change may be measured by statistical calculations or documented through interviews, observations, journals, and logs. Some examples drawn from the studies of the information search process show the application of longitudinal methods for observing a process over time in different situations (see Table 11.1).

Table 11.1. Application of Longitudinal Methods in Study of ISP

Problem	To observe process over time
	To observe process in different situations
Method	Within study—data collected at two or more points in time
	Across studies—similar data collected in different studies
	Case study—in-depth data collected within study and across studies

An example of data collected using within-study qualitative methods for revealing changes over time is taken from the initial study of the information search process with secondary school students. Changes before and after the formulation stage were revealed in comments from participants. One student commented that before formulation, "I was worried that I couldn't do a good job because I didn't know what I was doing." After formulation, "I felt pretty happy about it. I was beginning to find recurrent themes." Another student commented that before formulation, "I was confused and lost, because I like to know that things are in order." After formulation, "I was a lot more relieved because I had a goal. Once you know what you are looking for it is so much easier to go about what you are doing." These comments, elicited through longitudinal methods, would not have been apparent in data collected at one point in time.

An example of within-study quantitative methods is the large-scale study of more varied population of users in three library contexts using a survey administered at three points in the information search process. The findings revealed a change over time in thoughts and feelings to verify the model developed in the earlier qualitative study of students.

Longitudinal methods were used to study information seeking and use across a series of connected studies to observe the process in different situations, to verify and refine findings of earlier studies, and to extend the concepts underlying the results. The more quantitative approach incorporated repeating the use of a questionnaire survey with the same cohort after a four-year period of time had lapsed. Students were given a questionnaire at the completion of secondary school and again at the completion of their undergraduate education to compare their perceptions of the information search process. This comparison revealed that their sense of process had increased over the years.

Another example of the application of longitudinal methods across studies is the use of case study methods through semi-structured interviews at four- to five-year intervals. The longitudinal case studies provided evidence of change in perceptions of information seeking and use from secondary school to completion of an undergraduate degree, with the next interval examining early career information use and the next investigating transition from novice to expert use of information in the workplace. This analysis of change over time revealed new insights and questions, such as the relation of the user's perception of task complexity to the user's experience of the stages in the information search process.

The study of information seeking and use in the context of people's experience calls for extensive application of longitudinal methods. Longitudinal methods

- are not limited to one point in time,

- are useful for documenting change, and

- provide observation of process.

Unfortunately much of the research in the field concentrates on one incident of information seeking within a system or source at one point in time rather than extensive information seeking and use of multiple sources over an extended period of time. Longitudinal methods offer ways to gain insight into the process of using information that suggest new approaches to accommodating information seeking and use.

The Information Search Process As a Conceptual Framework

The series of studies described in this book revealed common patterns in users' experience in the process of seeking meaning from information. Users experienced the process of information seeking as a series of thoughts, feelings, and actions. Thoughts that began as uncertain, vague, and ambiguous became clearer, more focused, and specific as the process progressed. Feelings of anxiety and doubt became more confident and certain. Through their actions, users sought information relevant to the general topic at the beginning and pertinent to the focused topic toward closure. A task was identified for each stage; as were strategies for accomplishing the tasks and the mood or stance most productive for the user to assume at different points in the process. Formulation of a focus or a personal perspective of the topic or problem was a pivotal point in the search process. At this point, feelings shifted from uncertain to more confident, thoughts changed from vague to more clear, and interest increased. Patterns in users' experience were articulated in a model of the information search process describing typical tasks, thoughts, feelings, actions, strategies, and moods within six stages: initiation, selection, exploration, formulation, collection, and presentation. The model was verified in longitudinal case studies as well as in large-scale studies of diverse samples of library users. Further studies have examined the implementation of a process approach in school contexts and investigated the information search process in the workplace.

At initiation, when a person first becomes aware of a lack of knowledge or understanding, feelings of uncertainty and apprehension are common. At this point, the task is merely to recognize a need for information. Thoughts center on contemplating the problem, comprehending the task, and relating the problem to prior experience and knowledge. Actions frequently involve discussing possible topics and approaches.

During selection the task is to identify and select the general topic to be investigated or the approach to be pursued. Feelings of uncertainty often give way to optimism after the selection has been made, and there is a readiness to begin the search. Thoughts center on weighing prospective topics against the criteria of personal interest, assignment requirements, information available, and time allotted. The outcome of each possible choice is predicted, and the topic or approach judged to have the greatest potential for success is selected. Typical actions are to confer with others or to make a preliminary search of information available, then skim and scan for an overview of alternative topics. When, for whatever reason, selection is delayed or postponed, feelings of anxiety are likely to intensify until the choice is made.

Exploration is characterized by feelings of confusion, uncertainty, and doubt that frequently increase during this time. The task is to investigate information on the general topic to extend personal understanding. Thoughts center on becoming oriented and sufficiently informed about the topic to form a focus or a personal point of view. At this stage, an inability to express precisely what information is needed makes communication between the user and the system awkward. Actions involve locating information about the general topic, reading to become informed, and relating new information to what is already known. Strategies that open opportunities for forming new constructs, such as listing facts that seem particularly pertinent and reflecting on engaging ideas, may be most helpful during this time. Strategies that foster an indicative rather than an invitational mood, such as taking detailed notes, may thwart the process by seeking premature closure. Information encountered rarely fits smoothly with previously-held constructs, and information from different sources commonly seems inconsistent and incompatible. Users may find the situation quite discouraging and threatening, causing a sense of personal inadequacy as well as frustration with the system. Some people actually may be inclined to abandon the search altogether at this stage.

Formulation is the turning point of the search process, when feelings of uncertainty diminish and confidence increases. The task is to form a focus from the information encountered. Thoughts involve identifying and selecting ideas and forming a focused perspective on the topic. A focus in the search process is comparable to a hypothesis in the process of construction. The topic becomes more personalized at this stage if construction is taking place. Although a focus may be formed in a sudden moment of insight, it is more likely to emerge gradually as constructs become clearer. During this time, a change in feelings is commonly noted, with indications of increased confidence and a sense of clarity.

Collection is the stage in the process when interaction between the user and the library and information system functions most effectively and efficiently. At this point, the task is to gather information related to the focused topic. Thoughts center on defining, extending, and supporting the focus. Actions involve selecting information relevant to the focused perspective of the topic and making detailed notes on that which pertains specifically to the focus. General information on the topic is no longer relevant after formulation. The user, with a clearer sense of direction, can specify the need for pertinent, focused information to mediators and to systems, thereby facilitating a comprehensive search of all available resources. Feelings of confidence continue to increase as uncertainty subsides, with interest in the project deepening.

In presentation, feelings of relief are common, with a sense of satisfaction if the search has gone well or disappointment if it has not. The task is to complete the search and to prepare to present or otherwise use the findings. Thoughts concentrate on culminating the search with a personalized synthesis of the topic or problem. Actions involve a summary search in which decreasing relevance and increasing redundancy are noted in the information encountered. Organizing strategies, such as outlining, for preparing to present or otherwise use the information are applied.

Assessment, though not specifically designated as a stage of the information search process, frequently occurs after the task of the presentation stage has been accomplished. Reflecting back on recent experience in the search process increases self-awareness of the problems that were encountered as well as the successes that were experienced. This reflection may enable users to internalize their own search process and to assume a process approach in future situations of information need. Assessment includes the evaluation of use of time, sources, and mediation in the process of information seeking and use. At this stage the ability to articulate a clearly focused perspective that has developed during the process of information seeking is an indication that learning and construction has take place.

Criteria for Choices in the Information Search Process

The studies revealed a view inside the information search process in which the user is seeking meaning in the course of seeking information. From the user's perspective the primary objective of information seeking is to accomplish the task that initiated the search, not the collection of information as an end in itself. Seeking information is a means to accomplish a goal, not a goal in itself.

The process of information seeking from the user's perspective may be thought of as a sequence of choices based on four criteria: task, time, interest, and availability (see Table 11.2). The person in the midst of seeking information is concerned with the task to be accomplished, the time allotted, personal interest, and information available. These criteria offer an alternative way of understanding relevance judgments in the context of a sequence of choices. People in the course of information seeking were found to base choices on these questions: Task: What am I trying to accomplish? Time: How much time do I have? Interest: What do I find personally interesting? Information available: What information is available to me? One or more of these may predominate at any given time.

Table 11.2. Criteria for Choices in the Information Search Process

Criteria	Question
Task	What am I trying to accomplish?
Time	How much time do I have?
Interest	What do I find personally interesting?
Availability	What information is available to me?

There were particular points in the information search process when important choices were made that moved the process along to the subsequent stage. Some choices were found to be more important than others. Kelly described choices that provide clarification or changed perspective in a constructive process as elaborative choices. Elaborative choices were noted at two stages in the information search process, at selection and again at formulation. At these stages, users applied the four criteria for making what they judged to be the best possible choice for them at the time. The choices were based on the users' expectations of what will follow. These predictions are based on the constructs of the process of seeking information built in prior experience. Use of the four criteria at selection and formulation is described in the extended Information Search Process model in Chapter 3. The four criteria have important implications for a process approach to library and information services.

Task

The model of the information search process is a task model. It addresses people striving to accomplish a task that has a specific beginning (initiation), when the task is identified or assigned, and a discrete end, when the task is completed or otherwise comes to a close (presentation). The choices users make in the process are based on repeatedly returning to the question of what is to be accomplished through the information seeking. What is the proposed end result and outcome? This differs from models that encompass information seeking in the more generic context of everyday life, such as Dervin's sense-making. The model depicts information seeking and use within a task that requires information and construction over time to be accomplished. It is the task that prompts the information seeking and the task that brings the information seeking to closure.

In addition to setting information seeking within the situation of striving to accomplish an overarching task, the model identifies internal tasks to be addressed and worked through at each stage in the process. At initiation the task is to prepare for the decision of selecting a general topic. At selection the task is to decide on the general topic for research. At exploration the task is to investigate information on the general topic to get background and ideas for forming a focus, an angle, or a theme. At formulation the task is to formulate a focus from the information encountered. At collection the task is to gather information that defines, supports, and extends the focus. At presentation the task is to accomplish the overall task by applying the focus constructed in the search.

In these studies users were found to experience the thoughts, actions, and feelings within the stages of the information search process as described in the model in some situations more than in others. The studies of the workplace investigated the question of what information-seeking tasks prompt users to experience the changes in uncertainty and confidence described in the model. One important differentiation of tasks that seems to have an impact on users' experience is the degree of complexity a user has in accomplishing the task. The degree of task complexity, as Bystrom (2000) and Vakkari (1999) have discovered, seems to indicate a distinction. Routine information-seeking tasks that require little new knowledge to accomplish do not seem to elicit stages in information seeking. Complex tasks that begin with uncertainty and confusion and require considerable construction, interpretation, and learning are more likely to elicit stages as described in the model. Task complexity seems to be a key component of the information search process that warrants attention in designing process intervention in library and information services.

The concept of complexity is important for understanding the experience of uncertainty in the information search process. Findings suggest that it is an individual's perception of the complexity of a task that determines his or her experience of process and degree of uncertainty. Since it is the perception of complexity, not the complexity inherent in the task, tasks cannot be labeled in advance as complex or simple. A task in which considerable construction is required is likely to be considered to have a higher degree of complexity than a task that is considered routine, regardless of the inherent complexity of the task. Task complexity is emerging as an important concept for understanding when the stages of the information search process are experienced by users in contrast to information seeking that is more straightforward source location and question-answering endeavor.

Time

Time was found to be another important factor in the information search process that influences the choices users make. The process functions within the time frame of the task to be accomplished. There is a discrete beginning when the task is announced and a definite end to the task, a deadline, when time runs out and the task is finished. The time frame of the information task, whether it be hours, days, weeks, or months, is a critical element for users that influences their information-seeking behavior and the choices they make throughout the information search process.

Time has an important impact on information-seeking behavior. Students in these studies expressed a sense of wasting time at the beginning of the process that seemed due to their expectation that they should move into the collection stage after selection, skipping the essential stages of exploration and formulation in the constructive process of learning from a variety of sources. These novice information users became more aware of the pace of learning in the process of information seeking and more tolerant of the early stages of construction as they gained more expertise. Awareness that construction takes time gave them a sense of control over the pace and process of information seeking and use.

However, experts in different contexts had different reactions to time. For example, the securities analyst had less tolerance for complex tasks and the uncertainty that initiates the information search process because of the time pressure of the work context. He complained that it "takes too much time to get involved in uncertainty" that demands substantial learning and construction. The lawyers, on the other hand, expressed heightened interest and enthusiasm for complex tasks that required construction and creativity. They seemed to have more control of their time and were able to block out the time to construct their strategies for trying a case in the process of information seeking. Different perspectives on time are likely to influence a user's expectations, predictions, and choices in information seeking.

Interest

Personal interest was an important factor in the choices made, particularly in selecting a topic and formulating a focus, in the information search process. From the users' perspective, what they find of interest directs their path through the sources they encounter. What motivates users to search for information over a sustained period of time to accomplish as task? In this task model users are frequently motivated by an external prompt, an assignment of some sort that is imposed on the user and that the user is required to pursue. This external motivation was found to change to internal motivation as the information search process progressed through the stages of exploration and formulation, particularly where the user formed a focused perspective based on personal interest.

Interest was found to be associated with uncertainty in the information search process. At the middle of the process when uncertainty decreased, interest frequently increased along with personal knowledge. Interest increased after formulation, after a focused point of view had been developed. This was not evident in all cases, however. Only half of the participants in the large-scale study were found to form a focused perspective on their topic. This indicates that not all people construct new knowledge during information seeking even in the context of complex tasks. Limberg (1997) found that different students had different goals even when given the same information tasks. Some sought to gather facts, others looked for a right answer, and others sought a personal point of view that they could discuss and defend. These different goals led to different outcomes. It may be that some people do not form a focused perspective in the information search process because they are seeking to gather facts or to find the right answer and not intentionally seeking a personal perspective. In some situations factual goals and right answer goals may accomplish the task. However, the experts revealed the need to address the more complex tasks in the workplace with the objective to get an angle, to develop a strategy, and to create what Bruner called "products of mind." Participants who did form a focus revealed heightened interest and incentive, with evidence of pride of ownership in "my work" and "my ideas." Shifts in interest and the relation to motivation and incentive may indicate important elements for designing user-centered library and information services.

Information Available

People's notion of what information is available is another important factor that influences the choices they make. Questions such as what do I have at hand and what can I get to easily are one side of the availability issue. The other is the vast amount of information available though information technology. The issue of too much availability is a difficult problem confounding many information users. Several concepts that have emerged from these studies offer insight into the choices people make within their information environment.

The concept of enough involves the deceptively simple question, what is enough? What is enough may have seemed fairly straightforward when a person could gather all there was to know on a topic in a contained collection. The concept of enough is quite a different matter in the present information environment. Understanding what is enough is essential for finding meaning in the information available. *Enough* relates to seeking meaning in a quantity of information by determining what one needs to know and by formulating a perspective on which to build. The information search process treats the concept of enough as what is enough to make sense of the information available to accomplish the task at hand. Applying the concept of enough in each stage of the search process to services may assist users in determining what is enough to recognize an information need; what is enough to select a general topic; what is enough to explore for background and ideas; what is enough to form a focus; what is enough to define and extend the focus; what is enough to accomplish the task that prompted the information seeking; and what is enough to share what has been solved, learned, or created.

The notion of the relationship between uniqueness and redundancy of information is another concept that may offer insight into the user's dilemma in making choices within the process of information seeking. At the beginning of the information search process the likelihood of encountering uniqueness (new information) will be high and redundancy (familiar information) will be low. From the user's perspective these are two quite different types of information. As the process progresses and the person learns more about the topic, there is likely to be more of a balance between the two types of information. Ideally at the close of the process the ratio will be reversed, with uniqueness low and redundancy high. Therefore, uncertainty may be associated with high uniqueness at the beginning of information seeking and confidence with high redundancy toward the end of the process. This concept may lead to new ways of thinking about choices of relevance in information seeking.

A Principle of Uncertainty As a Conceptual Framework

An important element in theory building is to state findings and patterns revealed through extensive research as a conceptual premise. The conceptual premise proposed here for library and information services is in the form of an uncertainty principle.

Uncertainty, the predominant experience in the early stages of the information search process, is not being sufficiently addressed in library and information services. The uncertainty principle states that uncertainty is a cognitive state that commonly causes affective symptoms of anxiety and lack of confidence. Uncertainty and anxiety can be expected in the early stages of the process. The affective symptoms of uncertainty, confusion, and frustration are associated with vague, unclear thoughts about a topic or question. As knowledge states shift to more clearly focused thoughts, a parallel shift occurs in feelings of increased confidence. Uncertainty due to a lack of understanding, a gap in meaning, or a limited construct initiates the process of information seeking.

The uncertainty principle is expanded by six corollaries, each of which offers an explanation of a particular aspect of the information search process: process, formulation, redundancy, mood, prediction, and interest.

In the uncertainty principle, the constructivist view is articulated as a basis for information provision. Information seeking is described as a series of stages in a process of construction in which the individual moves from uncertainty to understanding. A process approach to information provision accommodates a series of dynamic stages of seeking meaning from information. The uncertainty principle offers librarians and information professionals a conceptual basis for diagnosing users' problems to determine appropriate intervention. Different types or levels of intervention are needed for the different stages of the information search process.

The axiom that information reduces uncertainty is not necessarily the user's experience in information seeking. In some situations information actually increases uncertainty. These studies reveal that prior to formulation users are likely to experience heightened uncertainty in the face of unique, incompatible, inconsistent information that requires construction and interpretation to be personally understood. It seems helpful for users to expect uncertainty to increase during the exploration stage of the process rather than thinking that increased uncertainty is a symptom that something has gone wrong. The expectation that information reduces uncertainty initially may be at odds with the user's experience in actual situations of information seeking. In contrast, the uncertainty principle proposes the expectation that uncertainty is likely to increase in the exploration stage. The tolerance of uncertainty is introduced as enabling the early stages of the information search process, when the experience of uncertainty may overwhelm the person and deter progress in the process. Uncertainty from the user's perspective is a natural experience in the process. If unexpected, the presence of uncertainty and particularly any increase in uncertainty can heighten anxiety.

These findings indicate the need for considering uncertainty as a natural, essential characteristic of information seeking rather than regarding the reduction of uncertainty as the primary objective of information seeking, as in the bibliographic paradigm. Uncertainty is a concept that offers insight into the user's quest for meaning within the information search process. If we think of uncertainty as a sign of the beginning of innovation and creativity, the goal of library and information services shifts from reducing uncertainty to supporting the user's constructive process.

Levels of Library and Information Services

The concept of levels of intervention within the two basic library services of reference and instruction provides a way of envisioning how different kinds of information-seeking tasks may be accommodated. Reference services are differentiated into five levels of mediation: organizer, locator, identifier, advisor, and counselor. Instructional services are differentiated in five levels of education: organizer, lecturer, instructor, tutor, and counselor.

At level 1, the organizer provides an organized collection, but no intervention in terms of mediation or education. The organizer level of intervention depends on the user's capacity for conducting a self-service search. At level 2, the locator intervenes with one source in a single encounter. The locator offers ready-reference intervention by responding to a single query with an answer in the form of a fact or a source. The lecturer, on level 2, provides instruction in a single session with the purpose of offering an overview of services and sources in a general orientation not related to a specific problem or topic.

At level 3, the identifier mediates by providing a group of sources related to a topic. In this standard reference intervention, a subject search is conducted in response to a problem statement derived from a reference interview. A group of sources related to the topic are recommended in no particular order. The instructor, on level 3, teaches about sources in one or several independent, single sessions. The purpose of the instruction is to introduce a particular group of sources or type of source, usually to address a specific problem or task.

At level 4, the advisor provides pattern intervention or a sequence for using sources. In a reference interaction the problem is stated, assistance negotiated, and sequence recommended. The tutor, on level 4, provides instruction on a strategy for navigating through a search. The tutor conducts a series of related sessions instructing on the sequence for using sources to address a particular problem or task.

At level 5, the counselor addresses the holistic experience of seeking meaning within the process of an information search. The counselor provides mediation by disclosing an evolving problem for redefinition through dialogue, and recommends strategies, sources, and sequence for each stage in the search process. Instruction at this level is embedded in the process and educates users to identify and interpret information as a search progresses.

Diagnosing for a Zone of Intervention

The concept of a zone of intervention has been introduced for diagnosing users' need for one of the five levels of mediation and education. The zone of intervention is that area in which a user can do with guidance and assistance what he or she cannot do alone or can do only with difficulty. Intervention in this zone enables the person to move along in the information search process. Intervention outside of this zone is intrusive on the one hand and overwhelming on the other. Intervention on both sides of the zone of intervention is inefficient and unnecessary. The concept of a zone of intervention is a new approach to analyzing users' information needs and calls for an active diagnostic role for librarians and information professionals. The critical element in diagnosis is whether users' problems create a source or a process information need or some combination of both.

The practitioner applies theory and experience to the professional art of diagnosing users' problems. Diagnosing users' problems to determine an appropriate level of intervention is a reflective activity in which the practitioner relies not only on the patterns and underlying principles of a theoretical framework but also on sound professional experience. In other contexts, Schon (1982) describes the reflective practitioner as one who has internalized the underlying principles of the profession and develops the ability for continued learning and problem solving throughout his or her career. Reflection-in-action is a "thinking on your feet" approach to solving problems frequently observed in the seasoned professional. An overarching theory, combined with an intuitive feel for the situation, guides the reflection-in-action of an experienced professional. In this way, practitioners can recognize and engage that which is shifting and turbulent in their practice. Reflective professionals need to redefine library and information services in this shifting and turbulent period. Reflection-in-action, guided by an internalization of the underlying patterns and principles in the process of information seeking, is a way to develop a new approach to services. Developing the role of the counselor in the information search process requires considerable reflection-in-action as well as extensive conversation, experimentation, and documentation among reflective practitioners.

Developing a Process Approach

Although the stages in the information search process, the uncertainty principle, levels of mediation and education, and the concept of a zone of intervention have been articulated here as a conceptual framework for process oriented practice, there is no neat package of interventions that can be handed to librarians and information specialists. The process intervention depends on the reflective practitioner who understands the dynamic process of learning from information and incorporates that awareness into all aspects of intervening with users. There are three important elements of process-oriented library and information services: (1) acknowledgment of stages in the search process, (2) establishment of dialogue as a strategy, and (3) identification of a zone of intervention.

Acknowledgment of stages in the information search process is an essential component of process-oriented intervention. The process model offers a way to conceptualize and articulate the experience of a person involved in an extended search. The mediator clearly understands the process of the user and the sequence of tasks to be undertaken. Expectation of uncertainty, which initiates the inquiry, and tolerance for confusion before formulation provide an invitation for dialogue and the establishment of a range of associated strategies

Establishing dialogue as a strategy is a second component in responding to users who need counseling in the process of information seeking. The need to discuss and talk about the topic and the process is a natural instinct to be brought into mediation practice. The reference interview may be extended to a conversation that offers the user an opportunity to tell a story about the problem. The concept of a narrative or story may be much more appropriate for articulating an information need in the stages prior to formulation than that of a formal query, request, or question. In this way, emphasis is placed on the inquiry instead of the query. The conversation sets the stage for an ongoing dialogue throughout the process. Both the user and the mediator expect continuing interaction rather than a single incident. Dialogue centers on the user's narrative and is directed, to a large extent, by the user, particularly in the early stages. The sources and mechanics of the search, and the presentation and product of the task, are not allowed to overshadow the basic interest and concern of the user. Dialogue as a strategy facilitates formulation as well as promoting more conceptual search techniques. Such interaction offers opportunities for expressing an emerging focus and developing personal perspective. The mediator may share in the user's discovery and learning in the process of the search. The mediator may participate in the intellectual engagement of the user and in the user's increased interest and personal involvement. Professional responsibility deepens along with competence in making a clear distinction between enabling guidance and intrusive interference.

The identification of a zone of intervention is an important component in responding to users' needs for process intervention. Intervention is not needed in every instance or in every search. Identifying those instances when intervention is needed and determining the level of intervention required is the basis of process-oriented services. In library and information services each of the levels of mediation and education may be integrated into common practice. Many people use the library as a self-service collection. In most instances independent access will remain the primary use of an information system. Location continues to be a critical service for direct, simple questions, and orientation is an important aspect of education. The identifier/instructor and advisor/tutor continues to serve those people whose problems are extensive and ongoing, but in the collection rather than the exploration stage. The counselor level of intervention, however, needs further development. Problems currently being addressed by the locator/ lecturer, identifier/instructor, and advisor/tutor may well occur in the zone of intervention better served by the counselor. The ability to identify where users are experiencing difficulty is essential for developing process-oriented intervention. The concept of identifying a zone of intervention can be incorporated into common library and information practice.

Encouragement and support are an integral part of intervention at the counselor level, along with a sequence of recommended sources and strategies for formulating, extending, and defining. Strategies include various forms of writing, charting, discussing, and, where appropriate, use of peer support and team efforts alongside traditional search techniques.

Strategies for Process Intervention

Six main strategies for counseling indicated in this research are collaborating, continuing, choosing, charting, conversing, and composing. Collaborating responds to a sense of isolation in the process of information seeking and offers opportunities to engage in a cooperative venture to enhance the process. Continuing encompasses evolving quests that are addressed over time rather than simple queries that can be answered in a single incident. Choosing as a strategy gives people a sense of control over their own search process. Charting enables users to visualize the overall process and to track ideas that evolve as they proceed. Conversing encourages users to tell the story of their information seeking that fosters development of ideas and actions that lead to understanding. Composing promotes thinking and formulating as information is encountered throughout the stages of the information search process. These six strategies enable librarians to counsel users through the entire process sequence of initiating, selecting, exploring, focusing, collecting, and presenting.

Counselors may call upon four basic abilities that underlie information literacy: recalling, summarizing, paraphrasing, and extending. Recalling is thinking and remembering certain features of what has been gathered and read. Summarizing is organizing ideas in capsulated form and placing the ideas in a meaningful sequence. Paraphrasing is retelling in one's own words the information encountered in the search process. Extending is taking ideas from information, making connections with what is already known, and applying new interpretations in the creative process of understanding.

Increased Uncertainty Indicates a Zone of Intervention

The Information Search Process model describes the experience and behavior of people involved in extensive research projects. People using libraries and information systems to learn about a particular subject or to investigate a problem or issue often have difficulty in the early phases of information seeking.

Even when they begin with great enthusiasm and initial success, many become confused and uncertain as to how to proceed after a short period of time. This is particularly noticeable with students who have been assigned a research paper but is not exclusively characteristic of students alone. Initial hesitation, confusion, and uncertainty are reported by people in all types of libraries and in the workplace. In fact, we have no way of knowing just how many people give up after initiating a search because they become uncertain and feel incompetent to continue, but the number is probably substantial.

This research into the user's process of information seeking began with the researcher's own experience as a librarian. A recurring problem was noted: No matter how well students were oriented to the library and its sources, there was a common pattern of behavior when they came to the library for the first few days of their research. They were confused and disoriented, often expressing annoyance at the assignment, the library, and themselves. This point, when librarians frequently first encountered library users, is the most difficult stage of the information search process. Rather than a steady increase in confidence from the beginning of a search to the conclusion, as might be expected, a dip in confidence is commonly experienced once an individual has initiated a search and begins to encounter conflicting and inconsistent information. A person "in the dip" is increasingly uncertain and confused until a focus is formed to provide a path for seeking meaning and criteria for judging relevance.

Recent studies of the information search process in the workplace reveal that the user's experience of the stages in the information search process is related to how much the person knows about the problem and the degree of construction that should be undertaken during information seeking. In more routine tasks, where the goal is to answer a simple question or to monitor periodic change, people do not usually experience stages in their information seeking. However, in more complex tasks, where the goal requires considerable learning, people are likely to experience a process as described in the Information Search Process model.

The dip in confidence seems to be a natural stage in the process. When the process is viewed as a process of construction, the work of Kelly, Dewey, and Bruner explaining similar situations in which people are actively engaged in learning becomes a useful framework for understanding the process of information seeking as well. Each of these theorists described the constructive process as occurring in a sequence of stages or phases to be actively worked through by the individual. Uncertainty common in earlier stages increases with the introduction of new information that conflicts with previously held constructs.

Advances in information technology that open access to a vast assortment of sources have not helped the user's dilemma and in many cases have intensified the sense of confusion and uncertainty. New information systems may deepen the problem, particularly at the beginning, by overwhelming the user with "everything" all at once when a few well-chosen introductory pieces might be more appropriate for initial orientation.

People experience the information search process holistically, with an interplay of thoughts, feelings, and actions. Common patterns of thinking, feeling, and acting are characteristic in each stage. These studies were among the first to investigate the affective aspects or the feelings of a person in the process of information seeking along with the cognitive and physical aspects. One of the most surprising findings was the discovery of a sharp increase in uncertainty and decrease in confidence after a search had been initiated during the exploration stage. However, this experience is one of the most recognizable to both librarians and library users when presented with the model. Users tend to think that they are the only ones to experience increased uncertainty before they become aware that this is a common occurrence in the information search process. Increased uncertainty indicates a zone of intervention in the process, as shown in Figure 11.1.

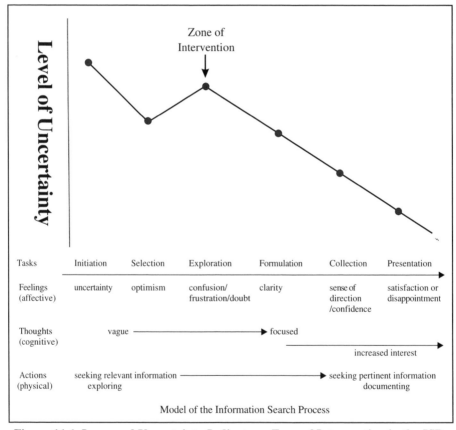

Figure 11.1. Increased Uncertainty Indicates a Zone of Intervention in the ISP.

Application in Library and Information Services

Strong validation of the research findings came with librarians' reactions to the model of the information search process as an authentic description of users' behavior and users' recognition of the model as an accurate description of their own experience. From the users' perspective the process may be thought of as a sequence of tasks, although somewhat recursive rather than strictly linear, to initiate, to select, to explore, to formulate, to collect, to present, and to assess.

Many of the different ways to test the validity of research findings have been discussed in this book. However, an important validity measure, often overlooked by researchers, is the sense of rightness of the people closely affiliated with the problem or activity under study, that "aha" of recognition of practitioners. Practitioner reaction is particularly important in evaluating research related to a field of practice such as librarianship. The sense of rightness of those in the practice of librarianship is a critical component for judging the validity of research findings. Therefore, it has been particularly gratifying that the sense of rightness about the Information Search Process model has been very high among practicing librarians (Kuhlthau, 1994).

The research findings have had important implications for librarians. In many cases librarians have come to acknowledge the process of information seeking and use, and the term "process" is more common in library vocabulary. Library services that formerly concentrated solely on the physical attributes of information seeking, such as locating and circulating materials, are attending to the more cognitive and affective attributes of using information for solving problems, for learning, and for seeking meaning. For example, reference librarians who have become aware of stages in the information search process describe important changes in the way they view people who approach the reference desk. They now listen for an indication of the stage in the process of the user and particularly note when someone is "in the dip" and needs some extra help to formulate a research focus. They are especially careful not to give too much too soon and to assist in pacing the use of sources.

Librarians planning instructional sessions describe being more cautious about offering one-shot sessions where students are expected to learn everything at once. Instead they are accommodating the user's constructive process by giving a series of instructional sessions spread over a period of time aimed at different tasks in the stages of the process. Once aware of the process, teachers also change the way they design assignments to give more time for exploring and formulating. They are acknowledging the learning process and finding new ways to assess and evaluate the creative construction of students.

The impact of the Information Search Process model on library services may be judged by "a sense of rightness" of those most closely involved in the process. Librarians and library users alike have acknowledged the authenticity of the model. The model serves as an articulation of the complexity of the process that forms a basis for counseling library users.

Challenges for Information System Designers

Although this research has had considerable impact on library services, there has been little impact thus far on design of information retrieval systems. In fact the concept of process, in the holistic sense that the user experiences, seems to be somewhat outside of the paradigm of information retrieval. User-centered information systems call for a broad vision of users as people actively engaged in tasks rather than the narrow view of information searchers at the time of interface with the system. The concepts emerging from this research may be useful for designing information retrieval systems that support innovation, creativity, and learning (Kuhlthau, 1999a).

This research reveals several important components of information seeking. From the user's perspective, forming a focus is a central task of the search process. Searching is commonly a process over time rather than a single event. Searching is a holistic experience rather than just an intellectual activity. Initially, searching often increases uncertainty rather than reducing uncertainty.

If we think of uncertainty as a sign of the beginning of innovation and creativity, the goal of information retrieval design shifts considerably. Can an uncertainty principle be applied to the design of information retrieval systems? Can systems be designed that are sufficiently open to accommodate exploring and formulating and do not close the person down too quickly?

The zone of intervention varies from person to person and from time to time. Can the concept of zones of intervention and levels of mediation be applied to designing information retrieval systems? Are information retrieval systems presently designed to work at all levels of intervention? Can mechanisms be developed that accommodate a range of different types of information-seeking tasks from routine to complex? Can mechanisms be developed that accommodate different stages in the information search process in complex tasks?

This research addresses information use as well as information seeking. It does not stop at locating information but is concerned with interpreting and using it. These ideas challenge some of the underlying principles of information retrieval system design, as they questioned the foundation of information provision in libraries. This research becomes more pertinent as researchers and system designers begin to turn their attention to the consideration of more user-centered approaches. User-centered systems should accommodate users beyond the interface, as people seeking information to create, learn, and innovate in the context of their daily tasks.

Ties between librarianship and information retrieval system design are important for providing a full range of services for information users. As an integrated field centering on the user, library and information science has great potential for solving problems of information seeking and use in the changing technological information age.

Developing Services and Systems for the Information Age

Library and information science as an integrated field has great potential for addressing some of the most pressing issues of the global information society. The field has developed by crossing boundaries of two distinct fields of study and practice, library studies and information science. The challenges of merging these allied fields into one have been considerable, with library studies grounded in humanities, social sciences, and culture and information science based in science, mathematics, and mechanics. However, it is this diverse foundation and orientation that comprises the strength of the integrated field for meeting a wide range of information problems that no other field systematically addresses or consistently solves.

Information technology has brought about major societal changes by producing vast amounts of information in a rapidly changing environment. An overwhelming amount of information coupled with volatility produces unpredictability in all aspects of life. Therefore, uncertainty is pervasive in the seemingly certain technological environment. The confrontation between the uncertain person and the certain system requires serious attention by librarians and researchers. The boundaries of research and practice should be fluid, with librarians informing researchers of what works and what doesn't work in actual practice and researchers informing practitioners of important findings, emerging conceptual frameworks, and theoretical perspectives.

Librarians are in the midst of redefining their role in the information age. Many of the services that were traditionally within the domain of the librarian are accomplished directly through the computer. Direct access for users is changing the role of the librarian in the technological workplace, school, and community. Users may have less contact with librarians at the very time when process intervention is increasingly required. There is a growing need for professional information counseling for seeking meaning and understanding from vast amounts of conflicting information.

The twenty-first-century library calls for services and systems that enable seeking meaning within an increasing amount of information. It is no longer sufficient simply to provide physical access to sources and information. In the technological information age, people require services and systems that facilitate understanding, problem solving, and decision-making in the process of seeking meaning. The challenge for the library is to further intellectual access for learning, working, and living.

References

Aguilar, F. (1967). *Scanning the Business Environment*. New York: Macmillan.

Allen, B. (1996). *Information Tasks: Toward a User-Centered Approach to Information Seeking*. London: Academic Press.

American Association of School Librarians (AASL). (1998). *Information Power: Building Partnerships for Learning*. Chicago: American Library Association.

American Library Association. (1980). *Policy Statement: Instruction in the Use of Libraries.* Council Document No. 45. Chicago: American Library Association.

Association of College & Research Libraries (ACRL) (2002). "Information Literacy Competency Standards for Higher Education." In *Standards Toolkit* [Online]. Available: http://www.ala.org/acrl/il/toolkit/standards.html.

Auster, E. and C. W. Choo. (1994). "How Senior Managers Acquire and Use Information in Environmental Scanning." *Information Processing and Management, 30,* 607–618.

Baldwin, N. and R. Rice. (1997). "Information Seeking Behavior of Securities Analysts: Individual and Institutional Influences, Information Sources, Channels and Outcomes." *Journal of the American Society for Information Science, 48,* 674–693.

Bannister, D., ed. (1977). *New Perspectives in Personal Construct Theory*. London: Academic Press.

Barry, C. (1994). "User-Defined Relevance Criteria: An Exploratory Study." *Journal of the American Society for Information Science, 45,* 149–159.

Bartlett, F. C. (1932). *Remembering: A Study of Experimental and Social Psychology.* Cambridge: Cambridge University Press.

Bates, M. (1979, September). "Idea Tactics." *Journal of the American Society for Information Science, 30,* 280–289.

Bates, M. (1986). "Subject Access to Online Catalogs: A Design Model." *Journal of the American Society for Information Science, 37,* 357–376.

Bates, M. (1989). "The Design of Browsing and Berry Picking Techniques for the Online Search Interface." *Online Review, 13,* 407–424.

Belkin, N. J. (1980). "Anomalous State of Knowledge for Information Retrieval." *Canadian Journal of Information Science, 5,* 133–143.

Belkin, N. J. (1984). "Cognitive Models and Information Transfer." *Social Science Information Studies, 4,* 111–130.

211

Belkin, N.J. (1990). "The Cognitive Viewpoint in Information Science." *Journal of Information Science. 16,* 11–15.

Belkin, N. J. and A. Vickery. (1985). *Interaction in Information Systems.* Library and Information Systems Research Report 35. London: British Library.

Belkin, N. J., H. M. Brooks, and R. N. Oddy. (1982). "ASK for Information Retrieval." *Journal of Documentation, 38,* 61–71.

Biggs, J. B. (1976). "Dimensions of Study Behavior." *British Journal of Educational Psychology, 46,* 68–80.

Blackie, E. and J. Smith. (1981). "Student Information Needs and Library User Education." *Education Libraries Bulletin, 24,* 16–23.

Borgman, C. (1984). "Psychological Research in Human Computer Interaction." *Annual Review of Information Science and Technology, 19,* 33–64.

Bruner, J. (1973). *Beyond the Information Given: Studies in the Psychology of Knowing.* Edited by J. M. Arglin. New York: W. W. Norton & Co.

Bruner, J. (1975). *Toward a Theory of Instruction.* Cambridge: Harvard University Press.

Bruner, J. (1977). *The Process of Education.* Cambridge: Harvard University Press.

Bruner, J. (1986). *Actual Minds, Possible Worlds.* Cambridge: Harvard University Press.

Bruner, J. (1990). *Acts of Meaning.* Cambridge: Harvard University Press.

Buckland, M. (1983). *Library Services in Theory and Context.* New York: Pergamon Press.

Buckland, M. (1991). *Information and Information Systems.* New York: Greenwood Press.

Bystrom, K. (2000). "The Effects of Task Complexity on the Relationship Between Information Types Acquired and Information Sources Used." *The New Review of Information Behaviour Research, 1,* 85–102.

Bystrom, K. and K. Jarvelin. (1995). "Task Complexity Affects Information Seeking and Use." *Information Process and Management, 31,* 191–213.

Choo, C. and E. Auster. (1993) "Environmental Scanning: Acquisition and Use of Information by Managers." *Annual Review of Information Science and Technology ARIST, 28,* 279–314.

Dale, E. (1969). *Audiovisual Methods in Teaching.* 3rd. ed. New York: Holt, Rinehart & Winston.

Debons, A. (1975). "An Educational Program for the Information Counselor." *Proceedings of the 38th American Society for Information Science Annual Meeting, 12,* 63–64.

DeMey, M. (1977). "The Relevance of the Cognitive Paradigm for Information Science," In *Proceedings of the International Research Forum in Information Science,* Copenhagen: The Royal School of Librarianship.

Dervin, B. (1982). "Useful Theory for Librarianship: Communication, Not Information." *Drexel Library Quarterly, 13,* 16–32.

Dervin, B. (1983). *An Overview of Sense-Making Research; Concepts, Methods, and Results to Date.* Seattle: School of Communication, University of Washington.

Dervin, B. (1999). "On Studying Information Seeking Methodologically: The Implications of Connecting Metatheory to Method." *Information Processing and Management, 35,* 727–750.

Dervin, B. and P. Dewdney. (1986). "Neutral Questioning: A New Approach to the Reference Interview." *Reference Quurterly, 25,* 506–513.

Dervin, B. and M. Nilan. (1986). "Information Needs and Uses." *Annual Review of Information Science and Technology, 21,* 3–33.

Dervin, B., T. L. Jacobsen, and M. S. Nilan. (1982). "Measuring Aspects of Information Seeking: A Test of Quantitative/Qualitative Methodology." *Communication Yearbook, 6,* 419–422.

Dewdney, P. and C. Ross. (1994). "Flying a Light Aircraft: Reverence Service Evaluation from the User's Viewpoint." *Reference Quarterly, 34,* 217–230.

Dewey, J. (1933). *How We Think.* Lexington, MA: Heath.

Dewey, J. (1934). *Art as Experience.* New York: G. P. Putnam's Sons.

Dewey, J. (1944). *Democracy and Education.* New York Macmillan.

Donham, J., K. Bishop, C. Kuhlthau, and D. Oberg. (2001). *Inquiry Based Learning: Lessons from Library Power.* Worthington, OH: Linworth.

Dosa, M. L. (1978). "Information Counseling and Policies." *Reference Librarian, 17,* 7–21.

Durrance, J. (1989). "Information Needs: Old Song, New Tune." In *Rethinking the Library in the Information Age, Volume II,* edited by A. Mathews. Washington, DC: U.S. Department of Education.

Durrance, J. (1995). "Factors That Influence Reference Success: What Makes Questioners Willing to Return?" *Reference Librarian, 49,* 243–265.

Eisenberg, M. B. and R. E. Berkowitz. (1990). *Information Problem Solving: Big Six Skills Approach to Library and Information Skills Instruction.* Norwood, NJ: Ablex Publishing.

Elkind, D. (1976). *Child Development and Education: A Piagetian Perspective.* London: Oxford University Press.

Ellis, D. (1989). "A Behavioral Approach to Information Retrieval System Design." *Journal of Documentation, 45,* 171–212.

Ellis, D. (1992). "The Physical and Cognitive Paradigms in Information Retrieval Research." *Journal of Documentation 48,* 45–64.

Emig, J. (1971). *The Composing Process of Twelfth Graders.* NCTE Research Report No. 13. Urbana, IL: National Council of Teachers of English.

Entwistle, N. J. (1981). *Styles of Learning and Teaching.* New York: Wiley.

Erdelez, S. (1997). "Information Encountering: A Conceptual Framework for Accidental Information Discovery." In *Proceedings of Information Seeking in Context.* London: Taylor Graham: 417–412.

Frannson, A. (1984). "Cramming or Understanding? Effects of Intrinsic and Extrinsic Motivation on Approach to Learning and Test Performance." In *Reading in a Foreign Language*. White Plains, NY: Longman: 86–121.

Ford, N. (1986). "Psychological Determinants of Information Needs: A Small Scale Study of Higher Education Students." *Journal of Librarianship*, 18, 47–62.

George, M. (1990). "Instructional Services." In *American Libraries: Research Perspectives*, edited by M. J. Lynch Chicago: American Library Association.

Glaser, B. C. and A. L. Strauss (1967). *The Discovery of Grounded Theory: Strategies for Qualitative Research*. New York: Aldine.

Goodman, N. (1984). *Of Mind and Other Matters*. Cambridge: Harvard University Press.

Hall, H. J. (1981). "Patterns in the Use of Information: The Right to Be Different." *Journal of the American Society for Information Science, 32,* 103–112.

Harada, V. (1999). "The Art of Collaboration." *Teacher Librarian, 27,* 9–14.

Hart, P. and R. Rice. (1991). "Using Information from External Databases: Contextual Relationships of Use, Access Method, Task, Database Type, Organizational Differences and Outcomes." *Information Processing and Management, 27,* 461–479.

Harter, S. (1992). "Psychological Relevance and Information Science." *Journal of the American Society for Information Science, 43,* 602–615.

Hollnagel, E. and D. D. Woods. (1983). "Cognitive Systems Engineering: New Wine in Old Bottles." *International Journal of Man Machine Studies, 18,* 583–600.

Hopkins, D. and D. Zweizig, guest eds. (1999) "Library Power Program Evaluation—Theme Issue." *School Libraries Worldwide, 5.*

Information Power: Building Partnerships for Learning. Chicago: American Library Association, 1998.

Ingwersen, P. (1992). *Information Retrieval Interaction*. London: Taylor Graham.

Ingwersen, P.(1996). "Cognitive Perspectives of Information Retrieval Interaction." *Journal of Documentation, 52,* 3–50.

Inhelder, B. and J. Piaget. (1958). *The Growth in Logical Thinking: From Childhood to Adolescence*. New York: Basic Books.

Irving, A. (1985). *Study and Information Skills Across the Curriculum*. London: Heinemann Educational Books.

James, R. (1983). "Libraries in the Mind: How Can We See Users' Perceptions of Libraries?" *Journal of Librarianship, 15,* 19–28.

James, W. (1890). *The Principles of Psychology*. New York: Henry Holt.

Katz, W. (1987). *Reference Services and Reference Processes.* Volume 2 of *Introduction to Reference Work.* 5th ed. New York: McGraw-Hill.

Kelly, G. A. (1963). *A Theory of Personality: The Psychology of Personal Constructs*. New York: W. W. Norton.

Kerlinger, F. N. (1973). *Foundations in Behavioral Research.* New York: Holt, Rinehart & Winston.

Knapp, P. (1966). *The Monteith College Library Experiment.* Metuchen, NJ: Scarecrow Press.

Krikelas, J. (1983). "Information-Seeking Behavior: Patterns and Concepts." *Drexel Library Quarterly, 19,* 5–20.

Kuhlthau, C. C. (1981). *School Librarian's Grade by Grade Activities Program.* West Nyack, NY: Center for Applied Research in Education.

Kuhlthau, C. C. (1983). "The Research Process: Case Studies and Interventions with High School Seniors in Advanced Placement English Classes Using Kelly's Theory of Constructs." Ed. D. dissertation, Rutgers University.

Kuhlthau, C. C. (1985a). "A Process Approach to Library Skills Instruction." *School Library Media Quarterly, 13,* 23–28.

Kuhlthau, C. C. (1985b). *Teaching the Library Research Process.* West Nyack, NY: Center for Applied Research in Education. (Second edition, 1994, Scarecrow Press).

Kuhlthau, C. C. (1987). "An Emerging Theory of Library Instruction." *School Library Media Quarterly, 16,* 23–28.

Kuhlthau, C. C. (1988a). "Developing a Model of the Library Search Process: Investigation of Cognitive and Affective Aspects." *Reference Quarterly, 28,* 232–242.

Kuhlthau, C. C. (1988b). "Perceptions of the Information Process in Libraries: A Study of Changes from High School Through College." *Information Processing and Management, 24,* 419–427.

Kuhlthau, C. C. (1988c). "Longitudinal Case Studies of the Information Search Process of Users in Libraries." *Library and Information Science, 10,* 251–304.

Kuhlthau, C. C. (1989). "The Information Search Process of High-Middle-Low Achieving High School Seniors." *School Library Media Quarterly, 17,* 224–228.

Kuhlthau, C. C. (1991). "Inside the Search Process: Information Seeking from the User's Perspective." *Journal of the American Society for Information Science, 42,* 361–371.

Kuhlthau, C. C. (1993). "Implementing a Process Approach to Information Skills: A Study Identifying Indicators of Success in Library Media Programs." *School Library Media Quarterly, 21,* 11–18.

Kuhlthau, C. C. (1994). "Impact of the Information Search Process Model on Library Services." *Reference Quarterly, 34,* 21–26.

Kuhlthau, C. C. (1996). "The Relation of Information and Uncertainty in Information Seeking." In *Proceedings of CoLIS 2 Conceptions of Library and Information science: Integration in Perspective.* Copenhagen: The Royal School of Librarianship: 367–376.

Kuhlthau, C. C. (1999a). "Accommodating the User's Information Search Process: Challenges for Information Retrieval System Designers." *Bulletin of the American Society for Information Science, 25,* 12–16.

Kuhlthau, C. C. (1999b). "The Role of Experience in the Information Search Process of an Early Career Information Worker: Perceptions of Uncertainty, Complexity, Construction, and Sources." *Journal of the American Society for Information Science, 50,* 399–412.

Kuhlthau, C. C., R. J. Belvin, and M. W. George. (1989). "Flowcharting the Information Search Process: A Method for Eliciting User's Mental Maps." *Proceedings of the American Society for Information Science, 52nd Annual Meeting, 26,* 162–165.

Kuhlthau, C. C. and S. Tama. (2001). "Information Search Process of Lawyers: A Call for 'Just for Me' Information Services." *Journal of Documentation 57,* 25–43.

Kuhlthau, C. C., B. J. Turock, M. W. George, and R. J. Belvin. (1990). "Validating a Model of the Search Process: A Comparison of Academic, Public and School Library Users." *Library and Information Science Research, 12,* 5–32.

Kuhn, T. (1970). *The Structure of Scientific Revolutions.* Chicago: University of Chicago Press.

Kwasnik, B. (1991). "The Importance of Factors That Are Not Document Attributes in the Organization of Personal Documents." *Journal of Documentation 47,* 389–398.

Limberg, L. (1997). "Information Use for Learning Purposes." In *Information Seeking in Context: Proceedings of an International Conference on Research in Information Needs, Seeking and Use in Different Contexts,* edited by Pertti Vakkari, Reijo Savolainen, and Brenda Dervin: 275–289.

Lindgren, J. (1981, Spring). "Toward Library Literacy." *Reference Quarterly,* 233–235.

Loertscher, D. (1982). "The Second Revolution: A Taxonomy for the 1980's." *Wilson Library Bulletin, 56,* 417–421.

Lynch, M. J. (1977). "Reference Interviews in Public Libraries." Ph.D. dissertation, Rutgers University.

MacMullin, S. E. and R. S. Taylor. (1984). "Problem Dimensions Information Traits." *The Information Society, 3,* 91–111.

Maher, B., ed. (1969). *Clinical Psychology and Personality: The Selected Papers of George Kelly.* New York: Wiley.

Mancall, J., S. Aaron, and S. Walker. (1986). "Educating Students to Think: The Role of the School Library Media Program." *School Library Media Quarterly, 15,* 18–27.

Marton, F. and F. Saljo (1976). "On Qualitative Differences in Learning." *British Journal of Educational Psychology, 46,* 4–11.

Meadow, C. T. (1983). "User Adaptation in Interactive Information Retrieval." *Journal of the American Society for Information Science, 34,* 280–291.

Mellon, C. (1986). "Library Anxiety: A Grounded Theory and Its Development." *College & Research Libraries, 47,* 160–165.

Miller, G. A. (1956). "The Magical Number Seven, Plus or Minus Two: Some Limits on Our Capacity for Processing Information." *Psychological Review, 63,* 81–97.

Mokros, H. (1990, March). Personal correspondence and conversation. New Brunswick, NJ, School of Communication, Information and Library Studies, Rutgers University.

Newmann, F., W. Secada, and G. Wehlage. (1995). *A Guide to Authentic Instruction and Assessment.* Madison: Wisconsin Center for Education Research, University of Wisconsin.

Pask, G. (1976). "Styles and Strategies of Learning." *British Journal of Educational Psychology, 46,* 128–148.

Pinelli, T., et al. (1993). "Technical Uncertainty and Project Complexity as Correlates of Information Use by U.S. Industry Affiliated Aerospace Engineers and Scientists: Results of an Exploratory Investigation." NASA TM-107693. Washington, DC: National Aeronautics and Space Administration.

Prentice, A. (1980). "Information Seeking Patterns of Professionals." *Public Library Quarterly, 2,* 27–60.

Ruben, B. D. (1990). "The Health Caregiver-Patient Relationship: Pathology, Etiology, Treatment." In *Communication and Health,* edited by E. Ray and L. Donohue. Hillsdale, NJ: Lawrence Erlbaum: 51–68.

Saracevic, T. (1975). "Relevance: A Review of a Framework for Thinking on the Notion of Information Science." *Journal of the American Society for Information Science, 26,* 178–194.

Saracevic, T. (1996) "Relevance Reconsidered." In *Proceedings of CoLIS Conceptions of Library and Information Science.* Copenhagen: The Royal School of Library and Information Science: 201–218.

Saracevic, T., H. Mokros, and L. Su (1990). "Nature of Interaction Between Users and Intermediaries in Online Searching: A Qualitative Analysis." *Proceedings of the 53rd ASIS Annual Meeting, 27,* 47–54.

Schamber, L., M. Eisenberg, and M. Nilan. (1990). "A Re-examination of Relevance Toward a Dynamic, Situational Definition." *Information Processing and Management 26,*755–776.

Schon, D. A. (1982). *The Reflective Practitioner: How Professionals Think in Action.* New York: Basic Books.

Shannon, C. E. and W. Weaver. (1949). *The Mathematical Theory of Communication.* Urbana: University of Illinois Press.

Shera, J. H. (1972). *The Foundations of Education for Librarianship.* New York: Wiley.

Spink, A., H. Greisdorf, and J. Bateman (1998). "From Highly Relevant to Not Relevant: Examining Different Regions of Relevance." *Information Processing and Management, 34,* 599–622.

Stotsky, S. (1990). "On Planning and Writing Plans—or Beware of Borrowed Theories." *College Composition and Communication, 41,* 37–57.

Stripling, B. and J. Pitts. (1988). *Brainstorms and Blueprints: Teaching Library Research as a Thinking Process.* Englewood, CO: Libraries Unlimited.

Sutton, S. (1994). "The Role of Attorney Mental Models of Law in Case Relevance Determinations." *Journal of the American Society for Information Science, 45,* 186–200.

Taylor, R. S. (1962). "The Process of Asking Questions." *American Documentation, 13,* 391–396.

Taylor, R. S. (1968). "Question-Negotiation and Information Seeking in Libraries." *College & Research Libraries, 29,* 178–194.

Taylor, R. S. (1986). *Value Added Processes in Information Systems.* Norwood, NJ: Ablex.

Taylor, R. S. (1991). "Information Use Environments." In *Progress in Communication Sciences.* Norwood, NJ: Ablex: 217–255.

Todd, R. (1995, Winter). "Integrated Information Skills Instruction: Does It Make a Difference?" *School Library Media Quarterly,* 133–138.

Tuckett, H. W. and C. J. Stoffle (1984). "Learning Theory and the Self-Reliant Library Users." *Reference Quarterly, 24,* 58–66.

Vakkari, P. (1999). "Task Complexity, Information Types, Search Strategies and Relevance: Integrating Studies on Information Seeking and Retrieval." In *Exploring the Contexts of Information Behaviour,* edited by T. Wilson and D. Allen. London: Taylor Graham: 35–54.

Vakkari, P. and N. Hakala. (2000). "Changes in Relevance Criteria and Problem Stages in Task Performance." *Journal of Documentation, 56,* 540–562.

Vakkari, P. and S. Serola. (2002). "Utility of References Retrieved for Preparing a Research Proposal: A Longitudinal Case Study." *The New Review of Information Behaviour Research, 3,* 37–52.

Van Rysbergen, C. (1996) "Information, Logic, and Uncertainty in Information Science." In *Proceedings of CoLIS Conceptions of Library and Information Science.* Copenhagen: The Royal School of Librarianship.

Vickery, B. C. and A. Vickery. (1981). *Information Science in Theory and Practice.* London: Butterworths.

Vygotsky, L. (1978). *Mind in Society: The Development of Higher Psychological Processes.* Cambridge: Harvard University Press.

Whittemore, B. and M. C. Yovits. (1973). "A Generalized Conceptual Development for the Analysis and Flow of Information." *Journal of the American Society for Information Science, 24,* 221–231.

Wilson, P. (1977). *Public Knowledge, Private Ignorance: Toward a Library and Information Policy.* Westport, CT: Greenwood Press.

Wilson, T. D. (1981). "On User Studies and Information Needs." *Journal of Documentation, 367,* 3–15.

Wilson, T. D. (1999). "Models of Information Behavior Research." *Journal of Documentation, 55,* 249–270.

Wilson, T. D., N. Ford, D. Ellis, A. Foster, and A. Spink. (2002). "Information Seeking and Mediated Searching. Part 2. Uncertainty and Its Correlates." *Journal of the American Society for Information Science and Technology, 53,* 704–715.

Yerkes, R. and J. D. Dodson. (1908). "The Relation of Strength of Stimulus to Rapidity of Habit Formation." *Journal of Comparative and Neurological Psychology, 18,* 459–482.

Yovits, M. C. and C. R. Foulk. (1985). "Experiments and Analysis of Information Use and Value in a Decision Making Context." *Journal of the American Society for Information Science, 36,* 63–81.

Yovits, M.C. and R. Kleyle. (1993). "The Average Decision Maker and Its Properties Utilizing the Generalized Information System Model." *Journal of the American Society for Information Science, 44,* 352–363.

Zuboff, S. (1988). *The Age of the Smart Machine.* New York: Basic Books.

Subject Index

Abstract media, 113
Academic library users, 29, 58–69
  sample, composition of, 58
Advisor, role of, 114, 117–18, 131, 201.
    See also Education, levels of
    intervention; Mediators, roles of
  effectiveness, 117–18
  limitations, 118
  pattern approach to intervention, 117
  underlying assumption, 118
Affective component of process, 6–7,
    23, 24–25, 64–69, 93, 97
  shifting of symptoms, as knowledge
    state shifts, 64–69
  uncertainty principle and, 200. *See
    also* Uncertainty; Uncertainty
    principle
American Library Association Council,
  122
Analysis of data. *See also* Case studies;
    Longitudinal methods;
    Longitudinal verification of
    process
  qualitative analysis. *See* Qualitative
    analysis
  quantitative analysis. *See*
    Quantitative analysis
  statistical analysis. *See* Statistical
    analysis
Analysis of variance (ANOVA), 55, 61,
  62
ANOVA. *See* Analysis of variance
  (ANOVA)
Anxiety in information seeking, 7, 30
  library anxiety, 7
  technology anxiety, 7
Apprehension, 38, 39, 41, 44

Assessment, 51, 166, 195. *See also*
    Closure; Enough, concept of;
    Presentation of information;
    Search closure
  by teacher, 31, 35
Assignment requirements, 42, 43, 101.
    See also Choices, criteria for
Assimilation, 18, 19, 26

Bibliographic instruction, 10–12, 120,
    143. *See also* Instruction,
    defined; Instruction services
Bibliographic paradigm, 1, 3, 4, 8, 9, 30,
    58, 93, 99, 105, 114, 115, 117,
    118, 119, 127–28, 130, 189, 200
Borrowed theory, 13, 89, 190
Brainstorming, 136, 146
Browsing, 120
Bruner, Jerome, 14, 16, 21–25, 41, 93,
    94, 112, 113, 163, 198, 205. *See
    also* Integrated perspective;
    Interpretive tasks

Case studies of information search
    process, 33–34, 74–75, 77–80,
    190
  benefits of, 33–34
  examples of case study research, 33
  interviews, use of, 34
  longitudinal studies. *See* Longitudinal
    verification of process
  prompts and questions, examples, 34
Central tendency, measures of, 61
Chaining, 120
Charting, 138–39, 204
Chi-square tests, 62

221

Author/Title Index

About the Author

CAROL COLLIER KUHLTHAU has been on the faculty of school of Communication, Information, and Library Studies, Rutgers, the State University of New Jersey, since 1985. She has served as chair of the department and director of the Library and Information Science Master's Degree Program. She has had many awards including the American Library Association Jesse Shera Award for Outstanding Research, the Lazerow Distinguished Lectureship, Department of Library and Information Science, University of California, 1995, the Educational Media Association of New Jersey President's Award, 1997, and the American Association of School Librarians Distinguished Service Award, 2000. Her publications include many books, including the highly regarded first edition of the current book and numerous research articles.